KILLER BEARS

MIKE CRAMOND

An Outdoor Life Book

Outdoor Life Books
New York
Charles Scribner's Sons
New York

For Maybelle,
because of whom my writing began — seriously

Published by
   Book Division
   Times Mirror Magazines, Inc.
   380 Madison Avenue
   New York, NY 10017

Distributed to the trade by
   Charles Scribner's Sons
   597 Fifth Avenue
   New York, NY 10017

Library of Congress Cataloging in Publication Data
Cramond, Mike, 1913
   Killer bears.

   1. Bears   2. Dangerous animals.   I. Title.
QL737.C27C73   1981   613.6′9   81-81093
ISBN 0-684-17285-2   AACR2

Manufactured in the United States of America

Contents

Preface

As a young boy in the early 1920's in West Vancouver, British Columbia, I was given a grizzly cub as a pet. That bear fostered a permissive— and even careless— attitude in me over the next 50 years. I felt that bears were not really much to worry about. Besides my experiences with that cub, I had fed bears and other wild animals by hand; I had driven bears away by yelling, throwing stones, and waving my arms; I had filmed bears close up; and I had hunted and killed bears that threatened me and mine. My research and investigations for this book caused me to revise my attitude toward bears: I'm still permissive of them, but I am no longer careless in their habitat.

While I was outdoors editor for the *Province*, a Vancouver news daily, from 1956 to 1978, I began accumulating a file of bear-related articles. These turned out to be predominantly about fatal and near-fatal bear attacks. Many included testimonies of reputed authorities on attacks. But the inconsistencies and apparent fallacies in these testimonies bothered me. In response I wrote newspaper columns designed to warn people of the hazards. My first related article, entitled "Never Trust a Bear," had appeared in *Outdoor Life* magazine in 1944. And I'd written another for *Outdoor Life* describing how I'd dispatched a bear that was at our baby daughter's crib on our front porch.

In 1973 my book *A Bear Behind* was published. From its prepublication manuscript the publishers had deleted the bear-attack material because it seemed too "indelicate" for the intended audience. I didn't object to the deletions mainly because I realized that these attack stories deserved to be a book themselves.

Then, some months before my retirement from the *Province* in 1978, book editor Chet Fish (a former editor of *Outdoor Life*) encouraged me to write a book on bear attacks. I then began the formidable research project which included 40,000 miles of travel, criss-crossing North America, to visit attack sites and to interview survivors, witnesses, biologists, and investigators. The evidence caused me to revise many notions I'd held regarding bear and human behaviors. In fact, it became most evident that no one has the answers that will prevent bear-man encounters from leading to attacks. As you will see in the case histories that follow and in the tabulations of hundreds of attacks in this book's Appendix, no action that you take when confronted by a bear will assure your safety. Much depends on your own personality, your wits, and your knowledge of bears. But far more depends on the mood and personality of the bear itself. What works for some people, on many bears, can fail for others. Quite simply, there is *no sure way* of gauging how an individual bear will react in a given situation. Thus, there is no sure defense against bears.

Still, there is much to be learned from this book. First, there are lessons on avoiding confrontations. Then to be considered are the widely varied bear reactions to human actions. As well, the stories show the fury and power that any bear can unleash, sometimes in contrast with a bear's surprising decision to cease an attack it is easily winning.

Although attack stories — by their nature — are dramatic and disturbing, I have avoided sensationalizing them. Yet I've been explicit enough to convince readers of the hazards involved in routine bear encounters. This, in turn, may help prevent more attacks.

In addition, I hope that these stories will somehow benefit surviving victims and families of victims, perhaps serving as catalysts to legislation that will help government agencies prevent attacks and encourage them to assist victims as they attempt to recover physically, emotionally, and financially from what is often the most trying ordeal of their lives.

My research continues. I would appreciate hearing from readers with reference to bear attacks they have survived or witnessed. Responses can be sent to me at 4875 The Dale, West Vancouver, B.C., Canada V7W 1K2.

Acknowledgments

First, with deep respect and affection, I wish to extend appreciation to those heroic victims who shared with me their experiences: Malcolm and Barbara Aspeslet, Mike Markusich, Louis and Marion Duckitt, Cynthia Dusel-Bacon, Jack Mackill, Ted Watchuk, Marianna Young, Mary Mattie Jack, Connie King, and Fred Sturdy.

Thanks go also to scientists and outdoors professionals whose advice and opinions furthered my work; among these people were Dr. Charles Jonkel, Laszlo Retfalvi, Dr. Cliff Martinka, Lorne O'Brien, Bob Frauson, and Dale Nuss. I am also indebted to newspaper and magazine people, among whom were Greg Sorenson, Paddy Sherman, Shirley Mooney, Tony Ebert, and Bob Henning. Thanks too to publications and news services that granted permission to reprint their stories; specific credits are noted in context.

Mike Cramond

1

One Big Sonuvabitch of a Grizzly

Poett Nook* is an idyllic circle of oceanside harbor on the Pacific Coast, just the kind of Shangri-la in which a man could hope to piece together the torn parts of his body, which a grizzly bear five years previously had all but dismembered and scattered on the frozen ground. It is a summer-business campsite and marina that Mike Markusich and his partner Len, who was his hunting companion at the time of the attack, are assembling at this westernmost point for adventurous tourists.

As I was tying up the painters of Buck Berry's fast 24-foot cruiser, he shut off the motor and dropped back to the stern. His finger was pointing across the transom to the nearby meadow.

"Hey, Mike! Look at that big bastard of a bear!"

Less than 200 yards beyond the craft's stern cockpit, a very

*Colloquially called "Poet's Nook."

1

large, squarish black body with a stubby head had its front legs set apart, feeding casually on the early May grasses. Against the emerald sheen of the meadow the bear's obsidian-black coat stood sharply defined not at all in the manner of a charcoaled stump. Although it did not move noticeably, the deeper hue, to an outdoorsman, was unmistakable. I looked up from the now turning animal to the surrounding hedge of 100-foot-high second-growth alders and maples and thought to myself, *How different it was from the settings natural to most silvertip grizzlies—like the man-killer that got proprietor Mike Markusich.*

Mike and I had begun talking to each other about bears a couple of years previously, when I was visiting Poett Nook in search of new chapters for my second book on chinook (spring) salmon fishing. Parts of our lives, although at different times, had been lived there in the same woods and waters, in the same pursuits—logging, fishing, and hunting.

When I first met Mike Markusich, his severely scarred face made me wonder about the cause of his injury. He looked as if he'd been caught by the tail-end whiplash of a logging haul-back cable—a fairly common mutilating injury among the Pacific Coast timber cutters. I asked him, and I was surprised by his answer.

"No! It was a big sonuvabitch of a grizzly that got me."

The cold shock of that statement left me silent for a moment. It was the first time I'd ever been able to talk to another man who had actually been attacked by a bear. My own first attack is authenticated by a witness. It was unprovoked, and it was a black bear. Unprovoked bear attacks are extremely uncommon. Bear attacks usually result from a wound or from intervention into the bear's territory.

The wording of my next question took a moment to form. Then, I thought, *He's a direct guy—a direct question will do.*

"Had you wounded him, Mike?" I asked.

"Hell, no! I didn't even see him—until he got me."

"That's unusual," I said. "But ambush is on record as a factor of some bear encounters. Were you hunting?"

"Yeah! We were after moose. I was with Len—my partner, the guy you were talking to on the bulldozer."

"Where did it happen?"

"Up in northern British Columbia," he said. "Near Mile 135, above Fort St. John."

"I read about that in the papers," I replied. "But I can't remember when it was."

"October 19, 1968. I got a good reason to remember."

We both laughed at that. Most people like to talk about their tragic, adventurous, or heart-rending experiences, often reliving them with a feeling of release. I had in mind a book on killings of men and women by both black and grizzly bears. The idea of a book on killer bears had developed after publication of a book about my own life among wild bears. Perhaps a talk with Mike Markusich was a good place to begin.

"Mike," I said to him, "I've got a book in mind—I'm a writer. Maybe you've heard of the one I wrote a couple of years ago —*A Bear Behind*."

"Yeah. I think I have. There's something about Vancouver Island in it, isn't there? Port Alberni and Campbell River?"

"Yes. I lived out here in 1944. Our son, Grant, was born in Port."

"Yeah?" he said.

I opened the subject again:

"What happened with the grizzly?"

Mike related the details of the encounter so vividly that I sat spellbound for nearly an hour and a half, listening. His narrative was shocking. He wasn't just lucky to be alive; his survival was a miracle.

A customer came into the lodge office, and Mike got up to serve him.

"I'll come back, Mike," I said. "I want to go into it with you —in depth."

"Sure, any time. Just let me know."

Well, two years somehow passed before Buck Berry, a mutual friend, arranged a weekend meeting with Mike Markusich. We'd meet during a break from spring salmon fishing at that remote, open Pacific fjord entrance. It was upon our arrival at the little harbor that Buck had noticed the bear feeding on the meadow.

About an hour later, Mike and I were sitting in the lodge

office with Buck and another man. They were having a beer when I asked Mike to tell me what he thought about the fact that grizzlies kill women more often than men—that is, women are usually killed but men more often survive.

His answer was immediate, unreflective.

"Women wear much lighter clothing than men," he said. "They mebbe fight back more'n a man would. If I wasn't wearing heavy wool clothing, the grizzly woulda torn me apart—more than he did. Yeah. I think it would mebbe be the heavy clothing a man wears."

His ready answer was a surprise. But perhaps there was a common element in all killings by grizzlies—something that would help other people.

"I think you hit it, Mike," I said. "What did you have on?"

"Well, it was cold that October. Weather came early. The rivers were froze up. I was wearin' a heavy wool mackinaw over a logging shirt and Stanfields [heavy long underwear], and a cap. That outfit might have saved my life. The grizzly tore a hole in my side that I figured I'd have to push my guts back into. If it would have been light clothing, they'd be hangin' out."

The other men and I were silent, awe-stricken. Then I took a pad and pencil from Mike's nearby desk.

"I want to take some notes about this," I said. "Give me some background. Where was it? And how old were you?"

"It was by the Beaton River, near Mile 135, the Alaska Highway. I was thirty-seven years old, just back from commercial fishing all summer and in good shape."

"You're about five feet nine. What did you weigh, Mike?"

"I weighed 187 pounds at that time. Two months later, I was only 147—when I got out of hospital."

"But, you *were* in good shape—hunting shape?"

"Yeah. Len and I camped beside the river in a pickup, and we'd towed up a four-wheel-drive unit. That morning a couple of the gas cans we'd brought along were leakin' and we needed some supplies. Len was goin' to drop me off at a spot that we'd looked at before—where Mile 135 Road circles back into the bush, crosses the Beaton River, then comes back to Mile 128.

Our camp was about eight miles back in from the Alaska Highway, so I had about five miles to hunt back on.

"Len was goin' on from where he'd drop me. He planned to look at some other country he liked, for moose. He was gonna come back to see if I was out on the road near camp, then go on into town for the things we needed. We'd been huntin' nine days without a moose.

"I told him not to worry if I wasn't on the road. Just go on. Even if I didn't make the five miles back to camp, not to worry. I'd just hole up in the bush with a fire overnight. There was no way I could get lost. I'd be following the course of the river all the time, goin' up on the ridge to look down on the little pocket deltas beside the river.

"A local guy had told me the moose were over the rut, and cagey now, hanging about in the brush along the riverbank. He was right. Soon after Len left, I was coming across moose tracks, some of them old. For a while, I followed the river down at the banks."

Mike Markusich paused for a moment and took a sip of beer. Then, in a motion habitual and casual to those who have survived head injuries that involve the loss of an eye, he brushed at his tanned cheek to remove the running tear below the artificial eye.

Watching him, I thought: *There isn't a damn thing pathetic about him. He doesn't feel sorry for himself. The scars and loss of vision haven't left him bitter.*

The rest of us were unwilling to break the silence, so Mike continued: "Down at the riverbank there was some heavier snow, from earlier, drying in patches. I guess I'd been hunting a couple of hours when I noticed where a grizzly bear had left its tracks.

"It had come across the river on the new ice. The water wasn't all froze up yet. It was goin' down, leavin' layers of ice at the point where it had frozen higher, some clear runnin' water in places. Not really good enough ice to cross on.

"I wondered about that grizzly. Jesus Christ! His tracks were big. I remember wishin' I had a steel tape to measure those paw marks. They looked like they might be fourteen or fifteen inches long on the back pads. That's a big bear!

"I looked for a good track, to try to find out how old they were. There was some in the snow, just where he headed up the bank to the hill I was going up next. I put my finger into the frozen crystals of snow in the hollows and pushed. I wanted to see if the ice was still like loose sand or if it had frozen back into the snow. If it's loose crystals, the animal might have just made the track. If it's frozen back to the bottom, either the sun has got at it or a thaw has come between the time it was made and the time you find it.

"The ones I looked at were solid—no loose crystals. So the track was probably old—couple of days at least. We hadn't had any thaw. It was about ten below at nights, not much warmer during the days."

He reflected on that fateful day.

"Yeah. When I fingered those ice chips, I thought to myself, *That's got to be one big sonuvabitch. I'd like to measure those tracks exactly. One of the biggest I ever saw. Wonder if he went on up the hill.*

"I looked back at where he'd crossed the river, and his tracks were clear on the ice. Then I looked up above on the sidehill. There was a thicket of jack pine a couple of hundred feet long, and I decided to go up there.

"I'd been hunting for about two and a half hours. There was a cat road nearby that was made by the oil-drilling companies or pipeline crews. It went right up the hill.

"I climbed to the edge of the jack pine thicket and crossed through the end of it so I could look down on the little pocket meadow along the riverbank. You could get up there above the moose without them knowing it and get a crack at them clear of underbrush.

"I came across another moose track on the other side of the thicket. It looked like it had been made quite some time earlier. But, when it's cold and clear, moose don't move much in the daytime. They may be lying down on the riverbank.

"I looked down, and there wasn't anything. So I moved back through the thicket and down the other side, to the open. There was only a few jack pine, fair size, like Christmas trees. Then you could see to the river.

"I remember thinkin' before I went up the hill: *The grizzly went up there. But if I go up, I'll keep my eyes open. If I can't put him down at seventy-five to one hundred feet, how much guts do I have?*

"I was packin' a Remington pump-action .30 / 06. That's got lots of power. It put a lot of big animals down before.

"That was when I heard him whoof—the first time."

Mike hesitated, remembering the sound. There was something I wanted to get clear. I broke in: "Just how far up the hill were you, Mike? And how far had you traveled after you saw the grizzly tracks on the low ground?"

"Well," he replied, "I had climbed about two hundred feet up, broke to the left, and ran into this old moose track about three hundred feet farther up. Then, into the thicket. And I looked to see if the grizzly track was anywhere around. I couldn't find it. If he did get up here, I figured he must have crossed on dry, hard ground. There wasn't any track.

"Later I asked the game warden, who was investigating. He said the grizzly had crossed on bare ground above me.

"Anyway," said Mike Markusich, "I came out on the low side of the thicket. There was a drop to the river. So I decided to go up again. The brush near the river was too thick to give me a clear look if there was any moose down there.

"I was just moving up into the thicket when I heard him make the first sound. Kind of a *whoof-whoof*. It's hard to explain what it sounds like. Then he roared and started his charge.

"I figured it was about forty feet away.

"I pumped a shell in and pushed off the safety.

"Jesus! I thought. *He's coming! And, I can't pick him up in the scope! I'll have to wait until he shows and then pull the trigger when he's in the clear.*

"That .30 / 06 rifle felt like a 22-caliber.

"I remember thinkin', *I wish I had an elephant gun like they use in Africa. He's too damn close!*

"I heard a twig or branch snap, right close to me, to the side in the thicket, where I couldn't see him. Then I did see the brown hide coming at me. But no head or shoulder.

"I thought: *Wait until you see him clearly. Don't panic! Shoot as soon as he's clear.*

"The grizzly let out a couple of roars, and I backed up two steps to swing around. My gun hit a Christmas tree and knocked a chip out of the stock near the receiver.

"I held my ground. I didn't panic.

"But on the second step back I must have hit a branch and tripped. When I started to fall, I held off pulling the trigger, thinking I wouldn't really go down.

"Then I was falling. It seemed like I was floating in space for a long time.

"I thought: *Christ! I'm not goin' to get a shot off! I'm not even gonna get a shot off!*

"The next thing I know, he had come so fast he had me by the foot. He just pulled me like I was a toy doll.

"Then he grabbed me by the thigh and shook me and tossed me, tore the hell out of my leg.

"It was really clear! I remember the third bite went into my side. And he threw me again.

"Then, I thought: *I got to get over on my stomach. If he ever gets at my throat, I'm a goner.*

"I rolled over twice after he bit me. He got me twice in the shoulders, but I don't remember feeling it. He got me in both shoulders, though, right through my heavy clothes and some rifle shells in my shirt pocket.

"No, I didn't feel those shoulder bites, though.

"It was when he bit me in the head that I heard the bones crack—like chicken bones. And I felt the second bite in the head. I don't remember the third head bite. The doc says he had his mouth right inside mine. Tore my palate and jaw loose.

"But I don't remember passin' out. I thought I was conscious all the time, that he'd just stood off from me a minute.

"I was lyin' face down in a patch of snow. I could hear my blood spurting out of my neck and jaw into the snow. It was going *pssst pssst* into the snow. Like a hose sound. It had to be a severed artery.

"Then, I thought: *Sonuvabitch! I'm gonna die. I can't last more than five minutes. Arterial bleedin'! I'll get that sonuvabitch. Where's my gun?*

"Still lyin' face down, I opened my eyes. At that time I didn't know I'd lost one eye. But I didn't move, just looked to see if I could locate my gun. I wondered: *Where's he at? I can't hear him breathin'.*

"Then I saw my rifle on the ground, about five feet away. I waited, listening for a snort or some breathin'. I said to myself, *I'm gonna die. All I wanna do is get one shot into that sonuvabitch.*

"I waited. And still no sound. Except that gushing blood. I thought, *The safety's off. I'll get him one shot, anyway.*

"Then, I raised my shoulders, got onto my knees, and lunged for the gun, all in one movement.

"I got it in the first grab and swung around, expecting to find him comin' at me. I was going to blast him once.

"No sign of him anywhere!

"Then, I was alone. I thought, *I'm gonna die and not get him.*

"I don't know. I wasn't scared to die. It just seemed that was gonna be it.

"I thought I was a damn fool. That grizzly suckered me into ambush. What the hell! How do I get out of this?

"I staggered up the hill and got onto the cat road. Went about a thousand feet before I came to a washout. It was about four feet deep. I thought, *I can't go down there! If I do, I'll never get out.* I remember looking down at my body and thinking, *Hell, my guts are hangin' out.* So I pushed back at the wound in my side.

"Then I went down in the ditch, and my knees folded. But I got out the other side. Hell! I could have jumped it easy, if I was all right. But right then it looked like a canyon. I was packin' the rifle, occasionally looking back to see if the grizzly was coming again.

"I looked down and seen my pantleg dragging, ripped open and catching under my shoes. *What time is it?* I wondered. *Mebbe if I get over this hill, Len might come by in the truck.* I saw the thong on my Big Ben pocket watch and pulled at it. I saw it was eleven-thirty in the morning. *Maybe too late to get to the road before Len goes by!*

"I just left the watch hangin' there. It was swingin' and

bumpin' my leg, but I thought, *I don't have strength to put it back.* So I just slogged up the hill—hopin'.

"I came over the hill still upright. I had traveled about 1500 to 2,000 feet when I came to a valve shack.

"Funny. The day before, we'd gone past on Mile 135 Road. I'd seen an oil guy attending those valves. But I hadn't gone around behind the shack, so I didn't know there was a cat road leading right to the river. Now, wondering how I'd go on, I was on that same cat road.

"Somehow I reached the road in front of the shack—right where I'd got a ride back to camp the day before from the guy who was turning the valves. I looked over to the right of the building, and there was a red box.

"*Jeez!* I thought. *That's got to be a telephone to the control center.*

"It was all I could do to reach it. Somehow I got my rifle barrel under the chunk of wood frozen in the latch and knocked it loose.

"The door flew open, but nothing was in there except a couple of bloody fire extinguishers.

"Then I thought, *I'll turn a couple of those big brass wheels on the valves and shut off the flow of oil. They'll come runnin' from the central station to find out what's wrong.*

"But I knew I was too weak to turn them.

"I thought, *I'll shoot some holes in the oil line and light a fire. That'll bring them fast.* But I couldn't feel right about doin' damage like that.

"I stumbled out onto the road. The air was so clear I could hear the big trucks on the main Alaska Highway nearly eight miles away.

"Then I thought of Len. Maybe he hadn't gone by on Mile 135 Road. I walked as far as I could go, about twenty-five feet each way on the gravel road, looking to see if I could find new tracks that would tell me that our Jeep had gone back. But there wasn't any tread that I could figure out.

"Looking down the way Len had gone to hunt, I figured I could go downhill that way, maybe find him comin' my way. But, if he'd already come back and left, there'd be no tomorrow. I wouldn't last. It had to be uphill. I thought, *If I go uphill and collapse on the road, they'll find me and know what happened.*

"There was also a pipeline road that led right to where we were camping. It was shorter, but they might never find me on it.

"Maybe I'd better build a fire, I thought. Then I realized it would take me half an hour to gather twigs that would burn up in five minutes. I decided to slog up the road as long as I could.

"I was bleedin' bad all over by now. I realized I couldn't go on any farther. At least I was on Mile 135 Road. A drill rig should be goin' by any time—perhaps.

"Then, I remembered four other hunters camped near where Len and I were. They were from Port Alberni, too, though we didn't know them. *Maybe they're in camp!*

"I'll signal with my rifle, I told myself. *That's it. Three close-spaced shots. Maybe they'll hear them and come.*

"The strap was hanging off the rifle. I knew the bolt was graphited slick, so it was easy to slip back and forth. I held the rifle down and pulled the trigger. It went off!

"I tried to pull back the pump-action handle, but it felt as heavy as lead. It was all I could do to work it. I pulled the trigger again. Nothing happened. Misfire!

"Maybe blood in the mechanism. Next time the same thing happened! I said, 'The hell with this!'

"Now I couldn't make spaced shots. I didn't have enough strength to reload.

"My eye was closing. I still didn't know I'd lost one.

"And, I thought, *I'm 120 miles from Fort St. John Hospital. They couldn't save me now, anyway. Not with all this blood I've lost.*

"There was a notebook in my pocket. I had made out a will before I'd left. I'd just bought a new house. I wanted my sister to have it.

"So they'd know what happened, I scribbled one word: *grizzly.* But, I looked at it and saw I'd spelled it *grissly,* and, I thought, *What the hell's the matter with me?*

"I was kneelin' in the center of the road when I heard a vehicle. He was coming downhill about three hundred feet from me when I thought, *Jeez, he'll skid on the ice and run over me.* Somehow I got up and moved to the edge. It was a station wagon. It went right on past me.

"I thought, *You sonuvabitch, I'll put one in your gas tank. That'll stop you.* But I knew the gun would misfire anyway.

"Then the car slowed down and stopped.

"I dropped my rifle and staggered up and opened the door. The driver just stared at me. I must have been some sight— all torn apart and covered in blood. He couldn't speak. Then he said in a small voice, 'What happened?'

"I thought, *Jesus Christ, don't faint! I need you!*

"Then, I thought, if he fainted, I could reach over and roll him off the seat. And, maybe drag myself over there and drive!

"My mouth was gone. I couldn't speak. He didn't see the word 'grizzly' I'd written on the paper even though I was shovin' it at him. I managed to get in. He started to drive to the drilling camp. I didn't know what to think. The airport was snowed in. Maybe he was trying to get me to a helicopter. The oil rig bosses used helicopters all the time.

"He drove about a thousand feet, when two pickups came toward us. I recognized them as those of guys from Alberni.

"I'd talked to them in the store at Mile 143 the night before. I had it in mind that I was going to get my driver to stop so I could go with them because they were going in the direction of the hospital. But he drove on.

"We got to the camp, and a bunch a guys come out and were staring at me. One said, 'Get him into the bunkhouse—right now!' They put me on the bed and one said, 'Get the cops!' Another said, 'Hell! Get the ambulance!'

"Then they phoned, and I heard them say the ambulance was on its way to some other place.

"One guy standing by me said, 'Jesus. He looks like he's been shot!' Another said, 'Looks like he was knifed!'

"I knew they hadn't read the note. I couldn't speak, so I motioned in circles with my hand.

"One said, 'Do you want to write something?' And, when I nodded, he got some paper and a pencil. I wrote what I thought was 'grizzly.' One guy said that a grizzly got me and they started talking about grizzly.

"The other guy came back from telephoning and said the ambulance was gone to another accident. Then somebody said, 'He wants to write something again.'

"I wrote, but I couldn't see by now. I guess it was the warmth in the bunkhouse closing up my face. The cold outdoors had slowed it down.

"One guy looked at what I'd wrote and said, 'He wants a helicopter.' Then, he said a little later, 'The cop said they couldn't get a helicopter.'

"I thought, *That's screwed it, right now!*

"I needed to get blood and be sewed up. They'd found a first-aid kit, and one of them said, 'Is that all we've got? Holy Christ!' I wrote, 'Cold.'

"They put blankets around me and closed the windows.

"One of them said, 'Hell, waiting for the ambulance! We coulda got him out ourselves!'

"They decided to do that. Loaded me into a truck. Two miles up the road, we met the ambulance comin'. There was a bunch of guys standing around me, then loading me into the ambulance. I wanted a needle. I was hurting bad. One guy was stayin' with me in the back. I wrote 'needle.' He said, 'I can't help you!' and shook his head. 'Sorry!'

"They stopped at the campsite where we were staying, called out to the guys, and said, 'Do you recognize this guy? Okay, one of you guys come with us.'

"Then the ambulance started movin'. That guy was really drivin'. Later, Len told me he passed the ambulance when he was comin' out to camp. It was *goin'*.

"We stopped at Mile 101 for gas. I heard somebody say, 'This guy's in really bad shape.' Then to me, 'It won't be long now.'

"I knew it was Mile 101, and that meant we still had fifty-four miles to go. A cop escort came along and went in front with a siren and lights.

"When I got into the emergency room in Fort St. John, I heard someone say, 'It's six-thirty, and nobody is around.' It was hot in there, and there were nurses all around me.

"Then the doctor came in. 'Who the hell's here?' he asked. Then he started giving orders. They were cutting off my clothes. One of the nurses told me after I was the worst case she'd ever seen. They started looking for my wallet to get my blood type. They started cleaning me up, and I guess they gave me a needle. But they coulda sewed me up everywhere and I wouldn't have felt it.

"I remember the doc saying, 'How'd you like the blood of an English lord?'

"And I thought, *Any old barnyard stock will do.* I wasn't in any condition to care.

"When I come to, I wanted water. I was in bed. I tried to get it across to the nurse, and she said, 'Not today.' Then, I guess it was the next day, she said, 'I'll get it this afternoon.'

"I didn't know my mouth was plugged full of bandages.

"Maybe it was the third day the doc said, 'We'll try to give him water.' And he started pulling the bandages out of my mouth. They were stuck to the bones. That was hell. My palate was gone. But he got most of the wads out and said, 'Okay, give him some water, nurse.'

"She gave it to me with an eyedropper. It hit the back of my throat and felt like I was getting a lot.

"Seven days later, the doc came in and asked me if I felt strong enough to fly to Vancouver. There wasn't anything more they could do there in Fort St. John. All they done was stitch me up on the outside. Mebbe a couple of hundred stitches—head, shoulders, leg, side, foot, and all.

"Well, in Vancouver I had surgery for two and a half months. Cost me a bundle. Insurance companies have a way of getting out of big claims. B.C. Hospital Insurance paid a lot of it.

"Anyone who ever gets badly hurt like I did should have special nurses for twenty-four hours daily. They cost like hell, but they were the difference in me being dead or alive. My relatives put them on for the first nine days. Specials know how to handle the machines. And they never leave you alone. I had a relapse when they left, but pulled out. I went down to 147 pounds. The regular nurses were wonderful, but they just have too many patients to lookafter."

I looked over at Mike Markusich, sitting on the chesterfield in his modern ranch-style home in Port Alberni. It was our third meeting. He looked healthy and pink of skin. His face was tanned, his arms and hands hardened from working as a logger. The scars about his face were certainly noticeable, but in no way ghastly or repulsive. He got up and picked a piece of torn shirt off a table, brought it over to me, and dumped out its contents into his hand.

The rifle shells were sturdy brass of .30 / 06 caliber. They were from the breast pocket of the shirt he was wearing when attacked by the grizzly. He turned the metal cylinders up to the light. There were indentations in the cases a quarter of an inch deep. You'd think they'd been pounded in with a hammer and punch.

He said, "Those were what the grizzly bit through to get at my shoulder. I don't know what would have happened if they hadn't been in the way."

The power of a bear's jaw is something the average mind can't conceive. It's common for bears to bite food cans open, squashing them like cheesecake to squeeze the contents into their mouths.

Buck Berry had seen the terrible scarring on Mike's side and hip. Buck had said, "Brother, it was torn up like you wouldn't believe!" The shells Mike held had definitely protected part of his chest.

I said, "Mike, how far away from the original attack site were you when you came to?"

He pointed to the six-foot-high potted New Zealand fern tree by the window of the living room and told me to imagine it was the tree that had almost knocked the rifle out of his hand and had broken the butt. Then Markusich pointed to a spot that corresponded to where the rifle had lain. Next he got up and went to the bedroom. He returned with the stock from his rifle and showed me the chipped-out section, where it fitted into the receiver. Then he put the stock down on the broadloom and lay face down on the floor beside the New Zealand fern tree.

He turned his head so that his remaining eye could pick up the rifle butt and said, "I could hear the blood spurting into the snow. . . . And the rifle was just about there."

I estimated the distance: about five feet. And the distance from the tree to the chesterfield, which Mike had indicated was where the grizzly first became visible as it emerged from the thicket, was less than nine feet. To where he tripped and fell, as he reenacted the encounter in his living room by taking two paces backward as he'd done after hearing the branch break, it was about twelve feet.

If you have ever seen a bear charge (and more particularly if you have faced that charge from fifteen feet), you would know that there was no way Mike could have escaped being mauled.

One grizzly came fifty yards at me, wounded and carrying 600 grains of expanded-lead slugs I'd delivered in three shots from exactly the same model rifle as Mike's—my Remington 760 ADL pump-action .30 / 06 rifle. That grizzly got to within nine feet before three shots added by the Indian guide finally put it down. That is roughly a thousand grains of lead at high velocity—*and ten times the distance.*

Attacked as he was from ambush at less than fifteen feet, Mike—even if he had managed to get in an unplaced shot—would have been mauled, perhaps torn completely apart by the enraged bear. Only a spinal shot would have stopped that animal. But that kind of shot isn't usually made in a hurry.

We sat and talked about bears. I asked Mike Markusich if he had shot any of the black bears that frequent the meadows within a few yards of his expanding summer campsite and marina.

He shook his head and pursed his mouth a bit wryly.

"No. I haven't had to, yet. But every summer I get worried about some of them campers. They go right over, like they was tame bears in a zoo, and walk up and take pictures of them. I did let a couple of shotgun blasts go over the head of one big bear, though."

His mood and thoughts seemed mild. I pushed a little.

"Did any of them ever come after you, Mike?"

"Not one of *those* bears. But one did up at the garbage dump. And I had to kill another one, when I was huntin' with another guy."

"Where did that happen, Mike? And when?"

He paused and leaned back into the sofa, fingering the broken rifle butt. He had explained to me earlier that a friend had removed it from the Remington .30 / 06 and replaced it with a new one.

"That was in 1960 on Grassy Mountain. A pal of mine and I were sittin' around doin' nothin', and I said, 'Let's go huntin'.' He was game. He didn't have a rifle, just went along for the hunt.

"He had a car. We went in on a road near Father-and-Son Lake. We'd been climbing about three hours when we came to a very steep ridge. It was a rock outcropping. There was a narrow sort of a path across the face—or we had to climb back and go around. It was several hundred feet of steep rockface, with sidehill below. I didn't want to go back, after coming up that far. So I was picking my way along it, with the guy behind me. Suddenly I spotted this old grandaddy bear with a gray face, right on the narrow trail ahead.

"He looked right at me from about fifty feet away.

"I went *whoof* to scare him. You know how sometimes they jump like hell and run? Well, this one didn't. He started comin' right at me. I yelled, but he still came, looking right at me.

"I had a Featherweight .270 rifle. There was no way we could get off the trail there. If I had tried, I'da rolled half a mile.

"The old grandaddy was comin'. And my yellin' wasn't doin' any good.

"He got to about forty feet. I pulled up on that gray spot on the chest. The bullet surprised me. It lifted him right up off his front feet, and he landed on his back.

"He started to kick on his side. The trail was so narrow I knew he wasn't goin' to stay on it.

"Behind me, Ron said, 'Go get him!'

"You just don't do that with a wounded animal. I waited while he was kickin'. Then, he gave a heave and rolled off the bluff. His body went bouncing down the rockface into nettles below. He slid out and struggled to get up. He did that a couple of times. And I thought, *Jeez, he's badly wounded. I'll have to go after him and finish him.*

"I went ahead a little, and then down the sidehill. Comin' to where he slid through bushes below, I found blood all over the place. Then, I came to a spot where it was too steep to go down.

I left him. It was no use. He'd die from all that lost blood. But I don't like to leave any wounded animal in the woods. I don't believe in that. But I lost him."

Mike Markusich's scarred countenance had a contrite look. I thought of a fellow policeman with whom I used to work. He told me he had shot seven black bears during one season—and *left them.* Flabbergasted, I had asked him why. His answer: "I hate those bastards." I worked with that man long enough to know that his only reason was that a bear had scared him while he was steelhead fishing. The contrast between his philosophy and Mike's was the difference in men.

My mind went back to the black bears on the meadow near Mike's Poett Nook campsite. Two years earlier I had camped there at the extreme edge, near the meadow. All that lay between my camper and the grassy clearing was a narrow creekbed that a wobbly two-year-old child could cross in seconds.

A sow bear with two cubs had been not more than 100 feet from my site one evening. I watched her carefully. She stayed on her side of the creek until nearly dusk. Then, with the cubs, she crossed the creek and climbed up a hill on the campsite side. During my three-day stay, I watched two other bears there.

I was looking at Mike, as I thought about those incidents.

"What about the one that came after you at the garbage dump?"

He grinned at the memory.

"I was just dumpin' some camp garbage. There was a big black bear about sixty feet from me, grubbin' around for somethin' to eat. He looked up at me as I got out of the pickup.

"I *whoof*ed. He just stared at me. I'd figured the sonuvagun would bolt. He didn't. I banged an oil drum hard. He started to come toward me. I banged the drum a couple more times. He was coming at me. I thought, *To hell with this!* I ran to the pickup, jumped in, and slammed the door. He was still comin'.

"I skidded the truck into reverse and swung around out of the dump. When I looked back through the rear window, he was standin' looking toward me.

"No. I never shot one of them at camp. But one night at

Poett Nook, on that meadow, I had a shotgun with me when one was too close to the campsite. I let a spray of pellets go on the water near him. He ran about twenty-five feet, then turned around.

"I yelled, 'Go on! Bugger off!'

"He stood there lookin' at me. I let another shot go near him. That time he started to move off, *slowly.* He wasn't too scared at all. I worry about them campers, though. You hear them say, 'Look at that cute little thing!' They're tryin' to photograph the small cubs beside the sow."

My thoughts went back to the time I fed a sow bear and two cubs, by hand, on the Yellowstone National Park highway. That was ten years after I'd been attacked by a bear in the wild. How nuts can we humans be? Mike was looking at me, perhaps wondering what I was thinking.

I said, "Mike, have you got any advice on how to avoid being attacked by a bear?"

He said, "I don't go cuttin' through deep thickets anymore! Not when I'm loggin'. Not when I'm huntin'. If I can't see into a thicket, I go around. I don't take any chances. Where I was loggin' today, there was a lot of bear signs around. Bears seem to hang around right where the loggin' is goin' on. Black bears are hard to figure out."

In the dying light of late afternoon, we went out on the porch. I wanted some photos of Markusich and his mementos of the grizzly attack. He held out the .30 / 06 shells to show the indentations of the grizzly's teeth. Half apologetically, he brought out the remnant of the padded cap he'd been wearing. The brim and sides were gone. All that remained was the center part of the hunting hat. In it were five slashes where the grizzly's teeth had penetrated hat and skull. He ran his fingers casually through the slashes.

"That's where his teeth went through," he said.

After the photos, we sat down in the living room. At my suggestion, Mike sipped a beer. He was aware that I'm a non-drinker—a twenty-year nonparticipating alcoholic. His thoughtfulness in holding off till I mentioned it registered with me. It filled out his character. But there was something I still wondered about.

Men of the woods and seas and those who live in outpost settlements or on farms have a reticence, close to shyness, with "city folk." I'm not a city man; I just look like one. But the fact that I was a reporter from a big metropolitan daily and a well-known book author in the province made Mike reserved with me.

I told him that my first pet had been a grizzly cub and that I had been attacked by a black bear in nearby Campbell River, as well as by a couple of wounded grizzlies.

We gabbed about personalities we'd both known in different decades. He mentioned George McGarrigle, a character I vaguely remembered from my territorial-police days in that area thirty-two years earlier. He laughed, as the old, hard-nosed logger came back to his mind.

"George was a tough old customer," said Mike. "He told me once not to worry about a bear chasin' me. Just to run like hell. The bear wouldn't be able to catch up to me. It would be slippin' in shit!"

We both laughed at that old saw. Mike shook his head ruefully. "I didn't get a chance to run on this one."

There was a winding-down sensation to the interview. I knew that I didn't wish to leave. Mike, too, seemed loath to end the session. He laughed reflectively.

"McGarrigle and another logger and I was out in some new loggin'," Mike said. "He saw a bear go in a hole under a big cat-face tree snag. Then he came over and called us two guys.

"It turned out that the stump was hollow for a ways. The bear was up inside the tree.

"McGarrigle said, 'Come on, you guys. Grab a club! If he comes out we'll nail him.'

"But the bear wasn't comin' out. The other guy poked a big stick at the black fur, and I seen that bear's paw hit it. It was so quick—like a flash—that you couldn't see the movement. It snapped the stick off like nothin'. That sort of got to me. Boy! That was quick and strong.

"McGarrigle said, 'Come on, you guys. Roll that big rock into the hole where he went in at. We'll plug him in there and come back tomorrow. Come on; roll that stone in there!'

"Well, we did. But I didn't like it. I thought, *Hell, if that bear comes out, it's goin' to be right at me!* McGarrigle was standing off to the side with a club.

"In fact, McGarrigle said, 'We don't need no rifle. I'll get him with an ax when he comes out. I'll hit him right between the eyes!'

"He was a tough old bugger. He'd've done it too. He was seventy-two years old and still workin' hard.

"The bear had gone up inside the tree. I looked up and saw its claws come through the wood of the 'cat-face' where there was a split and some rot."

I was curious. I couldn't remember what a cat-face was and said so.

Mike made a motion with his hand, as if next to a tree. He said, "It's a bald face that's kind of grown in at the edges where there's bark on it. It's where a tree's been scarred by something."

He went on, amused by his recollection. "That bear stayed in there, though! The other guy and I rolled a lot of big stones over the entrance.

"When we came back the next day, there was another hole right beside the first one, where another bear dug him out. Or maybe he did it himself.

"But when we were lookin' in the holes and up the tree trunk, I happened to look away. I saw two *big* black bears about a hundred yards off, watchin' us. They weren't two-year-old cubs, either. They were damn big black bears.

"I had a good look at them, and so did my pals. They were surprised at the size. McGarrigle had thought the bear was just a young one. It's a damn good thing for us he didn't come out!"

Yeah, Mike. Yeah!

2

The Inconceivable
Campsite Killing

Within the paved circuit and fully developed environs of Many Glacier Campsite, Glacier National Park, Montana, I stared down at painted section indicator No. 74. It was within 100 miles, a two-hour drive, of the wilderness in the Rocky Mountains in which I had killed my second grizzly bear. And right where I was standing, just five feet from the blacktop roadway, a lovely twenty-two-year-old woman, Mary Patricia Mahoney, had been killed by a grizzly bear. The bear dragged her in her sleeping bag from the tent where she and two other young women had been sleeping side by side. Then the bear carried the victim only a couple of hundred feet and partially devoured her.

It just could not happen!

A profound dejection came over me as I stared toward the fringe of coniferous trees girding the edge of the campground driveway, small timber left there to enhance the aura of "outdoor camping," which is so desirable to the city visitors who use the computer-controlled grounds of this modern national park. This wasn't really the wilds. It was a stage of development almost suburban, using the wilderness as its borders.

I leafed through my notebook and found the penciled, hand-drawn map I had received earlier that afternoon from District Ranger Robert Frawson at St. Mary's Park Station. A glance at the map gave me the needed direction. I strode southward in the now diminishing light toward where Mary Mahoney's partly devoured body had been found, only a short distance from Campsite 74, perhaps 200 feet into the hedge of trees.

It was nearing 5:00 P.M., and the campsite was deserted. The season had closed a week previously. The only remaining inhabitant—Park Ranger Terry Pentilla—still at the nearby rangers' cabin, had politely answered my questions about the tragedy of September 23, 1976. My schedule was tight on this trip two years after the tragedy, and I didn't wish to wait until the following morning. The sun was already well down behind the towering, jagged ridges of the westward Rocky Mountain summits over which I had just hurriedly driven my pickup camper. All was silent, the atmosphere still.

That same silence and twilight would prevail at the 6,500-foot place in this same range, where—many years before—outdoors painter-illustrator Bob Kuhn of Connecticut, big game guide Louis Capello of Windermere, British Columbia, and I had established our base camp for hunting. In that glacially eroded niche of a few square yards on the mountainside, we had found hummocks of dried grizzly dung on the grass and pine needles. Nevertheless, we had camped in that small, singularly flat spot in canvas tents. Scattered about the location were our provisioned saddle boxes and food, some of it in open pots in which it had been cooked. We had dumped refuse in a spot adjacent to the fire, to be burned later. Some of the refuse, partly burned, lay beside the burned-out campfire, awaiting the next lightings.

Yet, neither Louis—who had guided for fifty of his sixty-five years—nor I—who then had hunted and guided for twenty-five years—ever gave a single thought to the possibility that a marauding grizzly bear might enter our camp while we were there, either by night or by day.

It had taken us the better part of two days on horseback and on foot to reach that remote spot, partly because we'd literally had to hew our trail in. It was that remote in the heart of the Rockies. And on the morning of the fifth day of our encampment there, I killed a prime male grizzly bear less than half a mile farther along the slope.

Those recollections pulsed through my mind now as I stepped into the darkening cover of the trees at the site of the tragedy. My stride quickened as silence shrouded the scene. I glanced back and forth into the areas of shadow, almost furtively. I took a deep breath, wishing I had my old Mauser 9-mm pistol with me—but feeling utterly foolish about that desire.

In all God's truth, after sixty years in the outdoors, earning my daily bread there for thirty of them, I would have lain down in the open in a pair of blankets or a sleeping bag, just back there 75 feet, where Mary Mahoney and her companions had slept. And I would have gone to sleep feeling as secure as I would have in my own home.

Surrounding her campsite in tents and vehicles had been more than a dozen other people. The park ranger's cabin was just around the stand of trees a few yards away. And a large hotel-lodge complex and all its personnel and guests—trucks, gear, and all-night operations—were just a long block away. The campsite admissions wicket was within sight, only a few feet distant from the tent.

But, by contrast, the west end of the same campsite had just that week been closed to the public. Grizzlies had been seen in the vicinity, and a transport-type bear trap had been set. Official reports of the incident included that information.

As I moved deeper into the conifers, my gaze traveled instinctively toward that closed section. Every few steps, I did what I always do when hunting for game: I stopped and listened intently. During the previous week of the campsite's abandonment for the coming winter, wildlife had been afforded time to move in. Curiosity alone would bring any of them, even deer.

Just ahead of me was an unnaturally flat depression that ran in a straight, cleared line through the trees—the path of a sewage or water line. As I looked eastward along the swathed-out timber, I could see the corner of the ranger's white-painted outbuilding, only 100 feet away. In this forest stillness, I could have carried on a conversation in a normal tone of voice, from where I now stood, with a person at that building. Yet I was very close to where the grizzly bear fed upon the body of the young woman it had killed only a short distance to my right.

I moved another 20 feet southward through the sparse conifers. I was surprised to see a small stream. Beyond it was a clear view out over an expanse of grass and scrub-growth lands that reached all the way back to the wild lands and the summits of the overhanging mountains. The area was a natural forage lowland in which you could expect to find a grizzly sow with her summering cubs. Or it might be an area through which a grizzly bear would pass during its territorial meanderings.

I stared up at the blackening silhouette of those grand mountains.

The light on the horizon had lost most of its reds and saffrons, the sun well down. As I turned away from it, the blackness in the forest was immediately intensified and momentarily cut off my sight. While my eyes adjusted, I waited apprehensively and listened intently. The pine needles crushed softly beneath my leather soles as my steps quickened back past the spot where Mary Mahoney's body had lain. Almost breathlessly, I re-crossed the narrow swath of the pipeline, thence through the remaining skirt of trees to the edge of the blacktop. It was a distinct relief to look down that roadway and be able to see at least 100 yards in the twilight.

Walking back toward the cupola of the campground registration booth, I spotted the black and white No. 74 marker. This was the spot where five happy vacationing young women had bedded down. In my mind I could hear the muted conversations and happy giggles, then the screams and tumult, and finally the ominous silence.

My jaw clamped shut with some involuntary disclaimer.

Oh, hell, it just could not happen!

Not *here*.

Not a man-killer. Not a *man-eater.*

It was too monstrous to contemplate.

Two news items reached the Pacific Coast in that connection:

The Vancouver Sun: Thurs., Sept. 23, 1976

WOMAN MAULED TO DEATH BY BEAR

West Glacier, Mont. (AP)—A young woman was fatally mauled by a bear early today when she and four other women were attacked while sleeping in a campground in Glacier National Park.

Park officials identified the victim as Mary Patricia Mahoney, 22, of Highwood, Illinois.

Her companions were not harmed, officials said.

A park spokesman said Miss Mahoney was dragged from a tent only 200 yards from a ranger station on the east side of the park.

Officials said the pre-dawn attack occurred in one of the most popular campgrounds in the park.

Ed Rothfuss, chief naturalist, said the death was the third from bear mauling in the history of the park.

The Province: Friday, Sept. 24, 1976

PARK BEAR KILLS WOMAN

United Press International

East Glacier, Mont.—A Highwood, Illinois, woman was fatally mauled by a grizzly bear early Thursday while camping with four other young women in Glacier National Park. None of the others was hurt.

She was mauled and dragged about 300 yards from her tent.

The death of Mary Patricia Mahoney, 21, was the first caused by a grizzly in the park along the Montana-Canada border since two women were killed in the summer of 1967.

Ed Rothfuss, chief park naturalist, said rangers shot and killed two grizzlies shortly after Miss Mahoney was attacked. He said one bear treed two vacationing California State Parks rangers who were guarding the woman's body. Moments later, another grizzly appeared, and it also was destroyed.

In Yellowstone Park, Wyo., a female grizzly bear who mauled one man and had become a persistent food scrounger was shot, park authorities said. Although the 12-year-old bear was transported three times to remote areas of the park, she returned each time to the Fishing Bridge Campground, the scene of the Aug. 16 mauling.

Melvin Ford of Salt Lake City, Utah, was seriously injured while attempting to chase away her three cubs. Apparently the man did not see the mother bear, a superintendent said.

Perhaps the editors, upon reading the distances in feet mentioned in the reports, were inclined to use yards instead. How could they have conceived that the young woman was killed and partially devoured in the short distances from habitation and roads that such figures as 200 feet and 300 feet indicate?

Indeed, before I stood in the area of Campsite No. 74 and covered the short expanses between the killing ground and the feeding ground of the killer bear, I couldn't comprehend the way things had happened. And, when I walked those short, almost urban distances, the incredibility of the whole situation became even more intense.

I thought of what Dr. Charles Jonkel had told me the day before at his research offices in Missoula, Montana. He advised me to talk with Wildlife Biologist Cliff Martinka in the park headquarters of the West Glacier section of Glacier National Park. Now I clearly recalled Martinka's intensity about his computerizing of bear activities in the park.

Early that morning I had spent two hours interviewing Martinka and members of his staff. I had come away with very little about the killing of Mary Patricia Mahoney but much about the reasons for and methods of security in the park. It had become more apparent to me in mulling things over that there was some official concern about what publicity might do to the government's case if some form of suit or complaint were lodged in connection with the death of the young woman. The statute of limitations had only a short time before it would come into effect. No one would release any official reports of any kind to me on the Mary Mahoney killing, in contrast to what they had willingly given me in the case of Julie Helgeson and Michelle Koons, killed just ten years before, on August 14, 1967, also in Glacier National Park.

When I suggested going to the lawyers who were responsible for handling the reports and documents, park officials indicated that I would probably not get any official sanction. Such secrecy seems deplorable when you're trying to get at the truth. But when you consider how many lawsuits are filed each year, you can see the logic in the official reticence.

I went to a source open to newsmen: the offices of the *Hungry Horse News* in Columbia Falls, Montana. So many requests for copies of the papers covering the story had been received during the two years since the tragedy that no more were available. And the newspaper had changed hands, breaking continuity with the previous reporter-publisher-editor, Mel Ruder. I was able to reach him by phone at home, but he expressed no interest in being interviewed. He said copies of the story were all on file in the news office, and I could read them there.

Things began to look a bit hopeless. The issues in question had several extensive pages of pertinent coverage. And there was no nearby copying machine that would lend itself to full-page duplicating. I stood there a trifle stunned, wondering how I'd find another ten days free to return and spend the time to copy them by hand.

A man in a printer's apron came through the newsroom and seemed to sense my despair. I've noted such situations often in the news business. There always seems to be the "guy with the golden heart" who pops up at the right moment. He could ignore the situation and go about his own demanding duties. But he drops everything for a moment and opens the door.

"What copies do you need?" his voice asked behind me.

"Well," I said, "the three following the killing of Mary Mahoney—I need all three—to get the background and aftermath. The park people won't release their official reports."

He nodded, saying, "I know. We've had dozens of requests. There just aren't any copies left—for the public."

I sensed something in that last phrase, and said, "I'll pay for the use of somebody's personal copies, and I'll bring them back intact."

He looked at me for a second or two. "Wait here. I'll go and see," he said.

He opened a nearby door and went upstairs. A few minutes later he came back down and walked over to the counter. When I saw that he held three clean copies of the needed issues, I let out a long breath of relief.

"How much?" I asked.

Greg Sorenson shook his head emphatically, a little impatient with my citified, perhaps unintentionally cynical question. "Nothing but your promise to get them back to me in good condition," he said.

"Heck. I'll do that. But I'd like to reward you."

He shook his head and said, "Just get them back here, please."

He was gone into the printshop before my thanks were finished.

Pieced together from the *Hungry Horse News* issues of September 23 and 30 and October 7, 1976, and from a National Park Service news release of November 3, 1976, the story began to unfold.

The antiseptically unemotional news release of the NPS, which follows, was given me at their West Glacier headquarters—the only official document available on the tragedy. It should be read in order to help keep in perspective the events and circumstances of the tragedy.

FOR IMMEDIATE RELEASE

Richard J. Munro

November 3, 1976

BOARD OF INQUIRY CONCLUDES INVESTIGATION INTO DEATH OF GLACIER NATIONAL PARK VISITOR BY GRIZZLY MAULING

A National Park Service Board of Inquiry which investigated the death of a 21-year-old Illinois girl in a grizzly bear attack in Glacier National Park reported her death was the first such incident to occur in a major park campground and lacked any apparent explanation or motive, Lynn Thompson, Director of the National Park Service's Rocky Mountain Region said today.

"The evidence is that there were more people-bear encounters within the park this year, and in the Many Glacier area in particular, than in any previous year," the board said in its final report. "With increasing visitation in the park . . . this trend can be expected to continue, with the possible result of more management problems and more incidents."

The board of inquiry said Mary Patricia Mahoney of Highwood, Illinois, and her four companions had followed or exceeded all recommended safety precautions prior to the fatal attack in the campsite they shared in the Many Glacier Campground the morning of September 23. Some 14 other persons occupied other campsites in the immediate area. The girls' campsite was clean, with neither food nor other odorous materials that might have attracted the bear or bears.

The board said it is questionable whether the fatal attack on Miss Mahoney could have been avoided.

As general considerations, the board reported that:

• Because public safety is the primary responsibility of park managers, the fact that the grizzly bear is considered a threatened species under the Endangered Species Act of 1973 should be no deterrent to actions required to assure the safety of visitors. These actions should include the timely removal of problem bears, the board said.

• Glacier National Park's grizzly population appears healthy, with the probability of 30 new bears being added each year. The evidence also suggests an increased number of sub-adult bears (up to 3 years of age) while the overall population has remained relatively stable for several years.

• Some trails, campgrounds and other facilities in Glacier National Park may be located astride major bear travel routes, and it may be necessary to establish wildlife corridors or to modify developed areas to avoid the prospect of increased confrontation between bears and humans.

• The park's bear management plan should give consideration to management techniques, such as limiting or controlling human use in or closure of developed campgrounds, including such matters as regulating the type of camping shelter (i.e., hard-sided camping only).

• Increased vigilance and enforcement may be necessary as to park regulations pertaining to illegal camping, particularly relating to incidents of carelessness with food. This past summer, several persons were fined for illegal camping and trespass in areas closed because of bear danger in Glacier National Park. Grizzly bears raided several of these campsites and obtained foodstuffs.

"Based on this experience," the board's report says, "it is apparent that guidelines should be developed for bear-related closure and management of developed areas including campgrounds. Further, there may be a need for quicker analysis and interpretation of field observations and data so that they might be used in bear management actions."

The board of inquiry's formal conclusions included:

1.   The National Park Service and park employees involved have correctly followed Glacier's bear management plan. In the area of signing the Many Glacier area with bear warnings and in personally contacting visitors in the area concerning bears, the effort was exceptional when compared with the requirements of the plan.

2.   The five girls in campsite number 74 had a clean camp and also followed or exceeded the precautions one would take in avoiding conflict with bears.

3.   The aggressive behavior displayed by the bears when they treed (two men) near the scene of the mauling, their previous sightings and raids on camps, and especially their aggressive behavior toward the fishermen at Fisher Gap Lake (September 19, 1976) justified their destruction.

4.   The evidence is inconclusive as to which bear did the mauling of Ms. Mahoney or, indeed, whether the two bears destroyed were involved. Similarly, the available evidence does not suggest why the tent containing Ms. Mahoney was attacked by the bear in question. The evidence is that none of the known causes for such action by a bear (odors, food, etc.) were involved.

5.   We can only speculate as to whether any of the revisions to the Glacier bear management plan, discussed above, could have directly affected the circumstances in this incident since the attack and death of Ms. Mahoney are unexplainable. The board recommends that consideration be given to the revisions discussed under general considerations.

Chairman of the board was Kenneth R. Ashley, Associate Regional Director of the National Park Service's Rocky Mountain Regional Office at Denver. Members included Dr. Charles Jonkel of the University of Montana, head of the Border Grizzly Study Team; Dr. Richard Knight of Bozeman, Montana, head of the Interagency Grizzly Bear Study Team and a former member of the faculty at the University of Idaho; Chief Ranger Charles B. Sigler of Glacier National Park; and Edwin L. Rothfuss, Chief Park Naturalist at Glacier.

Having read this document several times, I still thought it held little information to explain the development and eventual circumstances of the tragedy. However, another document had these more pertinent facts.

On August 7, 1975, members of the Peterson family of Des Plaines, Illinois, were attacked by a persistent grizzly while they were on the Grinnell Glacier Trail. The bear attacked without provocation, first hitting Karen who was in the forefront of their early morning hike, when she startled it during its feeding alongside the trail.

Karen Peterson received multiple injuries, including fractured bones of the face and skull; Harold suffered a fractured and lacerated arm and other wounds; Seth had deep scratches on his back. The bear was a sow. The attack occurred within 5 miles of Many Glacier.

On August 27, 1975, William Disser, accompanied by Barbara Disser, at the foot of Upper Kintla Lake, near the Canadian border, was bitten on the left wrist. Barbara's left cheek was scratched by a black bear. Upper Kintla Lake is approximately 30 miles from Many Glacier.

On September 7, 1975, Michael Coppes, hiking near Rockwell Falls with Martin Evans, was attacked by bears that were eating in a huckleberry patch. Evans received several head and face lacerations, and Coppes received severe lacerations to the lower body. This site is within 5 miles of Many Glacier.

During the same year, Sarah Bishop, near Medicine Grizzly Lake, on July 5, was knocked down by a sow grizzly with two cubs. Dale Kreji, at Belton Hills, had his shirt torn off and his back scratched in an encounter on May 26, 1975, in which the bear, a sow, stole his lunch before retreating.

Such are the facts recorded in the "Summary of Grizzly Attacks, Glacier National Park." It documents incidents that occurred between September 2, 1907, and the fatal day of the attack on Mary Patricia Mahoney, September 23, 1976. From the perspective of hindsight, it seems there were evident warnings of impending attack before the Mary Mahoney fatality.

On July 7, 1976, while William Schweighofer was asleep in his tent at the lower campsite of Logging Lake, a grizzly bear sat on his tent, bit him, and then dragged him in his tent a short distance before departing. The victim received lacerations on one arm and shoulder. This incident occurred within 17 miles of Many Glacier Campsite, westward across the main bulk of the mountain range.

According to the September 23 issue of *Hungry Horse News*, on August 15, Pam Sue Wise, age seventeen, and Pamela Benda, visiting from Minneapolis, were hiking toward Ptarmigan Falls on their way to Iceberg Lake when they noticed a grizzly following them along the trail.

Dropping their packs, they climbed a tree. The bear stood on its hind legs, growling at the tree before leaving them momentarily. Then the grizzly returned to scratch the tree and growl, before finally departing for good. It was the third of such recent encounters with grizzlies on Iceberg Trail, none of which—fortunately—had resulted in injuries. This lack of serious injuries was sufficient reason to exclude these items from the aforementioned "Summary of Grizzly Attacks" published by the NPS.

On September 9, 1976, however, while hiking and purposely talking and making noises in accordance with official park instructions about avoiding problems with bears, Roscoe Black and Theresa Waden were attacked by a pair of three-year-old grizzlies. The bears jumped them from the side of the trail near Stoney Indian Lake.

Theresa Waden, a dining room hostess from St. Mary, and Roscoe Black were hospitalized. She had severe lacerations on one arm and shoulder and on her back.

Black, still on crutches from a severely bitten calf, was

released from the hospital earlier in the week that included the fateful September 23. Waden and Black received their injuries within 15 miles of Many Glacier Campsite.

On September 19, 1976, while reading a book near the outlet of Fisher Gap Lake, Karen Kuntz, twenty-one, of Glendive, looked up and saw two grizzly bears coming out of the nearby brush. Covering her head with her jacket, she was rewarded by having them only sniff at her and leave.

Her companions, also students of Montana State University, were Kerry O'Dell, 21, of Glendive, and Donald Brurud, twenty-nine, of Great Falls. Wearing wading boots, they were fishing at the upper end of the small lake.

At the appearance of the two bears, Brurud ran into the lake to escape them. O'Dell ran to a small tree and climbed it. The more aggressive of the bears rushed into the lake after Brurud while its mate passively watched the debacle.

The attacking animal got close enough to Brurud in the water to get its teeth into his waders as he kicked at it.

"I curled my toes," he later related, "and he just got the end of my boot."

Brurud's loud yelling caused the animal to return to shore. Then it went to the tree holding O'Dell and scrambled up the limbs on the opposite side. While the grizzly was still clawing at him, O'Dell dropped to the ground and fled into the lake beside Brurud.

The two young men then swam to the opposite end of the lake, and with Karen Kuntz hurried to the Many Glacier Ranger Station.

Their report was received there at 1:15 P.M. on September 19.

On September 19, according to reports in the September 23 issue of the *Hungry Horse News,* Ranger Reese of Many Glacier Campground "posted the [Fisher Gap Lake] trail as closed because of grizzlies, but a family with three little kids ignored the sign.

"Earlier in the day," the report continues, "Ranger Reese had a report of two bears in Many Glacier Campground. He checked and found two mature grizzlies, about 250-pounders, likely three- to four-year-olds. They went through the campground without incident, except to get some garbage that wasn't fully disposed of within the can.

"Roger Reese warned visitors, and later was joined by Ranger Lloyd Kortege from St. Mary. Saturday there was a report of bear damage to hiker packs at Ptarmigan Lake (within 10 miles of Many Glacier Campground)."

According to later published reports, which were included with the testimony of Ranger Robert Frauson, Frauson noted that "an 'Area Closed' sign tacked on the end of a bridge handrail by Reese on Sunday, September 19, had been torn off by a bear. There were teeth marks in the torn piece found under the bridge."

I cannot ascertain from officials at just what hour and date the western part of Many Glacier Campground was closed to campers and the bear trap set. But the *Hungry Horse News* item indicates it was Sunday, September 19, 1976. That would have been just three days before the registration of the five young women: Barbara and Patricia Tucker, Ellen Fineman, Jennifer Thompson, and Mary Patricia Mahoney, all of Missoula, in that fateful camp on the afternoon of September 22.

That they were conscious of the dangers or threats from bears during their camping trip was evident in the meticulous and wide coverage given in the *Hungry Horse News*. From that paper, on September 30, 1976:

Girls Ask About Bear Dangers

West Glacier—Veteran Seasonal Ranger Bob Graham at the park's west entrance recalls the five girls from Missoula entering Glacier, and asking him "about bears."

He remembers telling them that safe procedures included keeping food away from the tent.

At Babb, Oscar and Harvey Thronson, who operate the general store, mentioned the girls stopping there before driving into Many Glacier.

On the evening of September 22, 1976, the five young women visited the trailer of Ranger Fred Reese, acting campground supervisor, to inquire about the Grinnell Glacier Trail.

What were the difficulties to be encountered? And what was the bear situation? Reese explained to them that the trail was a 12-mile round trip. "The bear situation there," he said, "is that there's a sow with a cub and a single bear in the vicinity of the trail. You should hoot and holler a lot and be attentive. Never approach a bear. Always give them a wide detour."

Having listened to the directions and advice about their proposed hike, they left the Reese trailer at around 6:00 P.M. and returned to their two tents in Campsite 74, just beyond the near entrance of the campground.

At 7:00 P.M., Reese went to the occupied part of the campground in his nightly routine to talk with the campers. Eight groups of people occupied the area surrounding and close to the camp of the five young women.

All of the young women entered into discussions on safety from bears: suggestions about not cooking in a tent, about putting all food in the trunk of the car except at meal times, and about keeping no food in tents. The talk lasted about fifteen minutes. Other groups in the campground were interested in safety, and Reese informed them that there was a bear trap set in the west end of the campground and that the section was closed to them.

He explained that the bear trap had been set as an attempt to trap one of the two bears that had found food sources and had become a problem. The plan was to trap one of the animals and to separate the cooperating pair by transporting one of them to another district, thus alleviating the problem.

Later in the evening, Ellen Fineman and Jennifer Thompson retired to their tent. Barbara and Patricia Tucker occupied the adjoining tent with Mary Mahoney. The girls went to sleep after some quiet conversation.

Just after daylight, a clawing sound on the outside of the tent awakened Patricia Tucker. Mary Patricia Mahoney began screaming as a bear began pawing her.

Patricia Tucker implored her to lie still and be quiet, to play dead. Mary Mahoney became quieter and Pat Tucker squeezed her hand as the bear left momentarily. She and Barbara Tucker then pulled themselves deep into their sleeping bags, covering their heads.

Mary Mahoney was groaning in her sleeping bag nearest the tent door, through which the grizzly then returned. On its reappearance, the bear attacked Mary Mahoney, whose muffled screams and moans told of her pain. The tent was knocked down.

Jennifer Thompson and Ellen Fineman were awakened by the screams of their companions. They left their own tent and ran to their car. Once inside it, they began honking the horn.

After a minute or two of the strident horn-blowing, the screams of Mary Mahoney stopped, and the bear was seen moving away from the downed tent. It was dragging a sleeping bag toward the trees at the back of the tent site.

Within the next few minutes, Pat and Barbara Tucker untangled themselves from the fallen and torn remains of their tent and ran to the car. On the way, they pleaded with nearby campers—who were also awakened by the noise of the attack—to tell the ranger.

Shocked and unnerved by the sudden calamity, they were not aware that Mary Patricia Mahoney was still in the sleeping bag dragged off by the bear. In fact, in their shock and distress, they believed that she might have escaped and climbed a nearby tree.

Their testimony at a hearing the following morning alluded starkly to their beliefs:

Patricia Tucker—"I was in our tent when I was awakened by pawing. Mary Pat, the victim, was to my immediate right. She started screaming, because the bear was pawing her. I told her to play dead, but evidently she was unable to, because of shock.

"The bear, whose silhouette I saw, did not behave in any rational manner, but was frightened away when two of the party beeped their horn."

Barbara Tucker—"I woke up to sounds of a bear and buried myself in my sleeping bag and remained very still, but was continually being pulled toward the opposite end of the tent, where my friend was being attacked.

"She was emitting low screams, and my sister was telling her to lie still and 'play dead.' The tent had fallen down. Our friends in another tent escaped and ran for the car and honked the horn, which scared the bear. The two of us ran for the car and told some campers nearby to tell the ranger."

Jennifer Susan Thompson—"We were sleeping in the tent next to the one in which the woman involved was sleeping. We heard heavy panting (the bear) and our friend screaming.

"I was able to get out of my sleeping bag and run with my tentmate to the car, where we began blowing the horn. We saw the bear run off, after blowing the horn for one or two minutes!

"I saw him drag off a sleeping bag, but I didn't know if Mary Pat was in it."

Ellen Fineman—"I heard Mary Pat screaming and a bear around her tent. Jennifer and I got out of our tent and ran to the car where I started sounding the horn.

"I didn't see Mary Pat run. I saw the bear—young bear—run with a sleeping bag."

In the meantime Harry Mertz, one of the campground occupants, alarmed by the screaming girls, had run to the trailer of Ranger Fred Reese to inform him of the attack. At the time (approximately 6:50 A.M.), Reese had not yet risen. He hastily threw on some clothes and ran sockless to the ranger car, where there were first aid supplies. He drove to Campsite 74. He got out and talked with the girls, who were still inside their car. In response to his questions, they stated, "Mary Pat Mahoney is missing. She may have run away. There was a bear in the tent."

When Reese asked which directions may have been taken by the girl or the bear, they couldn't tell him.

Stu Macy, a vacationing California State Park ranger, hurried over and identified himself, asking if he could be of assistance. With Reese, he went back into the woods directly behind the campsite.

At a point just 25 feet from the collapsed tent, they discovered a torn and empty sleeping bag spattered with blood.

They continued searching southward toward nearby Swiftcurrent Creek. An apparent drag trail was interspaced with blood stains and torn pieces of flesh. It led to a bloodied T-shirt, but still no sign of the missing victim.

(At a point—later recorded by engineer Talber Scott, investigator for Glacier National Park—180 feet from the campsite was a section of scalp.)

Just 20 feet farther on, the shocked team of Reese and Macy came upon the face-down body of Mary Patricia Mahoney. There was no respiration or pulse. Unbelievably, a large section of her upper torso had already been consumed. There was no sign of any bear in the vicinity.

Reese and Macy immediately returned to the campground. Both of them alerted campers to pack up immediately and leave. The campground evacuation was complete by 7:45 A.M.

District Ranger Robert Frauson, unaware of the tragedy, was on his way to the Many Glacier installation. Reese reached him by phone at 7:20 P.M. when Frauson was at Shelburne Dam, at the park boundary. Frauson immediately sped the rest of the distance to Many Glacier.

I met Bob Frauson in October of 1978, outside St. Mary, where he lives. A big, angular man, he was busy repairing some fencing in the area of the recently closed-for-the-season information and control center for the St. Mary Campground of Glacier National Park.

A quiet, reserved man of middle age and husky physique, Frauson answered my questions politely. He said he had killed one of the suspected bears while in company with Ranger Kortege. He helped me draw a map of the tragedy site and said he was sorry he couldn't accompany me there.

Late that same evening, after driving up to visit the site of the tragedy at Many Glacier Campground, I went to Frauson's home. He told me the details of the aftermath. My mind could not seem to accept the timing: during the short time between the killing of the young woman and the killing of the two young grizzlies (all between 6:50 A.M. and 8:30 A.M.), a man-killer and man-eater had not only had time to feed but had also left and then returned to the scene! Frauson twice assured me that the times were correct. The events were on file in his report.

That report, though not available to me when I asked for it at West Glacier Headquarters, was ably reported by Mel Ruder and published in the *Hungry Horse News* on Thursday, September 30, 1976:

Statement by District Ranger Robert Frauson includes the following—

9/23/76 Thursday morning. Left St. Mary early about 7:05 to pick up rescue equipment for Great Falls Exhibit at Heritage Inn.

About 7:20 A.M. Fred Reese called me and said he had a DOA (death) at Many Glacier Campground. I said I was at Sherburne Dam, at Park Boundary, that I would be to the campground in a few minutes. . . .

When I pulled into the campground, there was a group of vehicles to the left with people running around. Two girls were embracing each other and were hysterical. Fred Reese said a girl was dead (Mary Patricia Mahoney) in the brush toward the creek.

There was a man (California State Park Ranger, Stu Macy) with Fred. I asked him if he could use a pistol. He said, "Yes." I gave him my .357 (loaded w/hollow points). Told Fred and him to guard the body and help the other campers as Fred had issued closure orders. (It was thought that there was one bear.)

The four girls were packing their camp. All other campers were notified earlier to pack up and move out. I got the girls' names and addresses from Fred and went to the Ranger Station at 7:45 and tried to radio Chief Ranger Sigler. The phone was also tried. Neither would work. I called Ranger Kortege at St. Mary Ranger Station to call Sigler and Coroner Riddle (in Browning).

Four girls came over to Ranger Station where Mrs. Pentilla gave them coffee and food. They were in shock, but doing well for the ordeal they had been through.

I talked to them about Mary's religion and best way to contact the family. They thought it would be best to talk directly to the family and not through a priest or friend.

Had trouble with the phone again, but finally got an operator who would stay with me. I contacted Mrs. Mahoney (She said her husband was at work) and told her that I had very bad news. I told her that her daughter had been camping with four other girls and was dead from a bear mauling, and tried to help her out. I told her I had contacted a priest (Father Talman) to administer last rites.

She wanted to know the names of the girls who camped with her daughter. I gave Mrs. Mahoney my name and phone number and to contact Chief Ranger for best information, since I would not be near a phone for a while, but we would do everything possible to help out, and our prayers were with the Mahoneys.

[*Author's note:* Nothing could be more illustrative of Bob Frauson's kindly character than that item.]

I had each girl call their home immediately, and talk with their families, and what their plans were.

I started to return to Campsite No. 74 in my vehicle when I received an urgent radio from Fred Reese that the bear was coming back to Mary's body. There was great confusion and hollering when I arrived at Site 74. I got out of my car and loaded my shotgun with slugs. Kortege radioed he was close, near Hall's house (nearing the campground). Fred Reese was shouting from the fire cache area, and there was still shouting from the direction of the creek.

It was difficult to know which direction to go. Then I heard Stu Macy call that the bear was at the body, and he up a tree over the body, so I went that way just as Kortege and Altemus arrived.

We (Frauson and Kortege) went through the heavy lodgepoles and brush. I sighted a bear off to my left at a fair distance and shot it in the shoulder. It spun around toward me. Then I saw a second bear to the left of the one that I had shot. I lost sight of both bears.

I called to Kortege that I had hit one, but there was a second bear. We pressed forward to the creek, but could find no bear. Thought they had crossed Swiftcurrent Creek. Kortege did not see any bears. Stu Macy joined us and we checked the gravel bar. We started a sweep back through the lodgepole with Stu Macy between Kortege and me.

Stu Macy saw a bear. I could not see it. Kortege shot, and I came around beside Kortege and also shot the same bear. The bear I had shot was beside the other bear where it had been sniffing about it.

The bears were both dark-colored silvertips. We checked to make sure they were dead. I put the two shotguns back in my car and picked up some yellow engineering tape, felt pen, and clipboard so Kortege and Altemus could flag and map the route Mary had been dragged. (I called a veterinarian to come and check the bears.)

We started at the body and worked back to Campsite 74. I

photographed in black and white and color 35mm. Fred Reese went back to interview the four girls at the ranger station. I had Clark Crane close off the road to the picnic area.

Crane said Mr. M had picked up garbage yesterday, I checked the bear-proof GI cans around the campsite and found the cans to be one-fourth to one-third full, but clean.

Kortege, Altemus, and I put Mary's body in a pouch at the site where she lay.

The report goes on with further details of the investigation.

Coroner Riddle arrived at the campground and examined the body and the scene of the tragedy. Mary Patricia Mahoney's body was removed, to be clinically examined and then prepared for burial.

The carcasses of the two bears were carefully examined by Frauson at the time of the killing, before they were flown to the technical laboratories in Bozeman, Montana.

On the evening in October 1978 that I visited Ranger Frauson's home, I asked him his opinion about the resultant conflict over whether either or both of the two bears killed had done the killing and the feeding.

He told me that his examination, with others at the scene, had shown flesh and blood residue between the claws of both bears. The laboratory reports indicated that one bear had human remains (blood and tissue) between its claws. The other bear had grizzly-type blood on its front feet and claws. This bear-blood evidence coincided with the fact that the second bear, when shot, had been standing guard over its fallen mate. When bear No. 2 had arisen on its hind legs as the rangers approached, Kortege's shot killed it.

I asked about the stomach contents of both bears. Was there any sign that either of them had consumed a quantity of human flesh?

His reply was that under laboratory examination, neither animal's stomach had shown any sign of human flesh. Nor had a diligent search of the surrounding area in the direction from which the bears had returned shown either bear scats (dung) or any other signs of leavings.

Frauson did, however, mention some evidence from a case

involving an Alaska bear. That bear had killed a man and consumed part of the victim. But the bear afterward had regurgitated. Apparently it had been unable to hold the human flesh in its digestive tract. It is possible that a young grizzly, unaccustomed to such a diet, might gorge itself and be forced to regurgitate.

Besides, Frauson noted, the exact measurements the Bozeman laboratory made of the space between the canine teeth of both Many Glacier bears coincided exactly to the millimeter with measurements of the punctures left by such teeth in the body of the unfortunate young woman. There wasn't enough concrete evidence to indicate the presence of a third grizzly in the vicinity, either at the time of the attack or before the return of the two animals directly to the body.

As far as Ranger Frauson was concerned, the evidence he was faced with in the finding of the body, the return of the bears to the body, the matching measurements of punctures and teeth, plus the human blood on the paws and claws of one bear was sufficient to conclude that *that* bear was the cause of Mary Patricia Mahoney's death.

It was only later, during the complete classification of these records, news reports, and official documents, that some qualification was given to the opinions about the two grizzlies.

The item, a portion of which challenges the conclusion, is the following news report on Page 5 in the *Hungry Horse News* of September 30, 1976:

"Ranger Kortege (the killer of the second of the twin bears) noticed that the snow fence near Many Glacier Ranger Station during the night (of Sept. 24?) had toppled and overturned some rocks near the station. It could have been by a bear. If it was a bear, he hasn't been seen."

A retrospective piece in the September 29, 1976, issue of *News, Kalispell,* written by G. George Ostom, includes this item:

"Then, when things got to the shooting stage, the mother bear retreated, only to return the following night to do the digging, rock turning, and tear down the snow fence."

The elapsed time from 6:45 A.M. (the approximate time of the attack) to the arrival of Rangers Reese and Macy at the body of Mary Patricia Mahoney, to Reese's return to the office (there contacting Ranger Bob Frauson at 7:25 A.M.) is actually only 40 minutes. If we subtract the time spent by Reese and Macy in getting to the tragedy, talking to the victim's companions, and then reaching the body (an estimated total of 15 to 20 minutes), we see that the animal in question had only 20 minutes in which to devour quite a large section of its victim and then leave the area.

In a period of about an hour and forty minutes (approximated times from reports: 6:50 to 8:30 A.M.) the bear or bears had killed, dragged, eaten and then had departed the scene before returning and forcing Ranger Macy and his fellow ranger up a tree. Yet, there is speculation that a third bear intervened at the site. This speculation is supported by the comparatively small amounts of consumed evidence in the stomachs of the two bears killed. Reese and Frauson's reports show Frauson being notified at 7:25 A.M., after which he drove to the campsite and phoned the parents about the tragedy, and then was called to rescue the treed rangers at the witnessed time of 8:30 A.M.

The following statement (attributed to Ranger Fred Reese) was made in connection with the return of the bears: "The grizzlies had come in fast to reclaim the body. I spotted one about 75 feet away, sort of circling me, but when I went to fire, the gun jammed. I got out of there fast—very fast."

Item from *Hungry Horse News,* September 30, unattributed: "The two grizzlies were near the body of the dead woman and were aggressive."

The fact that two experienced park rangers were treed by the animals doesn't leave any doubt about the grizzlies' aggressiveness toward humans or about the territorialism that is characteristically displayed by such carnivorous animals after a kill.

The time between 6:45 A.M. (attack) and 7:15 A.M. (consumption of flesh) is only 30 minutes. The time between leaving the corpse (7:15) and returning to it (8:30) is just 75 minutes. It is a very improbable period for a bear to completely digest and evacuate thereafter. It is also a short period in relation to departure and return from a kill. There is a possibility that one reputedly aggressive young bear was frightened off by the noise and commotion after its kill. Perhaps that bear went to the baited trap at the end of the campground, where its mate might have been. Then perhaps the frightened bear returned, reinforced by its litter mate. Remember the antics described earlier in the chapter by the fishermen who were chased into the water or treed at nearby Fisher Gap Lake.

In describing the attack, killing, and dragging of Mary Patricia Mahoney from her tent into the surrounding woods, all witnesses mention one bear. At no moment during that time did anybody see more than one bear. Ellen Fineman's testimony at the inquiry the next morning was: "the bear—young bear—ran with a sleeping bag."

There is no evidence that a larger bear was in the vicinity: not in accounts of witnesses and not in rangers' accounts, before or after the investigations were made.

Ranger Reese's closing of the westward section of the Many Glacier Campground and the setting of the bear trap in the closed section were purportedly done because of the appearance of two young grizzlies that caused no incidents as they traversed the camping area. That evidence, however, does place two young grizzlies in the specific area of Many Glacier Campground, within three days before the tragedy.

Added up, pro and con, 90 percent of the evidence points to the troublesome grizzlies of the Fisher Gap Lake episode and other local incidents as the guilty parties in the death of Mary Patricia Mahoney.

The remaining 10 percent of the evidence (lack of specific intestinal-tract findings) is more of a missing link than it is actual hard evidence of any unidentified third party.

3

Since the Day the Bear Almost Ate Our Baby Daughter

For thirty-two years, as I write these words, we have lived in a suburb of a city of half a million people. Our subdivision had got its start shortly after 1900. We had been in our home less than a year when a black bear came up onto our veranda, heading straight toward our baby daughter in her crib. It was a day we'll never forget.

But let's back up a bit.

Because of my reputation as an outdoors writer in *Outdoor Life, Rod and Gun, True, Saga,* and *Sports Afield* over a few years, I had been asked to produce an outdoor radio program. It was the first of its kind in Canada (one of the first on the continent) and was called "The Hunting and Fishing Club of the Air."

Radio has an insatiable maw. It uses material at an almost vicious rate. I did everything on the show from choosing the music and sound effects to writing and broadcasting the material. That, believe me, is the hard way. But even today very few people have enough knowledge and experience in fishing, hunting, and related outdoors subjects to produce an authentic outdoors program.

"The Hunting and Fishing Club of the Air" was rated second in popularity, above all but one other local radio program. I guarded that reputation with all my ability. The show's popularity came largely as a result of a continuous flow of fresh material, most of it from my own experiences and activities during the previous twenty-five years. My background provided a limited scope from which to draw a full 13 minutes of spoken broadcasting each week, however. Part of what helped me fill my air time was a system of local reports. These came from areas of sea, lake, stream, plains, hills, or mountains in which the recreations took place. I had a great circle of friends, including a number of game wardens, who funneled local reports to me.

The most difficult part of the program to produce was "the story of the week." It featured a true anecdote. That show made me a reputation as somewhat of an expert and brought me sundry requests for opinions and advice.

One of those requests was from a friend of a friend and concerned an early twentieth century drilling—an over-and-under shotgun-rifle combination. It had 20-gauge shotgun barrels and below a rifle barrel of 6 × 57mm caliber. Fitted with beautifully engraved metal, fine French walnut stock and forepiece, and a fantastic Bausch & Lomb scope, it was one of those European handmade pieces that give a man almost the same feeling as holding the reins of a good horse or the hand of a fine lady. The owner insisted I take the drilling home, examine it, and—if possible—test it. He had never shot it but thought he might. He was wondering whether to leave it to a son-in-law or sell it.

If he decided to sell, I offered him the opportunity to name his own price. I took the piece home with me to examine.

Our home in a Vancouver suburb is not a place you'd expect to encounter bears. However, the sea is just in front of us and the coastal mountains rise from the tide line, so there's only a rather narrow strip of settlement between our back lot and the

North Pole. In those days, it held perhaps a dozen homes, with many empty lots between them.

Much of this narrow skirt was and is timbered rock bluffs. To our southwest, and beginning just one narrow lane over from ours, is a forested parkland at least the size of Central Park in New York City. Our park is an admiralty reserve, about as wild as it was when the Indians used it as their campground.

Lighthouse Park, as it is known, remains a natural habitat and somewhat of a sanctuary for wildlife: deer, raccoons, western skunks, mink, grouse, bandtail pigeons, bear, and an occasional cougar. They all use it at will.

Our own property has several large dogwoods. It also had some 100-foot cedars and hemlocks until I felled or topped them. Across the road, those same coniferous species still rise to an impressive 200 feet. The timber continues in that size, interspaced with houses and some scrub woods during the first mile, right to the mountaintop. From there to the northern wilds, the only man-made break is an occasional highway or logging road.

This panorama of rock bluffs was, in 1947, still wild land. We locals annually hunted both grouse and bandtail pigeons within 100 yards of our rooftops. Bandtail flocks still load down my dogwood trees in autumn when the seeds are a ripe red. During one season back then, I kept count of eighteen buck deer that were shot within a two-mile radius. The most destructive pests we had in our rose garden were the does and fawns, which browsed (and occasionally still do) on these ornamental shrubs. Our own property lies directly in the crossover line that the deer take from the upper wilderness of the mountains into the sanctuary afforded by Lighthouse Park.

During the summer of 1947, several sightings of black bear were reported from this crossing and the small network of crescents and winding roads that make up our immediate neighborhood. In a couple of instances, a bear had disturbed the neighborhood dogs for several nights and the large animal had several times been seen ambling unconcernedly up the roadways. I received phone calls asking me to shoot it.

Perhaps my natural empathy for bears was the cause of my making a joke of the requests. I reassured the complainants that I'd lived in the district for a good part of my then thirty-four years and that many bears had passed by, or through, and even been in my own garden at night. I mentioned that no one had ever experienced any harm from those bears—except perhaps an overturned garbage can.

"Shoot it? No! Do it yourself," I said. "Or call the game warden or police."

That was the state of the neighborhood when my friend's friend asked me to try out his drilling. I gave the shotgun-rifle a cursory examination in our living room and picked up a couple of rifle shells and one 20-gauge cartridge. Then, on that early fall afternoon, I crossed the highway beside our property and scrambled up the granite bluffs leading to a section in which I knew the cliffs afforded a safe background.

Actually, I meant only to test-fire the two barrels, especially the magnificent scope-sighted 6 × 57 mm. section of the action. I sat down on a mossy granite hummock and held the beautiful example of gunmakers' art and craft, delighting in the intricacy of the engraving and the silver inlay. As I did so, I noted that the small receiver channel of the firing pin, which took the impact of the exposed side-hammer for the rifle barrel, was askew. It actually wiggled under the pressure of my finger and, when twisted, turned freely in its threaded seat.

Its owner had said the gun had been in the family twenty or thirty years but that he had not shot it.

I thought, *How lucky can you get?*

If the drilling had been fired in that condition, a logical probability would have been either a misfire, which was fine, or a blowback, which was far from fine. Whatever the possibilities, the rifle mechanism—until tightened with a wrench—would be either useless or dangerous to shoot.

With this in mind, I examined the firing-pin sleeve on the other side of the shotgun to find that it was securely screwed down. There in the bright sunlight I had a good opportunity to take the whole gun action down and to look closely at the inner workings.

My attention was on the lower barrel's locking mechanism when, in the direction from which I'd come, I heard a rustling of undergrowth.

Hah! A deer, I thought. *Wonder what it will do when it sees me.*

I remained quite still. Out of the well-worn, slit path through which I had entered the clearing came the head and shoulders of a black bear.

My gut involuntarily tightened in alarm, despite any beliefs of mine about bears being harmless. The animal was only 30 feet away, looking directly at me. To this day, I'm not too impressed by statements of scientists about the eyesight of dogs and bears. I find that they see quite well.

Right then, I think I broke the record for reassembling a gun with fingers suddenly turned to putty.

Damn! I said to myself. *What a time for a bear to show up.*

Suddenly, after moments of almost sullen unblinking study, the bear was walking right toward me.

I let out a shrill whistle, which only made the bear prick up its ears. My yell, which is a husky one, made it stop uncertainly. Then the bear resumed its approach, and I slipped in a single 20-gauge shotgun shell, realizing it held only tiny No. 7 bird-shot.

Oh brother! I thought. *Shades of my Campbell River attack!* (See Chapter 14.)

I brought the gun nearly to my shoulder and stood waiting as the animal advanced slowly but deliberately. Its head was moving from side to side, and the black hackles on its shoulders were upright. I don't remember any growl or snort. Just within 15 feet of me, the bear stopped, blinked its reddish-hued eyes as if unaccustomed to sunlight, and then sniffed at the air in an almost contemplative manner.

What to do?

In that split instant, I decided to wait until that black bear was within five or six feet of me. Then I'd fire the shotgun blast right into its face. If that didn't kill it, the blast could at least temporarily blind and stun it.

Its next move was a side step, then a quick turn toward the nearby shoulder-high brush. The hedgelike growth circled right in behind where I was standing. In the instant that the bear's hindquarters disappeared into the low brush, my legs came to life. I lunged down the trail up which we had both come.

Almost instantly, I looked back over my shoulder to check the bear's position. It had immediately circled the spot I'd been standing in and was coming out again just behind where I would still have been if I hadn't taken off.

Ambush?

At that time, I wasn't too convinced. Perhaps the bear was just curious about what a man was doing in its domain. Perhaps. But the quick circling into cover behind me would have provided it with an ideal opportunity for a quick rush. Today, I wouldn't bet my life on a perhaps, as I nearly did then.

I immediately thought of the incident as a good story of the week for my radio program. But when I got home, still in a bit of a sweat, I told my wife, Thelma, what had happened. She smiled, but her attitude was skeptical. If she—a city girl all her life—was doubtful, what would a weekly audience of outdoor people think?

Who wants to be publicly branded as a damned liar? I thought.

That weekend, I took time off from my real-estate job in Vancouver and headed home at noon on Saturday. I had to write my radio program for the following week. I did have reports to go over in that connection, but the main item was missing. The irony was that a bear story always brought good audience reaction.

Damn! I thought. *Why can't I think of a good one from the past?*

Here it was fall already, the hunting season was open, and my business commitments didn't leave much time for hunting and fishing trips. That was a disturbing situation, for much depended on such expeditions and their success. My managerial salary in real estate was not yet that high, and we had a new mortgage, a two-year-old son and a four-month-old daughter. If I couldn't get out hunting, there would be little prospect for story sales to national magazines. Those sales had often filled in the financial slack.

Besides, city life has always left me tense, a soujourn in the wilds being the most reliable release. Hell! What to do?

We had just finished lunch, and I was moping in my chair beside the lunch table. Thelma picked up the remaining dishes, put them into the hot water in the sink, and looked curiously at me.

"Why are you so far down?" she asked.

"I don't have a story for the weekly program. I'd give an eyetooth for one."

She stared at me thoughtfully.

"Why don't you go out and trim the hedges. You'll think of something. You always do."

"Trim the hedges, hell!" I shook my head in disgust.

Thelma walked off into the living room. Minutes previously she had picked up Grant, our two-year-old son, from the lawn and had put him in for his afternoon nap. Then she had fed Pamela, our infant daughter, and taken her out to her sun-crib on the front veranda. I was in the kitchen and could vaguely hear the infant's contented cooing sounds, those of a well-fed and adequately burped child, happy and contented before going to sleep.

I was self-indulgently nursing a disgruntled reflection upon the onerous duty of producing a radio program without a story of the week.

Suddenly, from the living room came Thelma's strained voice.

"Michael, Michael! There's a bear on the lawn!"

She was anxiously beckoning me from the end of the living room.

How like a woman! I thought. *No sense of timing in her attempts at humor.*

My answer was pettish.

"Thelma, please! For godsake, don't kid me. Not right now! I'm really worried . . ."

Her voice cut over mine with a higher pitch.

"There *is!* There *is* a bear! I tell you there *is* a *bear!*"

The anguished accents of her tone were getting to me. She wasn't that good an actress. My still hesitant buttocks lifted reluctantly from the kitchen chair. I walked casually into the living room, half willing to be taken on a daytime "quail hunt."

I stared directly over her shoulder, my eyes following her pointing finger.

"Now, where in hell is this bear? Jesus! . . ." The word died in a gulp in my throat.

Thelma's finger was lined up on a big black bear that was standing on its hind legs right in the nearest corner of our lawn.

I blinked and then shook my head in utter amazement. Not at midday! What in hell was it doing there?

During the twenty-five years I had then lived within a mile of that spot, I had not once seen a bear right down in the area of houses during daylight. At night, yes.

But, there it was! At practically high noon! On our lawn!

For a moment I was transfixed. The big animal was still on its hind legs like a circus bear. It swung its head about in a circle, its blunt, tan-hued snout extended, nostrils dilating as it sniffed the air.

It seemed to be trying to pick up the scent of our daughter, who could still be heard gurgling contentedly in her crib on the end of the veranda closest to the bear.

The distance between them was only 20 feet in a direct line.

My rifles! Where was the handiest one?

I ran through the hall. Kneeling before the closet in the bedroom, I reached into the shadowed light of its inner recesses. My hand closed over the familiar barrel of my old Ross .303 British army rifle. Another twist of my wrist flipped the nearby packsack upside down on the floor.

Meanwhile from the area of the French doors into the living room I heard the skitter of flying heels. Thelma was running out to pick up our baby daughter.

Before me on the floor among the jumbled miscellany of compasses, knives, cord, hooks, camera, emergency rations, shotshells, and cartridges, lay two brass shells. The hard, scratching sounds of a bear's claws climbing the granite base of our veranda stairs had spurted adrenaline into my veins. Again, I felt as if my fingers had turned to putty, but I managed to pick up two shells and cram them into the rifle.

The scratching of the bear's claws on the wood deck sounded

dangerously close as I lunged for the double, glass-paned front doors.

Christ! How long the time and the distance! I thought. *Has the bear got to Thelma and Pam?*

At the doorway, I saw my wife with the baby in her arms. She had swept Pam from the crib, the bear's head almost at her skirt. In that split second, Thelma ran toward me as I stepped out, rifle cocked and pointed toward the marauding animal.

As my wife, carrying the baby, swept through the doors, the bear's eyes came menacingly up to mine. I now stood between it and the stairs up which it had so quickly ascended. Then, as I turned to pull the door shut behind my retreating wife, the bear moved toward the head of the stairs, six feet away, directly in front of me. Its sidelong glance was malevolent. The bear's head was down and its shoulders hunched forward as it moved in its pigeon-toed walk.

"Lock that door!" I yelled at Thelma over my shoulder.

With the full intention of shooting, I raised my gun nearly to my shoulder. Then the realization struck me that if I missed, the bullet would go straight through our neighbors' kitchen window, only 60 feet away. Any member of that family of four could be sitting there having lunch.

The bear, meantime was moving resolutely toward the stairs. I held my fire. At the top step, it stopped and swung its head toward me, just five feet distant.

Again I felt the urgency to kill it before it made a lunge.

Once more, at point-blank range, the jab of conscience. The bullet might travel through or miss the animal, and the trajectory of a ricocheting bullet is unpredictable.

The bear and I stared at each other, both uncertain.

It turned slowly. Then defiantly, taking its time, it thumped down the several wooden stairs leading to the granite ones. At the bottom tread, the bear stopped, half turned, and glanced up at me. I realized I still couldn't shoot it without risking a ricochet off the stonework.

Then, with its hackles still erect, the bear slowly paced across the intervening 30 feet of lawn toward the high concrete retaining wall that carries the main highway above the front of our property at roof level, some 50 feet distant. At the high wall, behind our peach tree and grape arbor, the bear hesitated. It was just on the far side of the big dogwood, with a mountain-thick granite and concrete background. Here was my chance to kill it safely.

I'll never know what made me hold my fire. The animal seemed to be wondering whether it should have allowed itself to be bluffed out of its prey on the veranda. Its belligerence nettled me. Its attitude was similar to that of the bear I'd met earlier that week a few hundred feet farther up the bluffs.

I sighted, tentatively, just behind the shoulder where lay its heart.

The bear then began slowly to climb the wall. Then I was startled by the sounds of approaching feet behind me. My wife was again standing there, quite close.

"Jesus Christ, Thelma," I yelled. "Get inside!"

The bear was still close enough to get to both of us in seconds. The last thing I wanted was another complication. Stung by my angry command, Thelma moved back.

In that instant, the bear made a quick scramble for the top of the 20-foot wall. With its forepaws on the edge of the wall, the bear hunched itself in the manner of a man heaving himself over an obstruction of the same kind. Just as its shoulders and head thrust above the concrete guard rail, two cars sped past, traveling in opposite directions along the narrow highway. They passed each other right in front of the bear, the closer car not more than three feet from its snout. Startled by the vehicles, the bear let go and came back down the wall toward me.

The rifle at my shoulder roared.

"You hit it! You hit it!" my wife screamed as the bear dropped momentarily to its knees.

Thelma was still standing behind me, fascinated. This time I pushed her roughly through the open glass doors. My stomach was like jelly. I don't remember what my words were as I warned her, but they must have been strong enough to keep her indoors that time.

I lunged down the steps to the garden just as the bear struggled to its feet, roaring and squealing. It had covered most of the 20 feet between us. I picked a point on the top of its front shoulders. This had to be *it!* I didn't want a wounded bear within 25 feet of our thin glass front doors.

As the shell exploded, the muzzle of the rifle jumped.

The raging animal lunged three or four steps in my direction before crumpling and sliding head first to within about 10 feet of me. Then the bear rolled over on its side, legs kicking spasmodically. The gurgling final breaths spilled blood from the bear's mouth onto the lawn.

Suddenly, I realized I had no more shells in my gun. I knew of bears that had gone almost a mile carrying more than two bullets.

Thelma was once again at the top of the stairs, in a veritable trance of excitement.

"Did you kill it? Did you kill it?"

I leaped up the stairs three at a time.

"I hope to God so! You stay in the house, goddamnit!"

During the next few seconds, I was back at the closet rummaging for shells for the .303 British rifle. I couldn't find even one more. A stunning thought went through my mind. One of those two shells I'd fired at the bear had been given to me six years earlier, when a black bear had come after me at Campbell River. How odd a circumstance.

A moment later, a clip of .303 British army ammunition spilled out of a hastily dumped drawer of mixed shells. Slipping three of them into the rifle's magazine and one into the breech, I hurried to the top of the stairs and looked down.

The bear lay prone on the lawn, where I had left it, oozing blood.

It seemed only seconds later that people began to arrive. Then came the reporters and photographers. I hadn't yet phoned the police.

What irony. The bear story, which had been my compelling desire, was there, all right. But everybody else had it first. It became a national news item with a photo of me standing over the bear as the "hero."

What a laugh! While I was groveling over a spilled haversack of gear and looking for shells, my wife had run out onto the veranda, rushing along the wall between the bear and the railing, to pluck our baby from her crib. Reaching the child, she had rushed back past the bear just as I came out the door. I would have been far too late if her act had not come first.

The bear was within two feet of the crib and undoubtedly could have reached the child with a short lunge forward. When I arrived it was uncertain in its purpose, obviously startled by my wife's swift intervention.

The bear's stare at me, previous to its hunch-shouldered, pigeon-toed walk toward the top of the stairs, together with its sidelong glance at me, openly declared its lack of fear, if not its contempt.

Believe it or not, there is a transference of intent between the eyes of men and animals, as there is between two men. That bear apparently sought to make sure of my hesitancy to attack it.

When it came toward me again after the two cars passed, the bear was showing no hesitation, no fear. Fear would have been evidenced in a hurried trot. We'd been dealing with a man-conditioned wild animal.

Just over half a mile from our property is Cypress Creek, which was once a robust producer of migrant salmon; three miles farther along is the much larger Capilano River, a major spawning stream for salmon. Neither distance is too great for the daily trek of a bear (although the Capilano River was unlikely, because of fairly dense residential habitation). At that time of year, berries—the main summer and early fall diet of black bears—were becoming scarce. The seasonal patterns of the bear families are governed by the availability of food. In the fall, bears traditionally turn to river systems for an abundance of fish flesh. Meat-eating comes just as naturally to bears as does the hunger that causes it.

A fat baby is *meat*.

When the bear was first sighted by Thelma, it was at the exact spot on our front lawn from which she had just plucked our two-year-old son. Perhaps his scent had originally attracted the bear from the deep timber and bush across the street. This forested area is several hundred feet long and has a deep ravine, a perfect approach cover and a normal pathway of wildlife.

The bear, having picked up the first child's scent and then

having heard the cooing sounds of an infant on the high veranda nearby, followed the completely logical bear practice of rising up on its hind legs and swinging its head in a circle. The bear was trying to locate the origin of the sounds and pick up any airborne scent.

If I had been as alert as my bush experience should have made me, I would have run out and picked up the child— knowing full well that the animal's actions were directed to locating a meal. Perhaps personal fear was an element in my running to find a gun. I don't know, but I wouldn't discount the possibility.

However, a gun meant both defense and offense to me, mainly because of my upbringing as a hunter. Furthermore, my five years as a paid protector against human violence had helped condition me to strapping on a sidearm (which I did not ever draw, even in emergency) as a backup to whatever physical prowess I could claim (I had twenty-nine fights and training as both a boxer and a wrestler).

On balance, it seemed logical that my first reaction would be to get a rifle. It provided one sure way to dispose of a marauding animal. On the other hand, a rifle provided me and my family some reassurance in case the bear was just passing through.

The distance from the lawn, where the bear was originally sighted, to the crib on the porch was 20 feet in a direct line, but the crib was 15 feet above the lawn. The approach by way of the stairs was some 60 feet: across the lawn to the long stairway, around the corner of the balustrade, thence along the 20-foot deck. The normal time it would take for a person to walk that distance would be from 30 to 90 seconds.

As I sit writing this account in our den, with the rug which the bear's hide became on the floor beside the fireplace, I realize that I had never tried to record how long it took the bear to get to the crib. Whatever that period was came within one second of the time that I arrived at the doorway just as my wife left the crib with the child in her arms.

I decided to reenact the sequence with the old .303 British caliber Ross Rifle that killed the bear. According to a stopwatch, the little drama took me 28 seconds to reenact.

However, there was foreknowledge in the staging. If the time were doubled to allow for delay by uncertainties, the bear still came 60 feet in 60 seconds. I consider that quite fast, if the animal was scenting prey, then following a path across the lawn, up the unfamiliar staircase, and along the veranda.

Such timing and the distances covered leave me with absolutely no doubt that the bear's intention was to find and take the "morsel" that was causing it to scent the air.

But for my wife's heroic act, that black bear would have become another man-eater.

Just last week two of our neighbors asked, "Mike, what should we do about the bear we keep hearing is in this neighborhood?"

My answer, "Go to your police office first. Then phone the British Columbia Fish and Wildlife offices."

No, I have no intention of getting into this one—at all!

4

The Century's Worst
Attack Case

Stone Creek flows under the forestry access road in Ontario's Algonquin Park through a four-foot-diameter culvert, emitting a loud chuckle as it tumbles past dark boulders. Its amber, beaver-pond waters move down the small gradient and form minor rapids for 50 yards.

It is not a man's kind of angling stream. Really a creek, it has attracted boy visitors to that Ontario government park for at least a decade.

The wildlife tragedy that occurred just 250 feet up its brushed-in edges is the worst of its kind anywhere in modern history. Three youths—fishing rods in their hands, brook trout on their minds—either were stalked and ambushed or were confronted and killed almost instantly by a healthy, six-and-a-half-year-old male black bear. The bear had no previous record of rogue incidents in those highly utilized parks, roads, and public environs for camping, canoeing, and fishing.

60

In the nearby village of Pembroke, most of the downtown houses and buildings are of red brick and have white corniced windows. There are small hygienic-looking trucks with serving windows, vending hot, deep-fried potato chips in a distinctly homey, small-town atmosphere. This is the northern Ontario town that experienced the extraordinary 48-hour, 250-man backcountry search for three missing boys.

The 48-hour intensive search was for three lads who actually strayed no more than 400 feet from the car in which the fourth member of their party (and the only one who survived) was sleeping. That member was Richard Rhindress, age eighteen. His companions included fifteen-year-old George Halfkenny, the first to be killed. George was dragged 200 feet upstream and then half buried. His brother, twelve-year old Mark Halfkenny, was killed in company with his buddy, Billy Rhindress, who was subsequently partially devoured. All three bodies were found within 15 feet of each other, under a partial covering of rotten wood and earth, less than 200 yards from the point at which they had left the road to fish one bank of the stream. George Halfkenny had taken the right bank to try the swollen, fresheting springtime waters. Mark Halfkenny and Billy Rhindress went up the left bank a few minutes later.

Tired from a drive that had begun at midnight and ended at the park entrance at 4:00 A.M. the eldest boy, Richard Rhindress, went to sleep in the back of the car. He was within 400 feet of his brother William and the two Halfkenny brothers at all times, yet he didn't see them alive again.

Why did this triple tragedy remain hidden from an organized 250-man bush and air search by helicopter for 48 hours after the boys were reported missing by Richard Rhindress?

Why did a completely healthy and robust 275-pound black bear kill them?

Black bears generally are thought to be neither man-killers nor man-eaters.

Some of the answers may assist others in avoiding such a tragedy—perhaps not.

When I entered the flame-hued autumn deciduous forests of Ontario on October 5, 1978, I was accompanying Conservation Officer Lorne O'Brien, who had killed the man-eating bear. He was carrying a .30 / 30 rifle and asked me if I wanted an arm. He grinned when I replied, "If *you* couldn't kill a bear that came after us—well, I'm damn sure *I* couldn't."

We made our way along the brush and timber-covered bank of Stone Creek along the route George Halfkenny had taken. In the otherwise silent woods, the waters—even at their low autumn ebb—were quite audible.

O'Brien stopped a couple of minutes later, turning toward me and the stream. He inclined his head toward the small pond beside me.

The branches broken by the bear and boy during the attack six months earlier still dipped into the water. The creek was partially blocked by large black boulders, which formed a deeper pool in the slight slope. Other twigs were bent into the newly fallen leaves, and pine needles covered the loamy forest floor. Some of the signs of the struggle showed faintly but were almost blended with the soil of the tiny open spot.

I looked back into the woods, noting that from almost any direction a man or an animal could approach another, quietly and without being seen, to within 5 to fifteen feet. Having donned hip waders at the truck, I strode out into the center of the stream to scrutinize the scene.

O'Brien moved up to the creek bank, pointing to the deeper section of the stream.

"His rod was driven tip foremost into the stream bottom," said the conservation officer. "About twenty feet of line was trailing in the water. The lure was missing."

I nodded, asking, "You figure he was hit from behind?"

"Well, all evidence would make it look like that." He pointed into the pool where it flowed past my legs. "His glasses might still be in there—somewhere. They were never found."

I don't know why, but that statement shook me a little. Perhaps it was because the pool in which I was standing had been the focal point of the boy's interest. It was a typical little trout pond. I could imagine the youngster's deep preoccupation as he sneaked up to the opening in the bushes, gingerly sliding the rod tip out in order to drop his lure into the waters and avoid being seen by the trout. I'd done it a thousand times myself, boy and man, intently preoccupied with catching whatever lurked deep in those waters, oblivious of anything else. Into my mind came the vivid image of the bear hitting George Halfkenny from behind, right where O'Brien now stood.

Goddamn! The kid's glasses might be under my feet! I looked down into the amber waters. Nothing glistened. I waded out of the stream.

As I backed up to about 10 feet to gain a better perspective, Lorne leaned out over the stream. "His jacket was in the creek, caught on this branch."

He pointed into the water. If I had stood silently right where I was, a youngster intent upon catching a speckled trout in this pool would be unlikely to see me. Even a youth who had taken two courses in bush survival, such as the ones George Halfkenny had been put through by his father, wouldn't likely be in any way alert to sudden attack. I stared at O'Brien leaning toward the stream. He didn't look like anything but man. He didn't even remotely resemble another bear.

The reports I'd read said the bear might have mistaken the boy for another bear. That had seemed to me an inadequate explanation. It is not a known trait of bears to ambush their own subspecies. They are usually aggressively loud and dominating or else immediately submissive and evasive. Why had that reason been put forth?

That question, when I asked it of Denis Voight, an animal biologist who'd been studying black bears for two years with the Ontario Ministry of Natural Resources in its scientific center at Toronto, had brought to light some information.

I had asked him why a boy in normal colored clothing could be thought to resemble a bear. He had replied that the boy was in dark clothing. I shook my head and argued that his face and head would be light-hued.

Voight looked a trifle embarrassed.

"George Halfkenny, the first victim, was a colored boy, Mr. Cramond."

"What the hell! I hadn't heard or read of that! Why was it kept out of print?"

Voight was taken aback. He hesitated.

"The department," he finally said, "didn't feel it was relevant."

Voight remained silent. I could see that bureaucratic reasoning was determining his reticence. The department's concern over racial controversy could inadvertently have resulted in the loss of rather interesting evidence, it seemed to me.

If the boy was black of skin and wore dark clothing, some credibility might be given to the idea that he somewhat resembled a bear when stooped over. But I was not convinced that the attack could be blamed on that factor. Certainly I didn't believe it as I looked at O'Brien's silhouette against the sheen of waters.

Absently, I asked him what he had said.

"The boy's jacket was caught on this branch in the creek."

"It was water-soaked?"

"It had been in the running water for several hours."

Again a snag was undone in my mind.

The interview and reports had said that a tracking dog named Cloud Three—brought in by Ontario Provincial Policeman Ray Carson—had been given the jacket but had neither tried to seek a direction from the scent nor made any effort to pick up a ground trail. That, too, had confounded me.

I had asked Denis Voight what the dog did when given the jacket. He had answered with immediacy: "It just ran around in a circle, then defecated."

I wasn't surprised by the statement. Dogs, hounds, suddenly let out of the confinement of a vehicle and feeling the spirit of the chase, or hunt, often do just that. But they also defecate when alarmed. I had looked at Voight's young face. He wasn't being defensive. I made a suggestion: "Have you ever heard of a dog being afraid of a bear?"

His reply was immediate: "Yes, but that dog's stool was solid —typical of a dog that eats food like pure Purina—not loose."

I didn't say anything. Fear doesn't suddenly liquify excretia. It causes the stomach to contort and eject what is there. I thought the dog might have been affected by nervous fear. Any normal tracking dog could pick up a two-day-old bear scent if heavy rain hadn't fallen. And the dog might pick up the scent of residual bloodstains. It might also have caught the scent of the bear, where it was later found to be standing guard over the corpses and feeding on the remains. That could have made the dog nervous and fearful. I've been with too many cougar dogs on deer kills and hunting dogs on bird or animal scents to accept the notion that even if the jacket was water-cleansed the dog wouldn't find some faint scent.

O'Brien stood looking at me. He pointed away from the stream and strode into the brushy bottomland.

"The bear dragged him in here, over this log," said O'Brien. "You can see the rotted birch broken away here."

I looked down at the spot he indicated. Branches had been broken back from a rotten birch log, which was still encased in its more durable gray-brown bark. The earth about it was disturbed, a state that can last for years, until the deposits of falling leaves, rains, and snows compress the marks once more to the levels surrounding it. The disturbance was still evident. Particularly when it was fresh, the trail could have been readily followed *without the aid of a tracking dog.*

Why had it taken 48 hours to discover the boys' remains?

As O'Brien pushed his way through the bushes, around logs, and between trees, he was following the six-month-old drag trail—not from memory but by actually finding disturbed earth, broken branches, and dislodged rotted tree trunks. Some 100 feet beyond the site of the killing, we came to a more open portion of forest and shrubs, thence back to the stream. The water was shallower now. Boulders protruded enough for us to walk across the brook without wetting a foot. O'Brien crossed and stopped at the far side to await me. I crossed over, and when I looked back, I could see for 50 feet into the forest we'd just walked through.

No doubt about it. Anyone approaching from the side we were now on could see—and most probably hear—anything moving along the path taken by the bear dragging its first victim.

O'Brien moved about 15 feet into the fairly open forest and said, "Evidence—a lost running shoe—showed that one of the boys was killed here." He then moved approximately 10 feet upstream and stopped. "This is the spot that showed evidence of the other boy being killed here."

I looked back at the opposite bank again.

Even if the two youngsters had backed up, after yelling at the bear burdened with their companion, they would not have gotten much farther. A black bear—which species has been reliably clocked at 45 miles an hour—could quickly have reached them —both of them. Such a sequence seems especially likely if the two youngsters were—as youthful buddies tend to be—protective of a companion, particularly the brother of one.

My mind was now unfolding a much more logically possible full sequence of the events—the reason I had driven 3,500 miles from British Columbia.

Lorne pointed to the spot where the third victim had been killed. I went over, curious about a scrub alder that still had an ivory-hued wood section. I'd seen a photograph of that very alder and had been told it was three inches thick and had been broken off by the furious attack of the bear. That statement had struck me as barely credible. Bears have enormous power, as I well knew from considerable experience. But a three-inch alder tree broken off?

Upon first seeing the photograph of the alder, I pointed out that it had not been broken off, but was merely split at a fork, something a man could have done by putting his foot against it. Actually, the alder was not more than two inches thick below the crotch. I could, at sixty-five years of age, still cause such a split in a green alder. Lorne nodded in agreement when I revealed my thoughts.

We had had similar early lives. He was born in the backcountry of Ontario and had shot his first deer at age ten on the trapline of his dad, Percy O'Brien, in Victoria County. He had joined the Ontario government twenty-five years previously and had worked in the game department most of the time since. On our drive to Algonquin Park, he and I had talked about predator hunting.

During my years as a B.C. Provincial policeman, I had been

an ex-officio game warden and had spent eighteen months hunting cougars with the top predator hunter in that field. As a youngster I had followed the West Vancouver–Howe Sound trapline of Yoshi Furakawa with his son, Haro. The two of us set traps and skinned the resultant raccoons, skunks, mink, and otter. The rural conditions then had been much the same. O'Brien and I spoke the same language.

When I asked him how many black bears he had killed, he became a bit self-conscious.

"Well, over the twenty-five years, 250 bears," he said. "Some of them were wounded, others just troublesome. You get called in because the animal is causing a problem. You have to do what is necessary so that no one gets hurt. Some of them are right in the city."

He looked apologetic, as if expecting criticism.

I laughed, perhaps somewhat cynically.

"Lorne, I know how you feel. The goddamn public calls you in to handle what they can't, and then some sonuvabitch who would wet his (or her) pants if the bear just growled at him criticizes you and makes a big stink because you had to kill it. They don't realize that you'd prefer to let it go. I've been through it—often."

He grinned wryly, but didn't continue. I asked him how bad the bear problems had been during the past three or four years, the ones relevant to this tragedy.

"Well, Mike, 1974 was a high year. I had to destroy fifty-one black bears. In 1977, I destroyed seventeen. In 1978, only one."

We had been driving through the unimaginable flame-red, orange, and yellow of the thick Ontario forest, along a long stretch of gravel road into the park. The timber was shorter and denser than the predominantly coniferous forest of the Pacific Coast, where most of my hunting had been done.

I broke the silence with a question: "You say you gridded the forest by helicopter in your search around Stone Creek. Did you see any bears?"

His answer startled me: "Yes. We counted twenty-nine bears in three hours—searching over four square miles of area."

"You mean an area four miles square, Lorne?" was my astounded reply.

"No," he said. "It was an area two miles by two miles. Four square miles. There were a lot of bears in there. It's swamp and grass country, and the bears were out eating grass. There isn't much else for them in the spring. They feed most of the day."

I was thinking about that statement as he moved from the sites of the killings into a much darker area of the forest. There was a covered-in quality about the area: a rising bank over which the dense branches of coniferous trees blotted out most of the light. As he stopped, I noticed a piece of red plastic ribbon staked to the earth. He pointed to the darkest part of the gloom, where there was a bit of a bank overhang. There was another red marker pinned to the forest floor. Around it, the earth still bore the marks of a pacing and grubbing bear. Debris, which had been piled over one of the bodies, lay where it had been cleared off.

"One of the brothers lay here. The other one where you're standing. Young Rhindress's body was draped over that log—the bear feeding on it. The bear had eaten most of the lower body."

The horror of the story made the scene oppressive. Looking up from the third red ribbon marker toward the light of the sky, I turned and pushed aside the branches on the bank. We had come only 50 or 60 feet from the site of the killings on the creek bank. The bear had dragged all three bodies into this dark haven. Even while men searched the nearby forest and helicopters flew overhead, the bear remained on guard over the bodies. That was a very unusual behavior for either a black bear or a grizzly.

I turned to face O'Brien: "Where did you kill the bear, Lorne?"

He nodded and turned toward the low bank beyond the pile of debris.

"Up there," he said as he pushed his way into an opening in the forest. I followed O'Brien and was surprised to find a newly cut rough logging trail within 15 feet of the tragedy. Beyond an all-terrain vehicle's deep wheel marks, where its wheels had sunk into the mud, the green of swamp grass showed.

Lorne looked around the opening, a bit uncertain of his exact location in the clearing made by the vehicle. He walked back to a log, stood beside it, and peered at the details at the end of the swamp.

"The bear was by that log over there when I first saw him. This must have been where I was when I shot. This logging trail is new to me."

I looked over at the fallen log lying in the swamp, then back over my shoulder, down the path of the logging vehicle. Clearly showing above the trees were the wires and insulators of the hydroelectric power line, the crossbars like a grave marker. Hell! Only 400 feet from safety.

Those poor kids! How the hell could it all happen?

Our own vehicle was parked just down by that line of wires.

If I walked down there and O'Brien called to me, I could hear him. I could hear him if he yelled, screamed, or whistled. It seemed impossible that the sound of a shout would fail to penetrate the forest through that short distance of backwoods silence. Just how in hell could it all happen?

Canadian press accounts that I'd seen on the Pacific Coast contained information that was minimal and inaccurate. The bear killing was reported in the *Province,* Vancouver, in the following manner, in part:

Three Mauled to Death by Algonquin Park Bear
The injuries sustained by the youths were consistent with a bear attack. They were not consistent with a human attack.

The latter statement seemed cryptic as I had reread the item. It was one of the reasons for my driving across the continent. The account continued:

Authorities shot and killed a 350-pound black bear found near the bodies of George Halfkenny Jr., 16, his brother Mark, 12, and William Rhindress, 15, all from Canadian Forces Base, Petawawa, who entered the park to go fishing.

After an all-day search with a helicopter and tracking dogs, the search party found the bodies about 37 kilometers west of the huge park's northeastern entrance.

As searchers approached, the article said, they saw a black bear "sniffing" around the bodies, and a conservation officer killed the animal.

Now that I was on the scene, however, I was to find that the bear weighed 275 pounds, the search ended almost 48 hours after the youngsters disappeared, and the animal had actually stood guard over the bodies. I was also learning the reason for the phrase, "not consistent with human attack."

Pieced together from interviews with members of the Ontario Department of Natural Resources, news and magazine clippings, and conversations with the residents of Pembroke, there gradually emerged the story of youngsters' fishing trip that ended in the century's most tragic wildlife incident.

Richard Rhindress, at eighteen, was the oldest in the group of four. The boys got into the car in the middle of the night and drove the 30 miles to the park, arriving there about 4:00 A.M. That was before the regular staff at the entrance could check them in. For a while they moved from creek to creek.

Familiar with several streams in the park from having fished there with his father (Warrant Officer George Halfkenny of the 8th Canadian Hussars), George Jr. went off on his own. He and his companions had learned bush survival from his father, who had led a Canadian Forces Survival training expedition in the remote Yukon Territory. They had brought with them a knapsack with food and extra clothing. They were unlikely to become lost, particularly near a stream.

George caught four speckled trout and carried them, as youngsters will, in the pockets of his jacket. About noon, the three young anglers had lunch together. Then they fished some more.

At Stone Creek, about 5:30 P.M., George wanted to try again. He left the others at the car and walked up the side of the creek on which O'Brien and I would walk six months later. He went out of their sight and hearing into the bush and into the rush of spring-swollen waters. He traveled no more than a couple of hundred feet, to where O'Brien and I made our first stop.

Mark Halfkenny, twelve, and Billy Rhindress, fifteen, decided to try the other side of the stream for a last chance at catching trout. Richard Rhindress, the eldest of the group, expressed a desire only to stay in the car, to catch up on sleep lost during the previous night's trip to the park.

At 6:30 P.M. Richard awakened, got out of the car, and yelled for his brother and companions. When they didn't answer or return, he honked the horn and waited. Perhaps twenty minutes later, he got into the car and drove around looking for another possible exit from the creek.

Some time later Richard returned to the rendezvous site at the power-line crossing of Stone Creek. Then he went up the side of the creek that George Halfkenny had followed into the bush. He neither saw nor heard anything of the group. It is possible that he was within 100 feet of the bear and the dead boys, all of which apparently were by then on the opposite bank.

After returning to his car and honking the horn in the approaching darkness, thinking it might give the boys a clue to where to come out, Richard sensed something was seriously wrong. He left the area near midnight, returning to Canadian Forces Base at Petawawa. There he told his story to Mrs. Charlotte Halfkenny.

In response to her plea for assistance, Lieutenant Colonel Bob Billings, 8th Canadian Hussars, sent 200 men to search the area that night. By early morning there were 250 men in the vicinity of Stone Creek, none of them realizing they were looking for bodies or a killer bear. As Algonquin Park regulations do not permit the carrying of firearms without a special permit, all of them were unarmed, and those regulations apply even to game wardens.

Lorne O'Brien's departmental report reads as follows:

Mr. J. A. Simpson
Superintendent and District Manager
Algonquin Park

At approximately 1:47 A.M. May 14, 1978, I received a telephone call from Dispatcher Fortier, O.P.P. Pembroke. She stated three (3) boys were missing in Algonquin Park off the Achray Road at the main transmission line. They had gone fishing up a small stream and hadn't returned by 7:00 P.M. on May 13, 1978. She wanted to know if I knew where this was, and if I would go and have a look for the boys. I said I would.

I patrolled the area with Ministry vehicle 2433-75. I checked out the stream with a flashlight. It was raining and [there was] a low lying fog. I could not find any signs of the boys. I checked all the roads in the area. I failed to find any signs.

Approximately 5:00 A.M. I received a radio call from O.P.P. Pembroke to meet at the Military Police Headquarters, Base Petawawa. I went there, met with the older brothers of the Rhindress boy and heard their story. I left by army helicopter to the area where the boys were last seen. We looked for approximately three (3) hours with no signs of the boys. We returned to the Base.

I phoned Algonquin Park District Office and spoke to Mike Wasylkiw, letting them know the boys were lost. I picked up Gordon Hamilton, Conservation Office and returned to the area where the boys were lost. We searched until approximately 9:30 P.M. with no results and returned to Pembroke.

Approximately 6:00 A.M., Monday, May 15th, Officer Hamilton and myself returned to the area where the boys were reported lost, ran down all leads we could and checked with everyone we could that might have some information. We returned to Pembroke at 6:00 P.M.

At 6:40 P.M. I received a telephone call from O.P.P. Dispatcher Wagner that the boys were found dead. A bear was guarding the three bodies. They asked me to bring my rifle and they would pick me up by Army Helicopter at Brum's Field, then would fly me in to the area where the boys were found to shoot the bear.

I said I would be ready in ten minutes at Stafford Fire Hall. The helicopter picked me up and flew me into the area. We went straight to where the bodies were being guarded by the bear.

At this time there was a lot of noise with the Helicopter and two hundred and fifty (250) men on the road behind. The bear was with the bodies but walked away when we approached. The O.P.P. dog handler from North Bay stayed with me.

Approximately seven or eight minutes later the bear showed up to the south about sixty (60) yards where I shot it. He went down with the first shot; it was hit through the shoulders. He kept trying to get up and I shot him again firing a few times. It was difficult to see as it was getting dark.

It was a two hundred and seventy-five pound male black bear. The bodies of the three boys and the bear were transported to Pembroke at 12:30 A.M. The bear was transported by Stu Stock, Conservation Officer from Stonecliffe.

On the afternoon of May 17th we returned to the area with Ministry officials and O.P.P. Identification Branch to photograph the area where the boys were killed.

Lorne R. O'Brien
Conservation Officer
Pembroke District

May 19, 1978

During my own five years of investigative work, I had made hundreds of such reports to department heads, so the clipped understatement was familiar. No dramatics, no opinions, no rhetoric, just plain facts. *All* the necessary facts. And be tight-lipped to the press!

Well, I'd been on both sides. Five years as a cop had taught me not to discuss a case even with my wife (who is about the least likely woman to gossip or reveal a secret that I ever met). And twenty-two years as a newsman had taught me never to reveal any indication of a source of controversial information. In fact, I had learned to protect sources even under threat of prosecution or cajoling from editors.

I walked away from O'Brien, down the ruts left by the logging vehicle in the edge of the swamp. About 20 feet into the tall green swamp grass, a tree stump rose above the growth. Beside it, rotting on the damp soil, lay the log that had been the tree. Standing beside the stump, I turned back to O'Brien.

"Is this where the bear was, Lorne?"

He pointed a bit to my left, nearer the bank beyond which we had seen the three red ribbons in the "den."

"About ten feet from you, Mike. Just beyond that stump."

My calculations were estimated from years of experience in pacing off the point-to-point measurements to hundreds of fallen animals and birds, in an effort to gauge the effective yardage of both shotshells and rifle bullets. I was surprised.

"This is nearly sixty yards—in the dusk of evening. You could barely see a bear in this tall grass. That's a tough shot!"

"Well—I *had* to make it. We'd moved the bear off the bodies. It could have gotten away. That would have left us in a bad spot, not knowing, when we saw it again, if it was the bear that did the killing."

We walked back to the car, down the freshly scoured-out path of the logging vehicle. Once back at the vehicle I had a feeling of relief. A couple of forestry men who knew Lorne O'Brien had stopped by the truck. They kidded with us for a few minutes. Neither of us revealed our reasons for being there or what I did for a living. Minutes later we were driving west to an area of bushland in which berries were known to attract sometimes as many as 100 bears during that time of the fall.

I was looking out of the window on my side when I spoke: "Why did they suspect foul play in the death of George Halfkenny?"

O'Brien was silent for a moment, obviously judging his words.

"Well," he said, "there was a round hole in the back of his jacket when they picked it up. They thought it was a bullet hole."

"What kind of a hole was it?"

"It was just a hole like a cigarette would burn—or a spark."

"Hell, a bullet hole doesn't look like that."

"Yeah, I know. A bullet hole looks as if a nail had been pushed through the cloth, rough around the edges, the threads cut."

"What would make them think it was a bullet hole? Who did they suspect would kill the boys?"

"That I can't tell you. You will probably hear that story around town. But not from me."

I made up my mind to go into that phase when I got beyond the realm of departmental reticence.

"Denis Voight told me," I said, "that all three boys were killed instantly, without signs of struggle."

"Well, you saw it back there. A few feet apart. The tracks where the bear paced between the bodies are still there. We kept most of the men clear of that area during the investigation."

"Yeah. Voight also said that the scats of the bear had been examined, that the latest ones were pure protein, as from eating meat, the older ones normal spring grasses. He said the stomach contents were also identified as human flesh. That there were shreds of red wool along the track where George Halfkenny had been carried and dragged, showing the sequence of attacks. Did you find any other evidence to the contrary?" I asked.

"No. It all seems pretty clear," said O'Brien.

"Then why in hell did it take forty-eight hours to find them?"

O'Brien was silent for a moment before speaking: "It takes a bit of time to get departments acting together. I think Richard Rhindress was so shaken that he didn't get all the details straight at first. And that put some of us searchers off the track."

"What about Carson's dog, Cloud Three?" I asked. "Why didn't it pick up the track?"

"That's a tough one, Mike. The jacket was in the water."

"But what about the tracks, or scent, from the ground?"

He shook his head, remaining silent.

When I pointed out that some dogs are afraid of bears, he acknowledged that but didn't comment.

Finally he said, "What do you think happened, Mike?"

My answer had been evolving quite slowly.

"Well," I responded, "I now have a couple of clues that I didn't have before. And two things have bothered me all along. One: Why did it take forty-eight hours to find three boys just four hundred feet from their car? Two: Why did the animal kill them? Right now, I'd say that an army-type organized search by a body of men would place the searchers about fifty feet to fifty yards apart, keeping each other in sight or hailing distance. And, the search would start at the creek. That would place them off the creek banks, and they would be out of sight of the bear in that denning spot. They probably wouldn't even be actively looking for any signs for at least the first five hundred yards. They were searching for living, walking, talking persons. That would cause them to pass by the critical area right away. Does that sound right to you?"

O'Brien nodded.

"It's just about what happened. It wasn't until Ray Carson went in the second day, with Richard Rhindress, and covered the side of the creek you and I went up that they found the jacket. From that find they concluded that they were looking for bodies. The supposed bullet hole between the shoulder-blade section of the jacket threw them off. As the coat was turned inside out, the fish still in it, foul play was suspected."

The reports that I had examined before came together there.

At the instigation of Constable Ray Carson, two groups of men were organized at the road and sent to search shoulder to shoulder along both sides of Stone Creek, downstream and upstream. At 6:15 P.M. on the second day, there was a yell from the south side of the waterway.

"We've found the bodies, and there is a bear with them!"

Among the group of twenty searchers who had gathered at the scene was Warrant Officer George Halfkenny, father of two of the boys. The bear, faced by such a gathering of men, reluctantly abandoned its prey and moved off into the bushes.

Armed only with a police 38-caliber special, Constable Carson ordered the men not to follow the animal. All of them were unarmed. If the bear was driven from the source of its food, it could be lost. The party withdrew from the scene. The summons went out to bring O'Brien in with his rifle.

His report read: "We went straight to where the bodies were being guarded by the bear.

"At this time there was a lot of noise with the helicopter and 250 men on the road behind. The bear was with the bodies, but walked away when we approached. The OPP dog handler from North Bay stayed with me.

"Approximately seven or eight minutes later the bear showed up to the south, about 60 yards, where I shot it. He went down with the first shot, hit through the shoulders. He kept trying to get up, and I shot him again, firing a few times. It was difficult to see, as it was getting dark."

For stark realism in few words, Ernest Hemingway could not have been more frugal. Because I had once tracked a wounded black bear at dusk in similar surroundings, I was aware of O'Brien's lack of embellishment.

I turned from the enormous panorama of autumn's brilliant hues. The vehicle's windshield faced an open section of valley that lay below the dirt road. O'Brien was pointing to the small side road ahead.

"We'll turn in there. That section usually has a lot of bears during the fall."

Along the way we stopped several times. O'Brien would point to the bark of a poplar or birch, indicating the scratches and claw marks made by bears. Some marks were simply the holes where cubs had driven their claws through the bark, four imprints at a time, in order to climb the trees, probably at the urging of a parent. Other markings indicated where mature bears had climbed trees. Still other trunks bore the bite marks, which are not fully understood. And we saw the scratches at six to seven feet above the ground, which indicate a marker of some sort, perhaps a territorial signpost.

There were dozens of such bear-marked trees right beside the road. The evidence suggested a large population of bears. During perhaps 30 miles of bush travel, some of it on roads almost grown back to forest, we saw no wildlife except one ruffed grouse. But it was most apparent that Algonquin Park's black bear population was extremely large.

O'Brien turned the vehicle around at a beautiful lake surrounded with flaming colors. I got out and stared at the calm azure surface. Reflections of red, yellow, orange, green, and the black and navy of shaded conifers performed a rainbow dance on the rippling waters. O'Brien walked down from where he had turned the vehicle and looked out with me.

"This is a good fishing lake," he told me. "People get in here by canoe."

"Anyone ever report being bothered by bears?"

"None that I have heard about."

"Do you think bears will cause trouble in the future?"

"Oh, they're bound to create problems, particularly if people don't stay away from them. Most often, though, a bear will just take off. You know that, Mike."

But bears are all different. Each one has as definite a personality as each human being does: some shy, some brash, some vicious, some insane. I had close to thirty fights in my day, most of them brawls outside a ring. I didn't at any time seek a fight; I simply took on what was offered or couldn't be avoided. Some men just go looking for trouble. They are *mustachi,* or *macho,* or just plain bullying bastards; you name it. It is a quirk of their nature to dominate you if they can. Among the thousands of people you meet in a lifetime, you're bound to run afoul of such persons.

Bears are much like men.

We got back into the truck and headed back to Pembroke. Lorne O'Brien was not a talker. He is a quiet-looking man, and he acted that way. Yet he had killed 250 bears during twenty-five years of public service. When I had asked him what weapon he used for most of them, his answer had shocked me: "Oh, a lightweight twenty-two-caliber autoloader."

"For Crissake, only a twenty-two rifle?"

"Yes. Most of them have been at close quarters. You hit the animal in the ear or the eye. The bullet penetrates the brain, and the bear goes down like a log. You can't use a high-power weapon in the city or around houses. The bullet could stray if it went through the bear. Somebody might get hurt."

He shrugged his shoulders in a matter-of-fact manner. That was it. In a government department, you learn to do things in ways that avoid criticism from the public. To hell with personal safety. Lorne didn't say that or even acknowledge his own courage.

I put the next question obliquely: "Do you have any of the long-skulled black bears in Algonquin Park? Ones that have a narrow, almost wolflike head?"

"Yes. Most of the bears in Algonquin are that type—rangy."

"Are there many of the round-headed, full-faced ones—that look something like a grizzly head?"

"Not too many. But the one that killed the boys was more of that round-headed type."

That was interesting. There are no grizzly bears in the eastern portion of North America. Never have been. Their evolution to a separate species obviously occurred along the backbone of the continent at the Rocky Mountains. At one time I'd wondered if blacks and grizzly bears might, upon occasion, cross. An old bushman had told me of (while following his trapline) watching a grizzly stalk, kill, and then eat a black bear. Wherever the two species compete in the same territory for food, the black bears always hurry off when grizzly bears enter the picture.

I was conscious of O'Brien's glance at me when I asked about the nature of the bear. He broke the silence.

"You said you had wondered about what made the bear attack," he reminded me. "What do you think about it?"

His question was my own, to myself.

"Lorne, I think you could meet 50, perhaps 1,000 bears, and 49 or 999 of them would take off, perhaps stand curiously and examine you or even make a bluff rush at you. The 50th or 1,000th would, or *will*, take after you! And it might kill you. That goes for black or grizzly. I've been attacked from behind by a black bear. Killed another one when it came toward me. Had one come up on my porch after our baby daughter; that one also turned on me when I was letting it get away. And I've had two grizzlies, which I'd wounded with sloppy shots, both come after me. At least 50 of the bears that I actually saw took off in a hurry. There were maybe another 100 that I didn't see, but I heard them rushing off, leaving tracks that showed they took off in a hurry. I can't forget the one that came from behind—in full charge. And I didn't even know it was there until I saw the facial expression of the guy facing me."

He listened to my statements without comment. Finally he glanced at me, then back to the road. He spoke thoughtfully: "There is always the one animal you can't figure. Yesterday I killed that red fox you see in the back of the truck. It was attacking neighborhood dogs. It's probably rabid. I'm sending its carcass to the laboratory for testing. We've had a few cases of rabies reported lately."

I listened intently, shocked at the statement. "The bear that killed the boys wasn't rabid!" I said. "Voight at the Resources Center says the tests taken on the head were negative."

"Yes, they were negative. No rabies."

Where did that leave the situation? Official Ontario sources that had been in on the investigation had proclaimed that bears in Algonquin Park don't fish for or eat suckers from the creeks. They dismissed the idea that the bear first smelled fish; two fish were still in the pocket of George Halfkenny's jacket when it was found. Yet the animal ate human flesh. One scientist suggested that the boy, bending over, had seemed to the bear like another bear. "Bears," said the scientist, "have very poor eyesight. The bear might initially have been attracted to Halfkenny by the smell of fish in his pocket. The bear killed the boy very quickly. It may then have smelled blood and associated the boy's remains with food."

So goes the theorizing, logic—and lack of it.

It is known that a bear did kill all three boys. All three victims bore lacerations of the head, neck, and torso that matched the claws and incisor teeth of a bear. Portions of two victims were eaten. Human remains were found in the stomach of the killed bear. Two days of excretia in the denning area had positive evidence of man-eating. All that is certified by laboratory examinations.

Why were the boys killed?

Perhaps this is oversimplification, but the reason may have been *simply because they were there.*

George Halfkenny was on the edge of a creek that runs through forests where twenty-nine black bears were counted by expert observers in a low-flying helicopter in an area of 4 square miles—that is, 2 miles by 2 miles. The thirtieth bear (this one with the corpses was never seen from the air) hit its victims without warning. It hadn't (as some killer bears have) been in any manner charted or reported as a rogue bear. It wasn't ear-marked as a bear that had been transplanted. In other words it wasn't a bear that had given trouble elsewhere, been downed by tranquilizer gun, tagged in both ears with metal tags, and then released in another district. When such animals are killed, either the tags are in the ears or the ears show a notch where the tags have been torn from the flesh.

The natural-resources authorities very clearly specified that no such markings existed on the head of the bear Lorne O'Brien shot.

When I stood where Mark Halfkenny and Billy Rhindress were killed, it was quite evident that both of them could have witnessed the bear bringing the body of their companion up the opposite bank.

If the bear had been denning up (and earlier scientific examinations of scats indicated that it had left excretia with grass only in it) and had dragged the boy across the creek before the two other boys got there, it could have ambushed them from behind, as it seemed probable the bear had earlier done to George Halfkenny.

Perhaps they saw the bear and yelled at it or just stood stupefied with fright. The quickness of a bear allows it to cover a short distance in split seconds. They died within feet of each other and left a can of soda pop and a running shoe to mark the spots. If they tried to scare the bear away from their companion, they died heroic deaths, fruitlessly.

5

COME QUICK!
I'm Being Eaten
by a Bear

*The summer of 1977 was my third summer in the Yukon-Tanana Upland of Alaska, doing geologic field mapping for the Alaskan Geology Branch of the U.S. Geological Survey. I began working for the USGS in the summer of 1975, making helicopter-assisted traverses in the highest terrain of the 6,000-square-mile Big Delta quadrangle.

The second summer, the project chief and I found it necessary to map the geology by backpacking, usually a week at a time, since our budget did not provide for helicopter expenses. Then, in 1977 we were again funded for helicopter transport,

*Author's note: Cynthia Dusel-Bacon, author of this chapter, is a remarkable young woman. Her account of an attack by a black bear, when she was working as a geologist in the Alaskan mountains, is one of the most dramatic and well-written stories I have ever read.

The story appeared first in the February 1979 issue of my favorite magazine, Alaska. The copyrighted story is reprinted here with the permission of its author and Alaska.

after an initial month of backpacking. All five geologists in our group, after being transported by air to the field area, usually mapped alone. Although I was concerned about the added risk brought about by working alone, I did enjoy the solitude and the opportunity to be by myself in a beautiful wilderness area.

Every summer in the upland area we saw bears. The first one I saw was walking slowly along on the far side of a small mountain meadow. I froze. It didn't see me and disappeared into the forest. Another time I was walking through a spruce forest and saw a black bear moving through the trees some distance away. Again, I apparently was not noticed. The second summer while I was backpacking, I encountered a small black bear coming along the trail toward me. I had been busy looking down at the ground for chips of rock when I heard a slight rustling sound. I looked up to see the bear about 40 feet in front of me. Startled, it turned around and ran off in the other direction, crashing through the brush as it left the trail. This particular experience reassured me that what I had heard about black bears being afraid of people was, in fact, true.

During the third summer, I saw my first grizzly, but only from the air. Although other members of our field party had seen them on the ground, I felt fortunate to have encountered only black bears. Grizzlies were generally considered to be more unpredictable and dangerous.

I had hiked through the bush unarmed each summer, because our project chief felt that guns would add more danger to an encounter than they might prevent. A wounded, angry bear would probably be more dangerous than a frightened one. Consequently, she had strongly discouraged us from carrying any kind of firearm. We all carried walkie-talkie radios to keep in constant touch with one another and with our base camp. Everyone was well aware of the dangers of surprising bears or getting between a mother and her cubs. Whenever I was doing field mapping, I always attempted to make noise as I walked, so that I would alert any bears within hearing distance and give them time to run away from me. For two summers this system worked perfectly.

In the summer of 1977 we were scheduled to complete the reconnaissance mapping of the Big Delta quadrangle. Since it is such a large area, we needed helicopter transportation to finish by mid-September. At about 8:30 A.M., August 13, 1977, Ed Spencer, our helicopter pilot, dropped me off near the top of a rocky, brush-covered ridge approximately 60 miles southeast of Fairbanks. I was dressed in khaki work pants and a cotton shirt. I wore sturdy hiking boots and carried a rucksack. In the right outside pocket of my pack I carried a light lunch of baked beans, canned fruit, fruit juice, and a few crackers. My walkie-talkie was in the left outside pocket, complete with covering flap, strap, and buckle. I was to take notes on the geology, collect samples with the geologist's hammer I carried on my belt, record my location on the map, and stow the samples in my rucksack. Standard safety procedure called for me to make radio contact with the other geologists and with our base camp several times during the day at regular intervals. The radio in camp, about 80 miles south of the mapping area, was being monitored by the wife of the helicopter pilot. I was to be picked up by helicopter at the base of the four-mile-long ridge on a gravel bar of the river at the end of the day.

After noticing, with unexpected pleasure, that I was going to be able to use a narrow trail that had been bulldozed along the crest of the ridge, I started off downhill easily, on the trail that passed through tangles of birch brush and over rough, rocky slopes. The ridge was in one of the more accessible parts of the quadrangle. There are a few small cabins about five to ten miles downstream along the Salcha River, and a short landing strip for airplanes is about five miles from the ridge. Fishermen sometimes venture this far up the river too, so bears in the area probably have seen human beings on occasion. That particular morning I wasn't expecting to see bears at all; the hillside was so rocky and so dry and tangled with brush that it just didn't seem like bear country. I felt that if I were to see a bear at all that day, it would likely be at the end of the day, down along the river bar and adjoining woods.

I descended the ridge slowly for several hundred yards, moving from one outcrop of rock to another, breaking off samples and putting them in my pack. I stopped at one large outcrop to break off an interesting piece and examine it. A sudden loud crash in the undergrowth below startled me and

I looked around just in time to see a black bear rise up out of the brush about 10 feet away.

My first thought was, "Oh, no! A bear. I'd better do the right thing." My next thought was one of relief: "It's only a black bear, and a rather small one at that." Nevertheless, I decided to get the upper hand immediately and scare it away.

I shouted at it, face to face, in my most commanding tone of voice. "Shoo! Get out of here, bear! Go on! Get away!" The bear remained motionless and glared back at me, I clapped my hands and yelled even louder. But even that had no effect. Instead of turning and running away into the brush, the bear began slowly walking, climbing toward my level, watching me steadily. I waved my arms, clapped and yelled even more wildly. I began banging on the outcrop with my hammer, making all the noise I could to intimidate the bear.

I took a step back, managing to elevate myself another foot or so in an attempt to reach a more dominant position. By this time the bear had reached the trail I was on and was slightly uphill from me. It slowly looked up the hill in the direction from which I had come and then stared back at me again. I knew that in this moment the bear was trying to decide whether it should retreat from me or attack. Suddenly the bear darted around behind the outcrop and behind me. My next sensation was that of being struck a staggering blow from behind. I felt myself being thrown forward, and I landed face down on the ground, with my arms outstretched.

I froze, not instinctively but deliberately, remembering that playing dead was supposed to cause an attacking bear to lose interest and go away. Instead of hearing the bear crashing off through the brush, though, I felt the sudden piercing pain of the bear's teeth biting deep into my right shoulder. I felt myself being shaken with tremendous, irresistible power by teeth deep in my shoulder. After playing dead for several minutes, I came to the horrible realization that the bear had no intention of abandoning its prey.

"I've got to get my radio in the pack, I've got to get a call out," I thought.

My left arm was free, so I tried to reach behind myself to the left outside pocket of my rucksack to get at the walkie-talkie.

My heart sank as I discovered that the buckled flap on the pocket prevented me from getting out my radio. My movement caused the bear to start a new flurry of biting and tearing at the flesh of my upper right arm again. I was completely conscious of feeling my flesh torn, teeth against bone, but the sensation was more of numb horror at what was happening to me than of specific reaction to each bite. I remember thinking, "Now I'm never going to be able to call for help. I'm dead unless this bear decides to leave me alone."

The bear had no intention of leaving me alone. After chewing on my right shoulder, arm, and side repeatedly, the bear began to bite my head and tear at my scalp. As I heard the horrible crunching sound of the bear's teeth biting into my skull, I realized it was all too hopeless. I remember thinking, "This has got to be the worst way to go." I knew it would be a slow death because my vital signs were all still strong. My fate was to bleed to death. I thought, "Maybe I should just shake my head and get the bear to do me in quickly."

All of a sudden, the bear clamped its jaws into me and began dragging me by the right arm down the slope through the brush. I was dragged about 20 feet or so before the bear stopped to rest, panting in my ear. It began licking at the blood that was now running out of a large wound under my right arm. Again the bear pulled me along the ground, over rocks and through brush, stopping frequently to rest, and chewing at my arm. Finally it stopped, panting heavily. It had been dragging me and my 20-pound pack—a combined weight of about 150 pounds—for almost half an hour over rocks and through brush. Now it walked about four feet away and sat down to rest, still watching me intently.

Here, I thought, might be a chance to save myself yet—if only I could get at that radio. Slowly I moved my left arm, which was on the side away from the bear, and which was still undamaged, behind me to get at that pack buckle. But this time the pocket, instead of being latched tight, was wide open —the buckle probably was torn off by the bear's clawing or from being dragged over the rocks. I managed to reach down into the pocket and pull out the radio. Since my right arm was now completely numb and useless, I used my left hand to stealthily snap on the radio switch, pull up two of the three segments of the antenna, and push in the button activating the transmitter. Holding the radio close to my mouth, I said as loudly as I dared, "Ed, this is Cynthia. Come quick, I'm being eaten by a bear." I said "eaten" because I was convinced that the bear wasn't just mauling me or playing with me, but was planning to consume me. I was its prey, and it had no intention of letting me escape.

I repeated my message and then started to call out some more information. "Ed, I'm just down the hill from where you left me off this morning . . ." but I got no further. By this time the bear had risen to its feet; it bounded quickly over to me and savagely attacked my left arm, knocking the radio out of my hand. I screamed in pain as I felt my good arm being torn and mangled by claws and teeth.

It was then I realized I had done all I could do to save my life. I had no way of knowing whether anyone had even heard my calls. I really doubted it, since no static or answering sound from anyone trying to call had come back over the receiver. I knew I hadn't taken time to extend the antenna completely. I knew I was down in a ravine, with many ridges between me and a receiving set. I knew there was really no chance for me. I was doomed. So I screamed as the bear tore at my arm, figuring that it was going to eat me anyway and there was no longer any reason to try to control my natural reactions. I remember that the bear then began sniffing around my body, down my calves, up my thighs. I could read the bear's mind as it tried to decide whether it should open up new wounds or continue on the old ones.

I didn't dare look around at what was happening—my eyes were fixed upon the dirt and leaves on the ground only inches below my face. Then I felt a tearing at the pack on my back, and heard the bear begin crunching cans in its teeth—cans I had brought for my lunch. This seemed to occupy its attention for a while; at least it let my arms alone and gave me a few moments to focus my mind on my predicament.

"Is this how I'm going to go?" I remember marveling at how clear my mind was, how keen my senses were. All I could think of as I lay there on my stomach, with my face down in the dry grass and dirt and that merciless, bloodthirsty animal holding me down, was how much I wanted to live and how much I wanted to come back to Charlie, my husband of five months, and how tragic it would be to end it all three days before I turned thirty-one.

It was about ten minutes, I think, before I heard the faint sound of a helicopter in the distance. It came closer and then seemed to circle, as if making a pass, but not directly over me. Then I heard the helicopter going away, leaving me. What had gone wrong? Was it just a routine pass to transfer one of the other geologists to a different ridge, or to go to a gas cache to refuel and not an answer to my call for help? Had no one heard my call?

The bear had not been frightened by the sound of the helicopter. Having finished with the contents of my pack, it began to tear again at the flesh under my right arm. Then I heard the helicopter coming back, circling, getting closer. Being flat on my face, with both arms now completely without feeling, I kicked my legs to show whoever was up above me that I was still alive. This time, however, I was certain that I was to be rescued because the pilot hovered directly over me. But again I heard the helicopter suddenly start away over the ridge. In a few seconds all was silent; it was an agonizing silence. I couldn't believe it. For some reason they'd left me for the second time.

Suddenly I felt, or sensed, that the bear was not beside me. The sound of the chopper had frightened it away. Again—for about ten minutes—I waited in silence. Then I heard the helicopter coming over the ridge again, fast and directly toward me. In a few seconds the deafening, beautiful sound was right over me. I kicked my legs again and heard the helicopter move up toward the crest of the ridge for what I was now sure was a landing. Finally I heard the engine shut down, then voices, and people calling out. I yelled back to direct them to where I was lying. But the birch brush was thick, and with my khaki work pants and gray pack I was probably difficult to see lying on the ground among the rocks.

Ed was the first to spot me, and he called the two women geologists down the slope to help him. Together they managed to carry me up the hill and lift me up into the back seat of the helicopter. I remember the feeling of relief and thankfulness that swept over me when I found myself in that helicopter, going up and away over the mountain. I knew that my mind was clear and my breathing was good and my insides were all intact. All I had to do was keep cool and let the doctors fix me up. Deep down, though, I knew the extent of my injuries and knew that I had been too badly hurt for my body to ever be the same again.

They flew me to Fort Greeley army base in Delta Junction, about an hour's trip. There emergency measures were taken to stabilize my condition. I was given blood and probably some morphine to deaden the pain. An hour or so later I was flown up to the army hospital in Fairbanks and taken immediately into surgery. For the first time that day I lost consciousness— under the anesthesia.

My left arm had to be amputated above the elbow, about halfway between elbow and shoulder, because most of the flesh had been torn from my forearm and elbow. To try to save my right arm, which had not been so badly chewed, the doctors took a vein out of my left thigh and grafted it from underneath my badly damaged right arm, through the torn upper arm, and out to my lower arm. This vein became an artery to keep the blood circulating through my forearm and hand. Four surgeons continued working on me for about five hours, late into the evening. They also did some "debriding"—that is, removing hopelessly damaged tissue and cleaning the lacerated wounds of leaves, sticks, and dirt. I stayed at Fairbanks overnight and then was flown out at 3:00 P.M. Sunday for San Francisco.

By this time our branch chief had managed to notify Charlie, also a geologist for the U.S. Geological Survey, of my accident. Both were waiting for me when I arrived at the San Francisco airport at 1:00 A.M. Monday. I was taken immediately by ambulance to Stanford Hospital and put in the intensive-care ward.

Then began the vain attempts to save my right arm. For more than a week I held every hope that the vein graft was going to work. But a blood clot developed in the transplanted artery and circulation stopped. The pulse that had been felt in the right wrist and the warmth in my fingers disappeared and the whole arm became cold. Although another amputation was clearly going to be necessary, the doctors felt they should wait until a clearer line between good tissue and bad tissue became evident. Then they would amputate up to this point and save the rest.

But before that line appeared, I began to run a very high temperature. Fearing that the infected and dying arm was now endangering my life, the doctors took me into the operating room, found the tissue in my arm to be dead almost to the top of my shoulder, and removed the entire arm. Not even a stump of that arm could be saved.

As if this was not trouble enough, my side underneath the right shoulder had been opened up by the bear when it tore out and consumed the lymph glands under my right arm. This area was raw and extremely susceptible to infection. It eventually would have to be covered by skin grafts, skin stripped from my own body. But before the skin graft could be done, new tissue would have to be regenerated in the wound to cover the exposed muscle and bone. I stayed in the hospital for weeks, absorbing nourishing fluids and antibiotics intravenously and eating high-protein meals of solid foods. Slowly, new flesh grew back to fill the hole, and the plastic surgeon was able to graft strips of skin taken from my right thigh to cover the raw flesh under my right shoulder. The thigh skin was laid on in strips like rolls of sod, kept clean and open to the air for many days, until it "took." These operations hospitalized me for a total of six weeks.

During my long days and weeks in bed I had lots of time to review my experience and ponder some of the questions that had puzzled me on that unlucky day of August 13. Why didn't I simply bleed to death after the bear had so badly mauled both my arms and chewed through the main arteries in each? My doctors told me that because I had been in excellent physical condition and my arteries were young and elastic, the blood vessels constricted and cut off the flow of blood very quickly after the flesh was mangled. Even the open ends of the arteries closed themselves off and kept me from losing all my blood, and my life.

Had my call for help over the walkie-talkie really been picked up? Or was the helicopter merely making a routine run over the area when Ed spotted me on the ground? I learned later that my first call for help had been heard, by Bev Spencer, the helicopter pilot's wife. She understood it clearly, and immediately radioed her husband that I was in trouble. She gave him what little information I had been able to transmit about my location, and he started right toward my ridge. He had also heard my call, but not clearly enough to be sure of the message. But why did he leave my ridge after he flew over me the first time? Where did he go? Actually, Ed hadn't been able to spot me from the air the first time, and realizing that he couldn't fly the helicopter and look for me at the same time, he decided to pick up another geologist first. The second time over he did spot the bear, and me, from the air, but he also saw that the terrain was too rough for only two to get me up the ridge to a landing spot. So again he left, flying back to pick up a third geologist from another area. Finally, with two assistants, he made his landing and led the successful rescue.

But why did the bear attack me in the first place? I could see three possible reasons: The bear may have been asleep in the bush and I startled it; it may have seen me as a threat, not only to itself but also to any offspring that might have been nearby; or it was very hungry. I do not even consider a fourth possibility, one that often has been suggested as a reason for discriminating against women in similar situations. That is the possibility that wild animals, particularly bears, often are attracted by the scent of women's menstrual blood. But for the three summers I worked in the bush, I never had any trouble with wild animals, and on the day of the attack I was not menstruating.

Regarding the first possibility, which I believe is the most likely one, the bear may have been asleep in the brush and woke startled when it heard me hammering on rocks. It should have had plenty of time to collect its wits, however, as it stared at me and circled me before charging. Although the terrain seemed rather unsuited for a comfortable lair—large, rectangular blocks of broken-off rubble covered the ground and were almost covered by birch brush—such a hidden spot may have seemed ideal to the bear.

It is also possible that the bear was instinctively fearful for the safety of a cub in the area. I never saw any other bear that day, but the helicopter pilot, after he left me at the Fort Greeley hospital, went with Fish and Game officials to find the bear that had attacked me so that it could be checked for rabies. They did, and shot what they believed to be the guilty one— a 175-pound female. They reported the presence of a one-year-old cub in the area, but left it to take care of itself. If the mother encountered a strange creature in its territory and simultaneously noticed the absence of its cub, it could have reacted violently, out of fear for its cub. The fact that I saw no cub suggests the possibility that the mother bear didn't either, and may have felt, in sudden panic, that I had something to do with its disappearance.

The third possibility—that the bear was extremely hungry— could have been a factor, too. The post-mortem analysis of the bear's stomach revealed only a few berries and some "unidentifiable substance," which may have been parts of me. I hadn't noticed any blueberry patches on the ridge, so the bear could have been tired of hunting for berries and decided to try for larger game, since it came upon me, either unexpectedly or deliberately, at a distance of only 10 feet.

One fact is certain: that bear wanted me for dinner. Once it tasted my flesh and blood, it did not intend to let me get away. But I did get away. Furthermore, I'm up and around again. The bites on my head have healed, and my hair has grown back and covers the scars completely. My right side is covered with new skin; my left stump is strong and has good range of motion. I'm fitted with artificial arms, and I'm ready to resume my interrupted life as both wife and geologist. It will be difficult for me to operate a workable arm on my right side, where I have no stump, and to manage the use of the arm and hook on the other side, where I have no elbow. But with practice, I know that I will eventually be able to make my prosthetic devices and my feet and mouth do many of the things my hands did for me before. I plan to continue my job with the U.S. Geological Survey. Both Charlie and I have loved our work there, and our colleagues have been tremendously supportive of me throughout the ordeal. I'd like to stay with the Alaskan Geology Branch, perhaps specializing in petrography—the examination of sections of three-hundredths-of-a-millimeter-thick wafers of rock under the microscope to determine their mineral composition and texture. With only minor adaptations to the microscope, I should be able to do this work as effectively as I was able to do it before my accident.

I am determined to lead as normal a life as possible. I know that there are certain limitations I can't get around, having to rely on artificial arms. But I'm certainly going to do the best I can with all that I have left. And that's a lot.

Author's note: Having read this story twice over, I wrote to Cynthia Dusel-Bacon through Bob Henning, editor and publisher of the magazine Alaska *and heard quite promptly from her in her home in California. She told me that she was going on with her work as a geologist and thanked me for my suggestion that she should become a writer.*

My request for permission to republish her story was met with by her statement that she had previously promised a writer friend of hers, living in Alaska, the right to use the story in a forthcoming book he was compiling. She said that she first should consider whether the story's use in my book would interfere with his plans. Now that is true loyalty, the purest ethic, a trait unfortunately seldom witnessed.

During a later telephone call, Cynthia Dusel-Bacon told me that she was flying back to Alaska with her geologist husband to return to the scene of the attack. Surprised and fearful for her safety, I suggested that they take a double-barrel shotgun, loaded with slugs. She had stated that they were going armed with a high-power rifle. She listened to my explanation that a shotgun slug has immense shocking power wherever it strikes, that a high-velocity rifle bullet could possibly travel right through a bear, unless very expertly placed, that a shotgun slug anchors a large animal almost immediately by knocking it down. It is often the preferred weapon of government employees who are forced to kill problem bears. She understood.

Cynthia Dusel-Bacon inspires a strong desire in others to protect her, mostly because of her extreme desire to be self-sufficient. She is totally independent, unmarked by self-pity or indulgence, determined to be useful. And she is accomplishing it.

I spoke with her on the telephone just before this writing. She had just entered the front door, from her car, and had left her purse and keys in the rush to the phone. She asked me if I would mind waiting while she got her purse and closed the door —obviously alone at the moment. In seconds she was back, out of breath in her rush.

In answer to my, "How are you, Cynthia," her reply was "Great. Just great! I was just going to write you, Mike."

We talked for a minute or two. I asked her about her projected trip to Alaska. She was enthusiastic.

"Oh, we've been up there and back. It was a great trip! We spent 450 hours in a helicopter. My husband is doing geological work up there. We went back to the scene of the attack. It didn't look like anything at all, just a wild area with a neatly bulldozed road right past the spot. I was a bit let down."

Her words reminded me so much of geologist Ted Watchuk, who, bare-handed, fought a grizzly bear and later revisited the scene. He said, "I looked around, and it was just a section of ordinary bush and trees. I thought, 'Huh! No monuments or anything. Nothing is changed. Just the same as it was before we came.'"

She responded thoughtfully, "I know what he means. It was a dull feeling."

I asked her what she was going to do in the future. She laughed.

"I've got plenty to do," she explained. "We're finishing our new home. This week it is such a mess. I've been washing my dishes in the bathtub, with my feet—a bit of a struggle. But we're going to get our swimming pool, too. Dad and Mom are helping us—I'm going on with my geology career. . . ."

How could God not love her?

6

Greater Love
Hath No Man

There are two Glacier National Parks. One is the large, world-renowned Glacier National in the northerly Rocky Mountains of Montana, U.S.A. The other is the much smaller, less pretentious, and undeveloped Glacier National lying between the towns of Revelstoke and Golden in British Columbia, Canada. The Glacier in Canada is west of the Rocky Mountains, situated in the slightly less spectacular Selkirk Range, about 200 road miles north and west of the more widely publicized parklands.

Both, however, have almost equal infamy as the scenes of attacks and killings by indigenous grizzly bears.

Malcolm Aspeslet of Edmonton, Alberta, was nineteen years of age when he shielded his girlfriend, Barbara Beck, eighteen years old, by throwing his own body across hers in defense against a suddenly attacking grizzly bear. In searching through the annals of more than 500 bear attacks made during the past fifty years, I find no other example of such selfless courage.

Slightly built and quiet, Malcolm doesn't look like the romantic image of a hero. And he doesn't go around acting like a hero, despite several medals given him for bravery during the attack. His casual grin almost disguises the fact that he does look as if he has suffered a grizzly attack.

Barbara, now his wife, the mother of his two children, says, "He's an imp!"

You get just that feeling as you talk with Malcolm. He laughs easily about his known mischievous nature, saying, "Oh, yeah! I've had a lot of fun. Never did anything bad, just crazy things. A lotta fun. We used to steal Ol' Man McLean's watermelons. Put farm equipment up on top of barns on Halloween. Barb makes more of it than it is."

"He's an imp, all right! Don't listen to him, Mr. Cramond!"

To listen to Malcolm Aspeslet, now twenty-seven years old, a man and an indulgent father, you have to ask him questions. Unlike Barbara, who isn't usually recognized for the heroine that she is, he isn't a garrulous self-starter. He responds to prompting with factual detail.

I asked him about his background, his experiences with other bears. He laughingly related some of them.

"I was cooking at the Northlander Motor Lodge that summer. Bears used to come around regularly.

"There was this one black bear, an old sow, that you could tell what time it was by her visits. At exactly 7:00 P.M. she came around for handouts. She was there every day, never missed.

"Nellie, one of the lodge workers, called her Sarah. She was Nellie's pet bear. She used to pat her like a dog. Every night the old lady had a hunk of salmon or something for Sarah. She used to feed it to her by hand.

"Nellie wore the thickest glasses I ever saw. She used to say she couldn't see beyond her nose without them.

"She liked old Sarah. So that she wouldn't mistake her for any other bear when she came back, Nellie painted a turquoise ring around her neck, by hand, while Sarah was eating. The bear didn't pay any attention. She was kind of a pet.

"I had a funny experience with her—Sarah, the bear, that is —one day.

"The hotel kitchen had a big walk-in refrigerator that I had to get provisions out of. I was walking by it to get some other stuff and noticed the door was open. I gave it a kick and knocked it shut.

"That big, heavy door came back flying right off its hinges. Sarah was behind it. She came over it, in a rush like you wouldn't believe, taking a whole pan of bread with her. She went flying out the door spilling loaves of bread all around her.

"It was funny!

"Oh, yeah. It was a big freezer door. Boy! She was real strong!"

Barbara was laughing too as Malcolm talked. She nodded her agreement with the humor of the scene.

"There were lots of bears around the lodge during the summer," she explained. "Sometimes as many as seven grizzlies digging in the garbage dump. We used to drive down there at night, when we were off work, to watch them. They'd get into the cans and barrels. You wouldn't believe the small size of the hole they could pry themselves into and pull back out again, even the big ones.

"They'd spook easily at first—like when a car door opened or closed, or when you whistled or turned the car lights on. Then, gradually they became bolder, even came toward the car. We got out of there in a hurry when they did.

"But Old Sarah, the black bear, she didn't cause any harm. She used to come right up to the hotel door when she wanted to be fed. Like Mal says, she was a pet. Particularly Nellie's."

I asked Barbara if she was an outdoor girl.

"Oh, no. I climbed all the seven miles up that mountain trail to the cabin at the top, where Malcolm and I got it, in vanity boots—see?" She lifted the big album. "In this photograph you can see them. I sure slid around a lot in them to get up there and back!"

One-year-old Sherri, their daughter, was pointing her finger at the color photograph. It was a happy photo—one taken the day before they had been attacked on the trail. It showed a rough pathway, a typical mountain track. The mountains in the background showed snow-streaks well below the elevation to which they had climbed. Malcolm had snapped the shot of

Barbara. She was wearing a pair of those high-fashion street boots you see skittering across the pavements of any modern city.

I looked over at Malcolm. "Are you a bushman, Malcolm?"

"No. I like the outdoors, but I'm not a bushman. I lived some of my life on a farm. I had been up to the cabin on Balu Pass three times before. I trained for cross-country events."

I noted, "You must have been in good shape."

"Oh, it's not that much. We took our time. In fact, we saw a sow grizzly with two cubs down below the trail when we hiked in. I'd seen three bears during previous hikes. I yelled at this one to get her to stand up, so I could get a good look at her with the binoculars. She stood up after I'd yelled a few times. She was big. We went on up to the cabin."

He was silent for a moment. Barbara took the cue.

"I got after him for yelling like that at the grizzly. She was with her cubs about four hundred yards away. I was glad to go on up the mountain."

Malcolm was silent. I asked him if it wasn't cold on the first of October, too cold to be hiking up a 6,000-foot mountain.

"Oh, it had been a good summer, hot and dry. It wasn't cold during the day. At night I put a great big log into the iron stove. There wasn't any other wood, so I stuck the log butt-end down and let it burn from one end on the grate."

"What time did you leave the cabin the next day?"

"Oh, late, about ten-thirty. Barb didn't want to get out of her sleeping bag. Mebbe it was a bit cold in the morning.

"It was about five miles down the trail, on the way back, that it happened. About two miles from where we'd seen the grizzly sow and her cubs on the way up the day before.

"I just saw the two cubs down below the trail. Then the sow was within ten feet of us, coming at a gallop right at us. We got about three steps running, and I knew she'd get us. I pushed Barb down on the ground beside the trail and threw myself over her.

"The grizzly hit me with her paw and threw me about five feet away. Then it started biting at Barb. I got out my hunting knife and tackled it, jumped on its back while it was biting at her. It left Barb, stood on its hind legs, and started batting at me.

"I was stabbing at it. And I think I got the knife into its neck a couple of times. They never did tell me if they killed that grizzly.

"Next thing I knew, the bear swung its head and broke my wrist, sending my knife flying. Then it closed in and we went rolling over and over. It was rolling with me, down the hill. It was biting at me all the time. Then she bit at me a few times and just left me. I gave myself up for dead."

As he finished speaking, I looked at Barb. She took up the tale with animation.

"When it hit Malcolm, it also hit me and drove me about four feet along the ground. Then it was biting at my side under the shoulder. One bite got a slice out of my ear and neck.

"Malcolm was yelling at me to lie still, to play dead. I didn't know what else to do. Next thing I knew he was stabbing at it with his hunting knife, and it was on its hind legs batting at him —cuffing him around like a kitten does a ball of wool.

"I hid my face. I guess that was when they went tumbling over each other down the hill. Later I could hear Malcolm call my name, asking if I was okay. I didn't want to answer, because I thought the bear was still there. But it had taken its cubs and gone.

"I knew Malcolm was in bad shape. He was bleeding all over. I ran down the trail toward the hotel."

It was a startling story. I shook my head, looking at her tiny frame.

"That was two and a half miles away, Barbara! Bitten as badly as you were, wasn't that pretty tough to make?"

She looked up ruefully. "I didn't even know I was hurt badly," she said. "There wasn't any pain. I had heard the bones crunch up near my ear (couldn't stand the sound of dogs chewing bones for a long time after that), but I made it. I slipped and fell a few times and was a mess. But all I could think of was Malcolm lying back up there. I thought maybe he was dead.

"After I reported the attack to the lodge, they flew in a helicopter to get him. They took both of us to the hospital. I was out in four days. You can see the scars on my back when I wear a bikini. Malcolm was in the hospital for fourteen months—operation after operation. They took him first to Revelstoke, then to Edmonton. It cost a lot of money."

"How much?"

"I don't rightly know. Several thousand dollars. Malcolm and his parents have paid it. I had to work until the kids came. The government of Alberta didn't want to take responsibility, because Mal was on his mother and father's hospital plan as a dependent, but was working in British Columbia. But British Columbia doesn't want to recognize it because he was supposed to be from Alberta."

She was dangling little Dena on her lap, bobbing her up and down. Dena was chewing on the wet satiny edge of her clutched blanket. She wanted more attention than she was getting and gave a small cry. Malcolm got up and picked her off her mother's lap. The child smiled happily as he carried her over to his own easy chair. I looked over at the domestic picture, his terribly scarred face softened by his quieting words to the child where she snuggled to him.

I sat for a minute, thinking about the bureaucracy of the two governments: one rich in oil, the other rich in timber, fish, and oil, and with an overpopulation of public servants.

"What about the bills, Barbara. What have you done?"

"They were just too much, all those operations for Malcolm. We had to declare bankruptcy, to get enough to live on—this year."

"The hell you say! You have to pay all your own bills, Malcolm?"

He nodded. "Most of them. Alberta paid some of them. I need another operation, maybe get back the sight of my other eye. It's alive still. At first I said just take it out. They said there was a chance to have it come back. I can now see some light out of it. The nerves are all messed up."

I guess my own shock was evident in the silence. What could I say? Malcolm provided a topic.

"I met a nice guy, an East Indian, at a meeting, where we were both speaking to a group of anthropologists. He said, 'Why don't you just write a letter to the Queen and governments and tell them you are going to put your gold medals up for auction.' "

Malcolm's words held me silent. He nodded with a crooked grin at me.

"Who the hell would want to buy them?"

My own anger was too much. All I could say was "Goddamn them all—the cheap bastards!"

He shook his head.

"I don't know. They have done what they think is right, I guess. But I'm having trouble doing my work. My right wrist is weak. It's been broken three times, has some pins holding it together. I can't lift a hundred-pound sack of flour or sugar like I used to do when I was cooking. Then I've been in and out of the hospital for operations. They don't want to give me unemployment insurance. They say it is illness—not unemployment."

"Do you get any pension at all?"

"What for? From whom?"

"You don't get anything from any sources, a regular payment?"

Barb took over the point.

"We don't get anything—except that we pay a rent here in accordance to our ability to pay—income that is. It's a public housing development. We pay rent to live here."

My mind went back to the impressions I'd had while walking into the modern layout of neat side-by-side condominiums, the well-planned—if compressed—grounds, the paved areas and access. My own retirement pension wouldn't have allowed me to live there. It gave the impression that they "had it good," a nice semidetached home, freshly painted, modern. Their house was nicely kept, well furnished, a television set in the living room. In fact, when I entered their living room, the large book, knick-knack, and china cabinet that occupied most of one wall had seemed singularly attractive to me. My remark that it was very effective, that it looked as though it had been made by a Swedish or Nordic artisan—the curves and scroll design relieving the somewhat austere lines—brought a surprising answer from Malcolm. "I'm of Norwegian origin. I made it. I'm working for a company that makes furniture now."

I had been curious about that, the effect of his having the use of only one eye, the terrible injury to his arm, the near amputation where the grizzly had torn much of his right leg away.

"Don't you find it tough to work with machinery, Malcolm? I have a full woodworking outfit in my basement—saws, planers. The damn stuff needs two hands to handle, wood kicks back."

"Yeah. A saw kicked back on me the other day. But I make out pretty good."

"Has the government—Canada Manpower—offered to retrain you?"

"No. I'm hoping to get into sales, for the company I'm with."

"You said there was a possibility of regaining the sight in your left eye. What are you doing about that?"

"Well, there's a doctor in Scotland. They say he's the only one who would be able to do it. He's had a lot of success with such cases. No one over here will touch it."

"Will the Scottish doctor take your case?"

"Yeah, they say he will, if I can get the money to go over there. It's a matter of several operations, months in the hospital . . ."

Barbara saw me glance at her.

"I think he should go . . . but how? I'd want to be with him all through it, and who'd look after the kids? We don't have any money. But we'd go into debt to get it done. He *should* have it done."

My mind was saying, "You're damn right! You're damn right he should! And you shouldn't have to suffer the costs. It should be paid for him. Hell! He stands as the most widely decorated civilian hero in Canada! A living example of courage, and his rewards are disfigurement, disability, and debt. There has to be a way!"

I voiced some of this.

Malcolm and Barbara listened. They would do their part.

The day after the interview, I took out his file and reread the news items. The falsity of my own impressions from previous casual reading became evident.

On Saturday, October 2, 1971, the following item had appeared in the newspaper, the *Province*, Vancouver, British Columbia, for which paper I was then the outdoors editor.

TWO HIKERS BADLY HURT BY GRIZZLY

Revelstoke: A grizzly bear attacked and severely mauled two hikers, Friday, in Glacier National Park.

Rangers said it is possible the bear is the same one—a huge sow grizzly—that bit an American tourist a month ago.

Barbara Beck, 19, of Langley, was in serious condition in the hospital Friday night, and Malcolm Aspelet, 19, of Edmonton, was in critical condition.

The two were hiking on the Balu Pass trail, the same trail on which tourist Kenneth Gates of Minneapolis was bitten by a bear accompanied by two cubs.

Miss Beck suffered cuts to her head and shoulders but managed to walk 2½ miles to a hotel where she was employed, to report the attack.

She was in a state of shock and could only give enough information to wardens so they could locate her companion, also a hotel employee.

Aspelet suffered head injuries, broken ribs and leg lacerations.

He was found 90 minutes later, and was taken by helicopter to Revelstoke hospital, about 60 miles southwest.

The trail, which starts near the Trans-Canada Highway and runs through timber and country above the treeline, was closed by wardens.

Because of the condition of Miss Beck and Aspelet, further details of the attack were unavailable.

Apart from the misspelling of Malcolm's last name, Aspeslet, that news item was well written, informative, and concise. I remembered reading it and thinking perhaps I should once more write something in my news column that would inspire more caution in visitors to the backcountry. But I had done such items several times, so I just let this one go.

In the daily issue of the *Vancouver Sun* of October 4, 1971, the following item appeared:

For Surgery

BEAR VICTIM TRANSFERRED

Revelstoke: A hotel cook who was mauled here Friday by a grizzly bear has been transferred to hospital in Edmonton, his home town.

Malcolm Aspeslet, 21, is in satisfactory condition at the Edmonton hospital where he awaits plastic surgery.

Barbara Beck, 19, of Langley, is expected to be released from hospital here on Tuesday.

The couple, both employees of the Northlander Motor Hotel, were hiking in the Balu Pass when the bear charged over a hill at them.

Aspeslet pushed Miss Beck behind a rock bluff and turned to face the bear. Park wardens later found him conscious, but weak from loss of blood near the scene of the attack.

It took almost a year for the event to become newsworthy again. Malcolm made it again in the pages of the *Vancouver Sun,* dated December 7, 1972:

Will Marry the Girl He Rescued

BEAR-FIGHTER 'BRAVEST MAN'

A man who won a British bravery award for fighting a grizzly bear that attacked a girl hiking companion will marry the girl in July.

The wedding of 20-year-old Malcolm Aspeslet and his 19-year-old fiancée, Barbara Beck, is still months away, because Aspeslet is undergoing corrective surgery necessitated by his wilderness ordeal in B. C. 14 months ago.

Today Aspeslet, an Edmontonian living in Surrey, was awarded the Royal Humane Society's 1972 Stanhope Gold Medal.

It is the society's highest award, given for the bravest deed of the year reported to the Humane Societies of the Commonwealth.

Aspeslet was blinded in one eye in the attack, October 1,

1971, in Glacier National Park while he and Miss Beck were employed by a motor hotel near Revelstoke.

The corrective surgery is required to repair severe head injuries caused by the large sow grizzly.

Between operations, Aspeslet is employed as a cook at Fuller's Restaurant on King George Highway in Surrey.

In an interview, he said he received word of the honor this morning when his mother telephoned him from Edmonton.

He will be going back into hospital for further surgery December 22, he said.

Aspeslet said the Stanhope medal is the second award he has received recently—the first being a Carnegie Hero bronze medal about a month ago.

He said he was aware someone had entered his name for the Stanhope award, but he had "forgotten all about it."

Miss Beck, a Langley resident, was also injured in the bear's attack but to a far less extent.

The citation accompanying the award said the couple were hiking through the park when they were confronted by the bear and her two cubs.

Miss Beck was attacked, but Aspeslet jumped onto the bear's back, stabbing it with his hunting knife. He shouted to the girl to feign death while he rolled down a 20-foot embankment, struggling with the bear.

Park wardens found Aspeslet conscious but weak from loss of blood near the scene of the attack. After its initial fury, the bear returned to its cubs and left the area. As far as is known, it was never found.

Aside from his head injuries, Aspeslet suffered broken ribs and lacerations. He was transferred to a hospital in Edmonton and later came to B.C. for a continuation of corrective surgery.

In Edmonton, Aspeslet's mother, Geraldine Aspeslet, said her son's spirits have remained high despite the long process of treatment.

"He wasn't bitter about it at all," she said, "and that's been a great help to us."

The *Sun* took the story up again on December 8, 1972, with a well-written piece by reporter Dave Stockand:

BATTLE WITH GRIZZLY RECALLED
'Gave myself up for dead,' says hero

"She was coming at full charge, that grizzly. . . . I got my knife out and went after her . . . We went rolling down the hill, and right there I gave myself up for dead. . . ."

It sounds like a mountain man's boast from a century ago. But —in truth—the words are as fresh as yesterday.

They come from a conversation with Malcolm Aspeslet and his bride-to-be, Barbara Beck in Malcolm's Surrey apartment.

Malcolm has got to face it—he is a hero.

Thursday, he got word from London, via his mother in Edmonton, that he has been awarded the Royal Humane Society's 1972 Stanhope Gold Medal.

This is the society's highest award, given for the bravest deed of the year reported to the Humane Societies of the Commonwealth.

Earlier, Malcolm was awarded a Carnegie medal from the U.S.-based foundation for "an outstanding act of heroism."

His tale of grizzly terror and budding romance goes back to October 1, 1971, and a hike while he and Barbara were working at a tourist resort in the Revelstoke area.

On their time off they had gone hiking in the high country, stayed overnight at a cabin at the summit, and were hiking back toward the lodge when the grizzly hit.

Says Malcolm: "I was walking in front of Barb, and I saw two cubs down in a gully. And then, all of a sudden, I saw the mother coming straight for us.

"I just turned Barb around, pushed her to the ground, and fell on top of her. The bear threw me off and went after her.

"So I got my knife out—it was a hunting knife with an eight-inch blade.

"The bear left Barb when I started stabbing and came after me. We went rolling down the hill—I mean, she was rolling as well as I was—and right there at the end I gave myself up for dead.

"Then all of a sudden she left me."

Did Malcolm score any points with his hunting knife?

"She was on her hind legs but sort of leaning over and I got a couple of stabs into her throat.

"Then she swung her head, hit me in the arm, and broke my wrist; sent me flying. That's when I lost my knife."

As for Barbara, she recalls: "I just lay there, I was too scared to breathe or anything. Malcolm kept screaming to me to shut up.

"When I looked up—once—the bear was swatting Malcolm around like a kitten with a ball of wool.

"I didn't even know the bear had gone until Malcolm called my name to see if I was okay. And I didn't answer at first because I figured the bear was still there, and I wasn't going to move."

Barbara ran for help—"I just kept running, right back to the lodge."

After rangers in Glacier National Park had been informed, a helicopter pickup took Malcolm to hospital in Revelstoke.

Fourteen months later, Malcolm has the cheerfully battered look of a second-rate prize fighter.

He underwent a terrible savaging which cost him the sight of one eye, which will mean more trips to hospital for surgery. So the tentative wedding date is not until July.

Barbara and Malcolm met while working at the lodge. They were, says Barbara, "just going around" at the time of the grizzly attack. The decision to marry was made later.

Just how extensive were Malcolm's injuries aside from the loss of one eye?

He says: "Well, I lost my total scalp. I lost my right ear, the top of my left ear, a broken wrist, no facial nerve on my right side, no feeling whatsoever.

"I got some real nasty scars, claw marks and teeth marks underneath my arm where she chewed at me. I got a big chunk taken out just above my knee. . . . There was also a slash that just missed my jugular vein."

And yet no bitterness.

"I'd do it all over again," says Malcolm. "Wild animals, you just can't say what they're going to do.

"It just happened—just like that."

On April 10, 1973, the *Vancouver Sun* picked up the threads again:

GRIZZLY BATTLER CITED

The heroism of a young Langley woman who battled a grizzly bear and won was recognized today by the Royal Canadian Humane Society.

Barbara Beck, 19, who survived the attack near Revelstoke 18 months ago, is one of two British Columbians awarded the association's bronze medal . . .

Miss Beck and her fiancée, Malcolm Aspeslet, were hiking in Glacier National Park when the grizzly attacked.

Aspeslet, badly mauled while fighting off the animal, subsequently received the association's gold medal for his part in the incident.

Now the association has acknowledged that, "in concentrating on the heroism of the young man, we failed to realize the part played by Miss Beck."

The citation added: "Though badly mauled by the bear, she ran three miles to a forest ranger's post to get help . . ."

The romance of the subject as news came clearly to the public in Susan Martens's piece in the *Vancouver Sun*, July 21, 1973, when happier endings were evident:

---

39 Operations Later

GRIZZLY BATTLER MARCHES TO ALTAR

Malcolm Aspeslet's romance with Barbara Beck has weathered months of separation and 39 operations.

They are getting married today in an afternoon ceremony in Surrey.

Aspeslet made headlines in October 1971 when he saved Barbara's life by fighting off an enraged female grizzly—with an eight-inch hunting knife.

The two young people were working at a tourist resort in the Revelstoke area, and when returning from an overnight hike into the high country they encountered the grizzly and two cubs.

Aspeslet's act of courage has won him four bravery awards.

On August 2, Queen Elizabeth will present him with the Canadian Star of Courage. The couple will fly to Ottawa for the award.

"That's going to be our second honeymoon," said Barbara on Friday. Following the ceremony at Church of the Nazarene in Surrey, the couple planned a trip to Washington State.

At the end of the year they will again meet the Queen—this

time in London. Aspeslet will be presented with the Royal Humane Society's Stanhope Gold Medal, the society's award given for the bravest deed of the year reported to the Humane Societies of the Commonwealth.

He has also received the Royal Canadian Humane Society's gold medal and the Carnegie Hero bronze medal.

For her part in bringing aid, Barbara, who was also badly mauled, has been awarded the Royal Canadian Humane Society's bronze medal.

The couple carried on a romance by correspondence during the months that Aspeslet was in hospital in Edmonton.

Aspeslet recently underwent the last of a long series of corrective operations to repair severe head injuries caused by the large grizzly.

The attack has left him blind in one eye and, although extensive plastic surgery has rebuilt the right side of his face, it remains paralyzed as a result of nerve damage.

Barbara, now 20, is employed as a teller at the Surrey Credit Union, and Aspeslet will return to his job as a cook at a Surrey restaurant.

The jewel in the hero's crown was reported with humor and drama by Dave Ablett in the *Vancouver Sun,* Friday, August 3, 1973, as follows:

ALMOST DIDN'T MAKE IT
Hero Gets Medal from Queen

Ottawa—Malcolm Aspeslet of Surrey will long remember the award for bravery he received Thursday from Queen Elizabeth.

But he will also remember that he almost didn't get to Government House in time to get his award.

The flight that was to carry him from Toronto to Ottawa in the morning was cancelled because of the CP Air strike.

So, at 10:15 A.M. Ottawa time, when guests and other recipients of awards were gathering in the Government House ballroom to await the Queen, Aspeslet and his wife were still on a plane to Ottawa.

Aspeslet was to have been the first to receive one of the new awards directly from the queen. Instead, he was the last.

It was a proud moment for Aspeslet, who was badly mauled

by a grizzly in October 1971 while protecting his girl friend, Barbara—now his wife.

The queen engaged him in animated conversation, both as she pinned the award on him and later, in the Long Gallery of Government House when she sought him out to talk to him.

What did they talk about?

"Bears," said Aspeslet.

As the queen presented him with the award, Aspeslet said she told him that "when she read the citation she didn't believe such a thing could happen."

"I told her, 'It happened.' "

The queen, he said, also said she didn't think bears were that fierce, and he responded that they were "pretty fierce."

Later, mingling with the guests in the Long Gallery, Aspeslet said the queen told him about a bear she had received as a gift from the Soviet Union.

At one point, he recalls, she held out her hand to illustrate the paw of the Russian bear.

"I didn't realize she was so friendly," Aspeslet said.

Aspeslet was one of five who received the Star of Courage from the queen, including Irene Patterson of Trail. Ten others received the Medal of Bravery. They included Corporal T. J. Miller, who was involved in a mountain rescue on Mount Slesse in July 1972.

The queen also invested 15 persons into the Order of Canada established in 1967.

Gee! The hero meets and hobnobs with the queen, after marrying the girl whose life he saved. It is the epitome of boy meets and saves girl; girl marries her hero; the queen (king) gives him a gold medal and recognition. What the hell more is there to a story than that?

In one sense, it is a fantasy brought to real life.

Then, fade out, into the glory of the sunset!

My first evening with Barb and Mal (she insisted that I use the diminutives: "Everybody else does") brought it all back into focus.

First of all, it was a shock to find that thirty-nine operations had left Malcolm Aspeslet still quite badly disfigured of face, that he wasn't able to work at his regular job because the severe breaks and resultant pins in his right arm left it too fragile to lift 100-pound sacks of flour and sugar, and that the mauling of his right leg had left it weakened.

The Aspeslets don't dwell on their personal tragedy.

When Malcolm told me that he had some hope of regaining the use of his right eye, I asked him when?

He shrugged.

"The doctor in Scotland thinks it is possible. It will take several operations."

"When are you going?"

"Well, if we can get the money together . . ."

This was where Barb told me about their having to declare bankruptcy because of the extreme financial drain upon them. She had worked until the birth of the children. We talked about possibilities. It was evident that any such probabilities would have to come from newly aroused public interest and response. Mostly Malcolm listened to Barbara's replies to my questions. Occasionally he corrected a small detail. Her intense desire for his good was almost tear-jerking.

Finally, when I told them I intended to visit the scene of the attack as part of my research, he made a surprising statement.

"It's nice country up there. I went back a couple of years ago. Went back up the trail."

"You did?" I asked. "Why?"

"Just wanted to go back to where it happened—to look it over. I took a Labrador dog and a big St. Bernard along with me."

I interjected, "Wasn't that taking a chance? Some dogs are afraid of bears."

Barbara burst in, "Oh, those dogs up there put the run on them. They are used to the country, not afraid of bears."

Malcolm grinned self-consciously.

"Yeah, they put the run on a black bear while I was taking them up the trail. Put him up a tree. I was holding the leash with all the strength I had; they were pulling me along with them. The bear went up a tree."

He was grinning at me.

Barbara was right. Hero, schmero! He is an imp.

He's also suffering, very patiently.

7

What the
Statistics Reveal

During the course of gathering facts about bears and their conflicts with humans for this book, the questions of just what causes an attack and how it can best be avoided, were frequently discussed. Many of the people I queried were administrators, scientists, trappers, ranchers, hunters, and park, forest, or game wardens, those who, by the nature of their occupation, would most likely be qualified to make a statement or give an experienced answer. The victims who survived the attacks were also questioned for background information that could lead to conclusions as to why they were attacked.

The first references of any scientist or administrator are the statistics he has gathered.* Statistics sequester the advocate and allow no introduction of a contradiction that is not of a mathematical nature. Thus evolved the joke about statisti-

*Tabulated statistics appear in the Appendix.

cians: "A statistician is a person who drowned in a river with an average depth of three inches."

Nevertheless, statistics can be highly valuable when considering an unknown quantity.

The primary reference of a layman is in the recollection of his own experiences and those of others with whom he has associated. The recall of a person who is experienced in the field is often accurate and wise, and although unsubstantiated in print, it is nevertheless viable and usable. However, the recognized fallibility of human memory regarding exact detail is established. The insertion of vanity, braggadocio, humor, or dramatics is also apt to occur. Despite this, the opinions and statements of a layman have just as often belied the tabulations provided by statisticians and/or vice versa.

Another factor to consider: When first seriously beginning my bear research, I already had some sixty years experience in the outdoors, forty of them in factual and interpretive writing about that field, and twenty-five of them in daily contact with both the field and the sciences that seek to manage our lands and waters. This exposure helped me form opinions that were primarily based on a layman's knowledge and experience, but were also to a degree influenced by reading writings and compilations by both scientists and laymen.

Consultation, argument, discussion, and study of the scientific data that were available changed some of these opinions, solidified others, and provided new knowledge. Even so, many of the conclusions that I arrived at were, and still remain, tentative.

Thus, the table of statistics to follow is given as a first reference only.

Since 1929, which is about as far back as reliable sources go, there has been an increasing documentation of conflicts between bears and man. Using items that have been gathered from any and all reliable sources still leaves many gaps, however. For example, Yellowstone Park's attacks were not available and not tabulated; Eastern Canada Parks' attacks were uncalculated; and many of the details about recorded individual incidents were unprocurable. This leaves any summation from resultant statistics usable, but not infallible.

My files containing procurable data were first compiled into card reference, under name, date, place, source, and other pertinent classifications. The specific details of each bear-and-human conflict were then added to the cards.

Reliably reported, there have been 251 attacks and killings since 1929.

The first publicly accredited opinion that proved false according to the data was that grizzly bears are greater killers than black bears. The data prove otherwise when available statistics are used. As of 1980, black bears had killed twenty humans, grizzlies had killed sixteen.

Two multiple killings by black bears and two by grizzlies adjust this total to seventeen black bears and fourteen grizzlies. Two of the deaths from black bears occurred in the hospital, after the incident, and three of the victims were killed by bears in captivity, placing the positive data at twelve actual on-the-spot killings by black bears versus fourteen by grizzlies.

The next data to be considered involve those attacks that did not result in death, but did result in actual severe injury to the human and, on occasion, to the bear. Grizzly bears take precedence here, with a total of eighty incidents to the black bear's seventy-two incidents. All of the grizzly attacks took place either in the wild or in public parks, whereas four of the seventy-two black bear attacks involved captive bears. The inference is that grizzly bears, although less abundant, are more inclined to attack. This comparative statistic *does* indicate, however, that the black is almost equally dangerous to humankind, a commonly unknown and often denied fact.

Polar bears, often proclaimed to be the real man-seeking killer of them all, fall far down the list statistically, with only seven people killed, three of them in captivity, since 1929. In the realm of attacks, polar bears statistically fall well beneath the other two species as well, with only thirteen recorded attacks. Three of these were in captivity, however, so the in-the-field total is ten people attacked. To be usefully related to the statistics on other species, this statistic must be considered in light of the fact that polar bears have little exposure to humans. Only a few thousand people have encountered polar bears in the wild, compared to millions of encounters with black and grizzly bears. When this is all considered, the arctic bear is shown to be extremely unpredictable and dangerous.

A few of the bear deaths in the wild are authenticated only by well-considered evidence, but most of them are incontrovertible. Even killings in the parks have a similar doubtful factor, but they are usually qualified by human residue being found on, or in, the killed animal. Thus, some reasonable doubt does exist in occasional summations. Altogether, a large number of attacks and killings cannot be traced to a particular bear species.

According to the statistics, six people were killed by bears the species of which was, or is, still in doubt. Five of these occurred in the wild. The sixth was in a zoo, but that incident was unverifiable at the time of this writing.

There have been thirty-nine recorded attacks upon people by unspecified bear species, seven of which occurred in the wild and thirty of which took place in public parks. Although opinions of investigators at the time indicated the probable species of bear that attacked, there have been no verifiable data brought forward to confirm that opinion. For this reason, these incidents are not included in the individual species items; they are used as a specific, separate statistic.

The by-no-means-complete data that might show the sex of the bear as an indicator of danger does show twice the probability of attack by a sow bear with cubs to that of attack by a male bear of any species; that is, thirty-eight sows with cubs, and sixteen established males (by their destruction after attack). This does lend credence to the well-touted statements and opinions that sow bears are the more dangerous.

A rather surprising statistic that comes to light shows that, by an overwhelming majority, those who fought or used some sort of physical defense survived bear attacks. It shows that of eighty-one who chose to fight, seventy-three survived. Of those who were known to have lain still, fourteen survived and three died. Of those who ran, four were killed and eighteen lived. It must be recognized that these data are limited to verifiable actions only, and thus must be used only as an indicator.

Although hunting places the human in the specific element

of bears, it accounts for only twenty-one attacks and killings. This is over half the number of incidents that occurred while persons were merely hiking (a total of thirty-five). The hunting figure is just one less than the next highest unit, which is people actually in a tent; that count is twenty victims. Hunting also accounts for no more attacks than those that occurred to people actually inside sleeping bags, a total of fifteen. Bear watching and photography can be quite dangerous, both to scientists and laymen, with a total of twenty-one people injured. Three of these victims were killed in the line of scientific duties. The simple pastime of walking on roads, in campsites, and near civilization was responsible for thirteen confrontations. Five people were actually attacked while inside houses. Trapping, a profession that is associated with bait (food) and done in the wild areas used by bears, has only four casualties, but operating a farm or ranch accounts for seven victims. Prospecting or surveying has a fair danger ratio at nine victims, while merely being in a handy (to bears) vehicle has claimed the same number of injured. There were twenty other varied activities, some of which were left unclear in the reports.

These data show the alignment of statistical equation with popular beliefs.

Perhaps the most gruesome statistic to come to light is the fact that both black and grizzly bears are instantaneous man-eaters, that consume portions of the body while the human victim is still alive. In several cases, large sections of the victim were consumed within minutes of the attack (the persons were located while still breathing); continued consumption occurred; and guarding of the kill over several days took place. Of the total of thirty-six killings by grizzlies and black bears, at least eighteen victims were largely or partly devoured by the bear. Such feeding was almost equally split between the black and grizzly species.

There is no question that all bears can be man-eaters!

Although man-eating bears tend to be categorized by "experts" as being old, infirm, or wounded, the facts do not support this. Six of the black bear man-eaters were young bears in excellent condition, and at least two of the man-eater grizzlies were young bears.

Deprivation of their natural foods because of seasonal variations is not always a cause of man-eating, but must be considered as a factor. A hungry bear must be considered a more dangerous bear. A garbage or hand-fed bear is more likely to enter and pillage campsites, be they in the wild or in parks. (Note: Innumerable incidents of campsites in the wild being pillaged or ransacked by bears have been reported, but these are not used as a statistic here because they were not validated by an official report.)

Government-funded studies made by several scientists show that bears readily adapt to feeding at garbage dumps, from garbage containers, and around campsites. The plastic bags that are used to convey such garbage have become familiar items to many bears. Indeed, the many cases of people being dragged, bitten, clawed, or killed while in sleeping bags or tents lead to the conclusion that the bears' practice of tearing open garbage containers in dumps is definitely related to the tragedies. One veteran park superintendent, an investigator of many park attacks, tells of one grizzly that was so used to this method of getting food that it actually knocked down a girl hiker who was carrying a pack. While the pack was still on her back, the bear held her down with one paw, tore open the pack, took her wrapped food, and then left her lying on the trail without further damage.

Campers are commonly advised (and this advice is printed in some park manuals about bear encounters) to first shuck and drop any pack, whether it contains food or not, and thus allow the dropped article to temporarily distract the animal's attention. It is also recommended that you discard items of food or clothing while retreating (I know this works—having been forced to do it). But such an approved method does not assure even a momentary delay of the actual charge of a bear.

When a bear is in the attack position—normally down on all four feet, head thrust out, eyes on the victim—there is no known or proved deterrent except a high-powered rifle, shotgun, or handgun. In view of actual facts gathered from all sources, and despite avowals to the contrary, there were no justified qualifications given by any of the victims interviewed to indicate that a deliberate attempt to stare the bear down had the slightest affect in deterring its charge. Many of the victims were struck from behind, by both black and grizzly bears.

Thus, we come through the transition from calculable statistics to considered opinions of people who have had experience with bears.

Any person—be he trapper, seasoned hunter, bushman, park, forest, or game warden, or experienced scientist—who has closely studied any or all bear species, readily draws this conclusion: *All bears are to be considered dangerous and likely to attack with or without provocation.*

One of the elder statesmen among the executives of Jasper National Park, who had lived much of his service life in weekly or monthly contact with bears, was sunning himself on his lawn and was nipped on the rump (bitten deeply enough to break the skin, but not enough to be considered a statistic herein) by a wild black bear. The bear retreated under a stream of surprised and vehement ejaculations and oaths, and was thus marked for destruction by his orders. His name is withheld from publication, not by his request, but in deference to the dignity required in upholding his position as an executive.

Had that "attack" occurred in the wilds, and not in the environs of a housing unit in a national park, where a bear is admittedly somewhat out of its own element, the incident: (a) might not have occurred at all or (b) could have resulted in man-killing and man-eating.

If a bear has come that far in its stalk of a human in the wilds, case histories prove that the outcome is, more often than not, disastrous.

He faced the bear, and it left!

At least half a dozen cases show that determined women (more often than men) have "broomed" a bear away from child, house, or home, with whatever instrument was available, even with their bare hands beating upon it. Strangely enough, there is no creditable account of a woman having been badly mauled or bitten when such a counterattack has been used.

They faced the bear, fought, and it left!

In several cases, however, the mere moaning or screaming

of the victim has been alleged to lead to a continued or concerted attack and/or killing of the victim. Such cases have been well documented.

They struggled, or lay still, yet died!

Of these data, it must be remembered that all these attacks were initiated by the bear, not by the human.

This detail can help us understand bear attacks, their nature, and how to best avoid them.

If a person seeks out and wounds or otherwise intrudes into the domain of a bear (and this category includes photographing, trapping, hunting, tranquilizing, or otherwise observing), then the case is not a simple attack, but is an instance of provocation.

But when a human being simply presents himself into the realm of a free-roving bear, the element of provocation also has to be considered. A bear is by nature a dominant animal, which means it is territorial. Thus, anyone who intrudes within a boundary considered by that particular bear to be its territory is inciting the animal to resort to its natural tendency to either attack or retreat. One example given by an experienced warden indicates that a distance as far as 600 yards between him and a sow grizzly and its cubs caused the subsequent charge and the animal's destruction.

By actual, well-documented fact, most bears do retreat. On the other hand, some bears will attack without even being seen by the victim!

Although it is common legend that black bears are sneaky and will attack from behind (my own experience verifies that), the attacks by grizzlies have been proved in several cases to be by ambush. (For verifications, see the items on Harvey Cardinell, George Halfkenny, and Mike Markusich). This means that the probability of sudden, unexpected attack from cover is a logical probability anywhere in the wild.

Any species of bear will attack without warning, be it wild or tame. *Tame* means that the animal is under specific human control. Wild animals are not tamed; they are conditioned.

And this draws us inexorably to the Bambi, Gentle Ben, Smokey the Bear syndromes, a cause celebre that has been touted into millions of earned bucks and unearned fame, and has ultimately contributed to the exposure of many humans quite needlessly and recklessly, to supposedly "safe" close contact with bears.

Let's concentrate on one of the first and probably best known and loved exponents of tolerable, even enjoyable, bear-and-man relationships, the fabled Grizzly Adams. Actually named James Capen Adams, this man used to walk the streets of several cities with his acknowledged favorite in the 1850s. To quote him as chronicled: "I felt for her an affection which I have seldom given to any human." He spoke of the grizzly bear he called Lady Washington.

No doubt James Capen Adams genuinely felt that respect. And the animal of which he spoke, his constant companion of many years and savior of his life and limb, Lady Washington, was a grizzly bear that deserved that commendation.

But let's consider his other chronicled report of how Lady Washington got that way. In Adams's published words:

With grizzlies (his previous statement was in regard to black bears), there was much more difficulty, not only on account of their natural ferocity, but because they were more than a year old. From the day on which they were captured, we were compelled to keep them chained, and, although they became by degrees more familiar, they did not show any disposition whatever to acknowledge a master. Lady Washington, whom I had treated with the greatest of kindness, was particularly violent, and invariably would jump and snap at me, whenever within her reach. On one such occasion, when she nearly injured me seriously, I came to the determination to give her a castigation that would make her recollect me; and I called upon my comrades to witness, and if necessary assist me in, this first lesson of subjugation.

I stepped back into a ravine, cut a good stout cudgel, and approaching with it in my hand, began vigorously warming her jacket. This made her furious; it would, indeed, be difficult to describe her violence, the snarls she uttered, the frothing anger she exhibited—not that she was hurt, but she was so dreadfully aroused. [Author's note: Remember he was using a stout wooden club on a chained bear.] My comrades, in view of the danger, cautioned me to desist, but notwithstanding their fears and remonstrances I continued trouncing her back, until she finally acknowledged herself well corrected, and lay down exhausted. It is beyond question a cruel spectacle to see a man thus taking an animal and whipping it into subjection, but when a bear has grown up, untutored, as large as Lady was, this is the only way to lay the foundation of an education—and the result proved the judiciousness of my course. A short time later I patted her shaggy coat, and she gradually assumed a milder aspect, which satisfied me that the lesson had been beneficial, and that she would soon forget it. As she became calmer, I gave her a greater length of chain, and upon feeding her, she ate kindly and heartily, and gave good promise of what she afterwards became, a most faithful and affectionate servant.

It is quite obvious that a grizzly bear has both intelligence and a long memory—perhaps both qualities being even greater than were Adams's own—if such were his conclusions.

That year-old grizzly cub, his renowned Lady Washington, was savagely beaten into submission by a big man with a heavy club, and it was what today is scientifically termed imprinted, or conditioned, to a certain behavior.

A bear in the wilds (parks included) doesn't receive any such advanced tutelage by a bear "expert." There is little doubt that any such "trained" bear has been subjected to a form of conditioning, or imprinting, before it is paraded at the side of, or in the company of, any human. Even a domestic puppy must be subjected to training that often involves at least some form of violence; training is seldom accomplished by simple, mild perseverance and completely gentle love.

No one should expect a wild bear to show even the remotest degree of fidelity, trust, or obedience.

Anyone who vouches for such possibilities, let alone probabilities, is showing a concerted degree of either stupidity or a desire for personal attention or gain.

To trust a bear to react in any specific way to the behavior of a human is a fallacy. No bear can be trusted to react in any specific manner when confronted by a human. Many tragic instances (251 recorded since 1929) are on record to support my position.

The last truth is that if you go into the domain of a bear, wild or otherwise, you must expect to be attacked, possibly killed, and/or eaten.

There is no single method or manner in which a human can be sure of surviving in bear country, with or without a gun, even a gun that is actually loaded, cocked, and ready to be fired in an instant.

And that is a reliable conclusion.

There is one other conclusion. The chances of a confrontation are millions to one—but, *the chance is there.*

8

A Grizzly with a Grudge Against the World

Item: *The Province,* January 16, 1970

GRIZZLY KILLS, EATS HUNTER

Special to *The Province*

Fort St. John—A big game guide was killed and partly eaten Thursday by the grizzly bear he was hunting in the dense forest 35 miles north of here.

The guide, Harvey Cardinal, 40, of the Doig River Indian Reserve, was found dead in 6-below weather, his leather mitts still on his hands and the safety catch on his rifle still engaged.

Senior conservation officer, John Mackill, who went to the scene with RCMP [Royal Canadian Mounted Police] after Cardinal's body was found by friends, said it is the first time he has heard of a grizzly eating a human instead of only mauling or killing.

Tracks in the snow showed that the bear had stalked Cardinal

123

from behind and killed him without a struggle. The tracks also indicated it was a "very large animal," Mackill added.

Because of the ruggedness of the area and the extreme cold, Mackill plans to hunt the bear from an Okanagan helicopter today, hoping to spot either the animal or its tracks.

RCMP said Cardinal had begun hunting the grizzly Wednesday, after its tracks were spotted on the trapline of one of Cardinal's friends.

When Cardinal had not returned home, Thursday morning, a group of his friends organized a search and found his body in the Rose Prairie area.

Mackill said it is unusual that the grizzly was not in hibernation. It may have been suffering some sickness or injury that kept it on the prowl, he said.

That story, from my former newspaper the *Province,* is one of the most complete news items among over 500 such clippings. It did not, and could not, foretell the tragedy that was to occur in connection with it. The whole thing happened during a six-week period while I was fishing in the Sea of Cortes off the coast of Baja California, Mexico. The conservation officer, Jack Mackill, was an old friend of mine, and unfortunately I did not even hear of the incident until it was too late to even visit him in hospital.

But nine years later, early in May 1979, while investigating attacks by bears in the Chilcotin District, I learned from friend and conservation officer, Leo Van Tyne, that Jack was living at Pine Valley, a small village just north of Williams Lake, and that Jack was now retired from the force. He stated that Mackill had been in charge of the investigations of a couple of grizzly attacks and that he had been hurt during the Harvey Cardinal case at Fort St. John.

The Cardinal case was one I wished to investigate because of the unusual circumstances: an experienced hunter being killed without warning and the immediate man-eating activity of the animal.

Later in the afternoon, I reached Williams Lake and called Jack at his home in Pine Valley. He stated he was coming into town to shop with his wife. Why not come out to the house around 6:00 P.M. when they would be back?

Just after 6:00 P.M., I pulled into the driveway of the well-kept ranch-style house. Through the windows, I saw Jack—familiar, tall, and straight—move toward the door.

His brown, hard hand was as firm as ever, and there was a quiet smile of welcome on his cleanly shaven face.

"Hi, Mike. It's been a long time."

"Too long, Jack."

"You remember my wife, Phoebe," he said as he turned to the pleasant, pretty, motherly woman who came into the living room as we went to sit down.

Yes, I certainly did. She and Jack had been more than hospitable and helpful to me while he was stationed at the Rocky Mountain villages of Invermere-Windermere. I had first met them there more than thirty years previously. Neither he nor his wife had changed as much as I had expected.

"You look good, Jack."

"I feel good."

"No repercussions from that helicopter accident?"

He grinned broadly at the remark.

"No. As one of my friends said, when he heard I was hit in the head by a helicopter blade, 'Hit him in the head, did it? That wouldn't hurt Mackill. You'd have to hit him in the ass of the pants. That's where his brains are!' "

All of us laughed. I had to acknowledge that I had received similar remarks when I had suffered a serious head injury and concussion many years before.

I noticed a slight white scar showing through Jack's jet black, closely cropped military haircut. The scar was barely visible even at that. I commiserated.

"You damn near bought the farm, from what I now hear. And I didn't even hear of it at the time. I was in Mexico when it happened."

He shrugged. "It was close enough."

We sat talking about some of the former places, people, and times we had known. The last time we had met was during a departmental case in which a friend of mine had been implicated. I had stood witness to the good character of my other friend. Jack had been a witness on the opposite side. It was a sensitive situation, and there was no way we could have met on common ground at that point. I somewhat hesitantly brought up that subject.

"Jack, he was always a good guy to me. I simply told the Court what I knew. It was the *other* side. I felt badly, but thought it was better to stay away from you during the day of the hearing. Then I didn't see you afterwards."

He smiled quietly.

"Mike, I knew exactly how you felt. There wasn't anything else you could do. You did what you thought right. I was simply on the opposite side. Never thought about it afterwards."

And that is typically Jack Mackill, the one I knew. I nodded my assent.

"I was wondering about the Harvey Cardinal case," I said. "As I explained on the phone, I'm researching cases for a book. Most people don't think of bears as man-eaters."

He nodded. "That's right, Mike. I didn't."

"What happened?"

"Well, we received a report at the office that the Indians at Doig River Reserve had found the body of Harvey Cardinal, frozen and partly eaten. That was on January fourteenth. It just didn't seem possible that a grizzly, or *any* bear, would be out at that time: below-zero weather and ice.

"I contacted the RCMP, and we went out to investigate the death. Cardinal was a big game hunting guide, an experienced hunter. One of the men in the village who had a trapline, had told him about finding grizzly tracks along his line. Bear pelts were bringing a good price. Cardinal set out in forty-below-zero weather to the area. He was carrying his rifle with one shell in the chamber.

"He left on Wednesday morning. He wasn't back that night, so several of the local men went out in the morning to look for him. They found him, partly eaten, and grizzly tracks all around. They came in and called us.

"When we got out to the area, it was easy to follow Harvey Cardinal's tracks to the spot. It was quite apparent what had happened. He was following the grizzly tracks in the snow. He was just past a small, head-high mossy hummock when he got it.

"The grizzly had been lying behind the mossy hummock and had heard him coming. When he was just six feet past it, the bear circled behind the hummock into his tracks and hit him from behind. It ambushed him without warning."

"Sounds like a black bear's tactic, Jack."

"Yes, it does. They are more sneaky, it seems."

"He didn't have a chance?"

"Apparently none whatsoever. When we got to him, he was a good deal eaten. Most of his abdomen was gone, up into his chest. It was a funny thing. He had his arms up behind his head, like you lie back with them—like this."

To illustrate, Mackill put his arms up with hands clasped at the back of his neck. Surprised at the illustrated body position, I shook my head.

"The news item said he was hit in the back of the head. I suppose the position was a reaction to pain, or an attempt at protection. Most of the people I've talked with tell of putting their arms up that way. But, to *stay* that way . . ."

Jack took a deep breath at the memory.

"It was surprising. He still had his gloves on. So he didn't get a chance to use his rifle. In fact, it was lying near him, the safety still on. He was frozen stiff. We picked him up and put him into the vehicle and brought him in.

"The next day we went out in the helicopter because the tracks led into deep brush and heavy forest, and the snow was crusty. The bear would easily be able to keep away from a search or hunting party."

When he paused, I mentioned the *Vancouver Sun* and the *Province* news pieces on the ensuing events, asking him if those accounts told the way it happened. He nodded.

The Sun, Vancouver, B.C., January 17, 1970

Grizzly Shooter Slashed By Copter

Sun Staff Reporter

Fort St. John—A conservation officer was seriously injured by a helicopter rotor blade Friday after the shooting of a man-eating grizzly bear.

Jack Mackill, 55, walked into the rear rotor of the copter when he stepped out of the machine in a muskeg clearing after the 600-pound animal was tracked down and shot from the air.

Mackill was flown to Vancouver and was in fair condition in Vancouver General Hospital today following surgery for head injuries.

BODY EATEN

Game branch officials said they are sure the grizzly that was felled by high-power rifle slugs and buckshot was the one that killed hunter and guide Harvey Cardinal, 48, whose body was found half eaten Thursday.

Fish and Wildlife branch biologist Fred Harper, who was on the predator hunt, with Mackill and conservationist Gordon Gosling, told about the hunt and the accident.

Mackill, who lost one eye in a war injury, stepped out, went to the rear of the machine and was struck by the blade.

Harper said the others yelled in vain to warn him away.

Harper said the group searched for four hours in the Okanagan Helicopters Ltd. turbo-prop machine before spotting the bear in dense forest near the Doig Indian reserve 35 miles north of here.

They had to return to Fort St. John to refuel before attempting a shot.

"Then, it took us a full hour to flush him out onto the muskeg where we could get a good shot at him," Harper said Friday.

The grizzly, a "good average bear" of about 600 pounds, seven feet tall, was first shot at close range with a shotgun using quarter-inch pellets.

"That should have killed him but it didn't. So we shot it several times with a high-powered .375 H & Magnum rifle," Harper said. "Then we hovered over it and shot some more buckshot into it to make sure it was dead."

After the accident, Mackill was flown back to Fort St. John in the helicopter—which shook from the bent rotor—followed by a plane. He was then flown to Vancouver in a stretcher on a scheduled C P Air flight. A doctor and his wife accompanied him.

Harper said the bear was probably injured or had a deficient fat reserve—which would have kept it from hibernating. This, combined with a shortage of game in the area, could have led it to attack Cardinal.

Conservation officials will go with a snowmobile and sled today to retrieve the bear carcass, which will be skinned to discover why it attacked.

January 19, 1970

GRIZZLY HAD GRUDGE AGAINST WORLD

Special to the *Province Sun*

Fort St. John—The grizzly bear which killed and partly devoured a man near here last week probably hated the world—with good reason.

It was old and fight-scarred, had broken teeth, a serious gum infection, a piece of its right front paw torn out—and it was hungry.

These findings were made during autopsy on the bear Sunday, after it had been tracked by helicopter and shot in rugged wilderness about 40 miles north of here.

Fred Harper, a regional wildlife biologist for the Peace River district, said about a dozen men went into the bush on snowmobiles Saturday to haul the bear to Fort St. John.

"We hung it overnight to thaw," Harper said, "because when we found it, the temperature was 40 below."

Harper said the grizzly, an old male over six and one-half feet long which weighed about 575 pounds, had several long and deep scars on its face.

"They were very bad wounds. The only thing that could do that is another bear. He was a fighter and in pretty bad shape," he said.

Harper said the bear's stomach contained part of a shirt, human hair and intestine.

"He was obviously hungry, but fat as a pig with two or three inches of fat on him. We don't know why he would have been out in the winter and not hibernating."

Harper said the bear's head will be sent later this week to the University of B.C. for rabies tests.

He said the bear was first seen last week by two Indians cutting firewood near the Doig reserve.

"They told Harvey Cardinal about it and since grizzly hides are valuable this time of year, Harvey went out Thursday to get the bear."

But when Cardinal, reputed to be a good hunter and an

excellent guide, failed to return, a search party Friday found his partially-eaten and badly mauled body.

Beginning where the body was found, Harper and Gordon Gosling, [John Mackill] chief conservation officer for the area, began following the bear's snow tracks Friday in a helicopter flying at almost tree-top level.

When they spotted the bear, the two men felled it with a heavy-caliber and a slug-loaded shotgun.

The hunt, however, almost claimed another human life.

Conservation officer John Mackill suffered serious head injuries when struck by a rear rotor of the helicopter after getting out of the craft to inspect the dead bear.

Mackill is in fair condition at Vancouver General Hospital after weekend surgery.

Both stories gave good coverage. I mentioned one of them to Mackill.

"It says here you lost an eye in a war injury? Where'd they get *that* from?"

"I did lose one," he replied.

"The hell you did! I never knew that!"

I was looking right at him, and neither one of his eyes showed any sign of being glass. His reputation for eyesight on a rifle was well known. I couldn't believe it.

"The lens was removed by surgery," he said.

"Well, I'll be damned. It doesn't show it. I didn't know!"

"It was part of the problem, I guess. We shot the bear from the helicopter because we couldn't get anywhere near it on the ground. The brush and trees were too dense. It could hide within a few feet, and a man on the ground couldn't get a shot at it. When the bear went down, the pilot put the copter down on a patch of icy snow as close to it as we could get. Both of us got out, one man on each side, Gosling and I."

He paused reflectively, putting his hands up beside his head.

"It was below-zero weather. I was wearing a cap pulled down, and my collar up. We wanted to be sure the bear was dead. It was about fifty feet away at the back of the machine. I walked away from the main rotor, then cut back toward the bear. I guess I misjudged the distance while thinking about the bear, because I cut back too soon. The rear propeller was still spinning, and it hit me."

My sympathy was with him. I expressed it.

"I've been knocked down a couple of times," I said. "There's a blinding green flash—sort of—in front of your eyes."

"That's right! I went down face first in the snow. I can thank Gosling for saving my life. He ran to me and turned me over, kept me from suffocating. I remember him saying, 'Let's get this guy out of here. *Right away!*' I was bleeding into the snow. Someone said, 'Christ, he's still alive!' "

I was surprised at the clear recollections of which he spoke.

"You weren't unconscious?" I asked.

"No, I never did lose consciousness. I was conscious all the way to the hospital. I remember the pilot saying in the aircraft, 'Don't let him get blood in his eyes,' and wondering about that."

He paused and welcomed a visitor from next door into an easy chair. After the introductions, we talked about head injuries.

I told him I'd spent two and a half hours on the operating table when my cheekbone was kicked up into my eye socket by a logging boot when I was down on the ground and that the surgeon had told me afterwards, "Mike, I had a couple of new young nurses in the operating room with me. I asked them if either of them had been in on a head injury previously. When they said they hadn't, I said, 'Then, don't be surprised if you see a lot of blood. But don't be alarmed. In head operations, the patient bleeds profusely.' You didn't disappoint them. You put on quite a display for them, all over the operating room." Pausing, I mused, "It seemed a funny thing to tell a guy."

Jack grinned.

"Yeah. I remember one of my nurses afterwards," he said. "The propeller blade had smashed a hole in the side of my skull. The doctor told me he had taken forty-seven bone fragments from the area and that I was lucky that the metal hadn't penetrated any farther into the brain case. It was only a fraction of an inch from there. The nurse had said to me, 'Jack, I don't know if *I* have any brains, but I know *you* have. I've seen yours!' "

In Jack's living room now, his visitor was eyeing the two of us with some degree of wonder.

He said, "You old guys! You should get together and write a book."

Jack laughed. "Mike is," he said.

Saying he'd check with Jack on the beaver pelts he was trapping, the visitor left shortly afterwards. I asked, "Who was that guy?"

"He's a conservation officer here," Jack grinned.

The young man hadn't said anything to reveal it, and it was a complete surprise, because Jack and I had been discussing some amusing and revealing departmental experiences.

"Jeez! I thought he was trapping with with you," I exclaimed. "I hear you are getting as much as three hundred bucks a pelt these days."

"Six hundred for lynx, Mike. The guy who told you three hundred—that's what he's paying as a dealer."

"Hell. We used to think forty bucks was a lot of money."

"Yeah. I remember!"

"Tell me, Jack. What was the condition of the bear that took Cardinal?"

His response was immediate.

"It was fat, but it had its eyeteeth broken off near the gums. The others were loose, and some were filled with puss. It had a bad cut over its nose, some old scar tissue around its head, and a torn paw. It was probably a fighter and suffered the injuries that way." He paused to speak to his wife. "Phoebe, have you got the album handy?"

She had been looking through the thick household album while we had been talking. She found the required place and showed the page to Jack. "Is that the one you want?"

He nodded and she brought it over to me.

On the first page was a color shot of one of the government men on the investigation, holding up the grizzly's head and paws. The claws were startling: all of six inches long!—ivory white and stained with blood—Harvey Cardinal's blood. On the next page was a section of the bear's carcass cut away. At least three inches of heavy, creamy fat covered the muscle structure—not a starving bear. The third photo was of a friend of the family beside a taxidermist's mount of the head, under which was a sign: MAN-EATING BEAR.

I asked where the photo had been taken.

Jack replied with some amusement. "Down at a hotel. Phoebe wouldn't let me keep the head here. The fellows had it mounted and gave it to me, but she didn't want it in the house."

He was laughing, and so was I. Phoebe remonstrated, showing some degree of disgust.

"I certainly didn't want *that thing* around *here!*"

I looked at the photo of the mounted head again.

"That's a prepared skull used in taxidermy. Those aren't the real teeth. You said they were broken."

Jack was still smiling at his wife's outburst.

"No, Mike. The real skull is in the department's offices."

We talked about other grizzly cases he had been on. He spoke of one attack, but couldn't remember the victim's name. I asked him where it had taken place. I could, perhaps, look it up in my files. He said, "Up near a pipeline, north of Fort St. John. In the late sixties."

A chord in my memory was touched immediately.

"Was it Mike Markusich?" I asked.

"Yes. By gosh, that was his name."

"Isn't that a coincidence? It was the first chapter I wrote and sent to my editor. Mike Markusich didn't know what happened with the bear, still doesn't. In fact, he didn't know who the game warden who handled it was. Did you go out on it?"

"Yes, I did," Jack said. "Markusich walked right by where the bear was lying on its moose kill."

"You're kidding! He didn't know that. Neither did I. He just thought it had ambushed him. Did you kill it?"

He shook his head.

"No. We looked over the area pretty good. That bear was so surprised it had 'killed' a *man* that it took off in twenty-foot jumps. Honest. You could see the reaction in the tracks. There were the bloody marks of the mauling, where Mike lay. Then the bear just headed out like they do when they're frightened. The jumps would clear the width of this house. Not just a few, either. It kept up that pace for at least a quarter of a mile, straight away and uphill from the scene. It was as if it suddenly realized its victim was a man. The man smell got to it, and it took off. We followed it a half-mile, and it was still running at top speed. We came back during the next couple of days, but there was no sign of it returning to the moose kill. There was no use going after it. It just got right out of the country, as if it was that scared."

I was surprised at the implications of the statement. It was the summation of an experienced bushman, one who was brought up in remote wilderness. Tracks tell very explicit tales. They often conflict with the story told by participants in an incident. Or they confirm it incontrovertibly.

My next remark was exploratory: "Mike said the bear came so quickly he couldn't react."

"Yes, it was close to the edge of the bush as he came along. They move so fast it is unbelievable. A man hasn't a chance. Think of Harvey Cardinal—right on its track, hunting it. It smashed his skull from behind."

Jack stopped for a moment, recalling something to do with the incident. "You know, people don't realize just how fast or strong a bear is, Mike. That bear that killed Harvey was suffering from an infected head, yet it went down to the creek nearby and drove its paw *right through three inches of ice.* Into the water underneath. It took a drink after eating the corpse. Drove a hole through three inches of solid ice, in January, with a blow of its paw. Hell! A man would need a sledgehammer to do that!"

I was listening intently, wondering. When he stopped, I asked another question: "Do you think Smokey the Bear, Bambi, and those TV commercials give a wrong impression? Do people get a false idea of what bears are like?"

He nodded thoughtfully.

"Bears are like people," he said. "Each one is different. The one that hit Markusich was so frightened by what it had done that it ran. The one that killed Cardinal ate him. You can't make any clear-cut rules."

"I'm glad to hear you say that, Jack. The 250 cases I've studied show just that lack of pattern developing."

Jack and Phoebe and I sat talking. I told him that the chapter on cutthroat trout in my book *Game Fish Angling in the West* had been written about the two days I'd spent back in Jack's small cabin deep in the Rocky Mountains, thirty years before. Had he read it? He grinned and replied that he hadn't been sent a copy. We both laughed. Phoebe remembered that she and Jack and the kids used to go there each summer. It was so remote and so beautiful. She recalled my being out there, and my expressing my enjoyment at the time. It was a pleasant recollection for all of us, warm old thoughts. It made me recall the words of an old Indian guide, which I then related: "He said, 'Me, I got sixty-five years these mountains in my heart.' "

It was a surprise to hear Jack say, "That was old Louis Capello."

"Oh, for godsake, Jack! I'd clean forgotten. You arranged for old Louis to guide Bob Kuhn and me into the Rockies behind Invermere. How stupid of me! That was the trip on which I shot my first mountain grizzly."

"Yes, I remember. You were with that well-known outdoors painter, Kuhn. It was quite a while ago."

9

They Tried to Outrun It

A favorite memory of mine concerns a backroad along the northern end of Okanagan Lake in British Columbia. I had some excellent flyfishing there and always intended to go back. A fishing buddy of mine, Bob MacMillan, ran a sporting goods shop in Penticton, some 80 miles south of there.

"Mike!" he said. "You're going north to Vernon. The grasshoppers are just about at their height now. Go through Vernon and switch back along the lake on the west side. There's an Indian reservation there, along the lake shore. Just go to the chief's house and ask for fishing permission—they're good guys. They'll even tell you the best spots. The grasshoppers get blown offshore on windy afternoons, and the rainbows come up for them. Here, take some of these grasshopper flies. I've done great with them. Wish I could go with you."

It was good advice, and I followed up on it. Bob had also said that the lee side of any point that formed a calm back-eddy from the wind would produce a good rise.

He was right. There were rises regularly. Some were feeding squawfish of up to three pounds. But every third or fourth rise was a fighting rainbow. In the course of three hours, and six bays tested, I had six rainbows ranging from one to three and a half pounds, a very agreeable surprise to me. I also kept five of the largest of the squawfish—chub, that is. Although in the past I had often found chubs taking my flies right along with trout, their name and the disgust of anglers toward them had always kept me from eating them. I would usually kill them as pests, leaving the carcasses for the predators. On this trip, I was going to cook one and try it. The chubs didn't look bad lying beside the trout in the car trunk between two wet sacks and green leaves.

Thanks to Bob's advice, the day had been a very good one. The lake's shores had been almost idyllic for an angler—undeveloped and remote, with a brilliant sunlit sky, a peaceful and wild landscape, and fish willing to take my offerings. My thankfulness was something that just had to be expressed.

On my way in to find the fishing, I had stopped along the dirt road where it turned down from the hills and passed an isolated farm cottage on the Indian reservation. The owner of the cottage had come out to the dusty road to tell me where to fish and had wished me luck.

He again came out to the road when I stopped on the way out. A man in his forties, summer-tanned, he flashed a genial white-toothed smile of interest.

"How you make out, mister?" he asked.

"Thanks to *you*, very well! I thought you might like some fish."

"Sure, I always like fish."

Lifting the trunk lid, I pulled back the upper sack, proudly exposing the twin rows of fish. He drew back his head with obvious appreciation.

"How you get that one?"

"A grasshopper fly, fished slowly on the surface."

"You do *good*, mister."

"Well, you take what you want," I said. "I'll be giving most of them away, anyway. I'll just cook maybe one for supper."

His tanned fingers slid into the gills of three of the chubs. I was surprised, although Indians do have an appreciation of foods that other people often ignore. As he lifted the three large chubs, my curiosity got the better of me.

"You like those best?" I asked.

"Sure, squawfish good to eat."

I was making an effort to cover my grin at his use of the term "squawfish," which I had been too timid to use. I tried to hold his eyes with mine, but had to look down at the fish. I spoke somewhat uncertainly.

"Don't you like rainbow trout?"

"Sure! I like rainbow trout!"

There was an awkward moment before my senses came into control.

"Then why did you take—uh—squawfish?"

"Hell! White man don't give Indian *rainbow trout!*"

We were now holding each other's gaze, eye to eye. This was a real man. I pointed to the rest of the catch.

"This one does. You take the big rainbows."

He looked at me for a long moment, grinned, and put out a hard-palmed hand, which I gladly gripped. He smiled appreciatively.

"Mister, you come back anytime. Mebbe get deer in September."

There was something about that friendly brush of years ago that very vividly remained with me. The warmth of the man, the utter simplicity of his thinking. There had been a lesson in humility for me: "White man don't give Indian rainbow trout!"

He sure as hell doesn't. He has done his best to take them away. Yet, we learn. I carried the memory with me and occasionally told the story to illustrate the differences between thinking people and people's thinking.

Never did I dream that my feet might be drawn back to that place as a scene of indescribable tragedy. Nor did my reading of the published news accounts of the death of Suzanne Duckitt in any manner connect that location with the scene of my earlier and happier memories.

That connection was most shockingly renewed Good Friday, April 13, 1979, when I visited Louis and Marion Duckitt at their little farm in Maple Ridge, just 40 miles from my own home. The Okanagan Lake waterfrontage they lease as a summer home is right on the property of Joe Lawrence, the kindly Indian who had first chosen the squawfish.

I had asked my wife Thelma to come along with me. My hope was that a woman-to-woman talk might soften the harshness of interview. As the four of us sat in the Duckitts' spacious family room, Marion Duckitt told the story in a clear, precise manner, the experience obviously relived a thousand times.

I looked over at Louis Duckitt. He was sitting silently in his easy chair opposite me. He had spoken very little, his eyes downcast. His mien reminded me of my phone call to their home the week before. I had asked if they would be hurt by discussing the circumstances, if they wished to give an interview. Marion Duckitt had said, "I'll ask Lou. Maybe he can talk about it now."

Three days later she had telephoned to say, "Yes, Mr. Cramond. Louis can talk to you about it now. When would you like to see us?"

My question about exactness of location of the tragedy was being answered by Marion. Suddenly the whole scene fell into place as being the idyllic fishing spot I'd held so long in my memory. It was up that road, past Joe Lawrence's home, that ten-year-old Suzanne Duckitt had hiked with her nine-year-old companion, Jennifer McHugh, to fix up the play fort that she had found on the hillside above.

A black bear killed Suzanne.

Now, twelve years later, it was somewhat less difficult for Marion Duckitt to talk about it. Her voice was even, but subdued.

"It was just a normal summer-camp August day, Mr. Cramond," she said. "There were certain chores that had to be done, as it was Tuesday morning. I'm a graduate nurse, and I guess I'm a bit fastidious about camp habits—perhaps overly hygienic. Apart from grounds-keeping and cutting wood for the fires once a week, our youngsters, Phillip—who was twelve then—and his sisters, Suzanne—she was just ten—and Gayle was six—had to bring buckets of water from the lake. I would regularly douse the interior of the outhouse, and its pit, with the water.

"Around nine in the morning Suzanne came and asked permission to go up the mountainside to their 'forts' with her friend Jennifer. She had a peanut butter sandwich, a bottle full of water, and a chocolate bar for an early lunch. I told her to be back home by twelve-thirty, as it was going to be a very hot day, and that they could all go swimming. And then I suggested that they take their younger dog, King, with them, as Cindy, their old Labrador, had a bad heart and shouldn't be allowed to climb the big hillside in the heat.

"For some reason, unexplained, Suzanne locked both dogs in the cabin, to keep them from following, then tripped off with Jennifer. Phillip and one of his pals were still doing chores. They left ten minutes later."

Marion Duckitt explained that like most of the Okanagan Lake shores, the hills behind their summer camp rise steeply through grassed slopes, usually browned off in August, past isolated patches of small brush and some small groups of coniferous trees, to a more solid cover of mixed timber at the mountaintops. The two girls were headed for the small plateau, about 1,000 feet above, where the boys—both Indian and white—cooperated in building forts and playing war games.

On the way up, Jennifer, who had come to the lake only a week previously and had heard about bears prowling around and knocking over the garbage cans, asked her friend if there was any danger of bears up the mountain. Suzanne replied that there were bears around the area, but that she had never seen any of them.

They climbed to the summit of the hill, where Suzanne had found a caved-in fort, and decided to fix it up.

As Marion Duckitt talked, I thought of Jennifer McHugh's own words, reported in the news at the time:

"We decided to fix it up (the fort). But before we started to do it, we climbed up on a rock to look down at the lake.

"I heard a sort of rattling in the bushes behind us, and when I turned around, the bear was right there.

"It wasn't more than four or five feet away, just looking at us. Suzanne said, 'Let's run!' And we both started running and screaming, but we couldn't scream too hard because we were so scared.

"Suzanne was right behind me, and we ran across the hill, but she turned and started running right down the hill.

"She let out this real odd scream, as if the bear had got her, and she stopped completely.

"I didn't hear another thing after that.

"I hid in the bushes and didn't see anything more."

Horrified by the sudden attack, Jennifer then ran down the mountainside to the home of the Duckitts. Marion Duckitt heard the girl's tale of the attack with stunned disbelief. She told herself that Suzanne was all right, that she had just taken another route home. They would find her as soon as they got a short distance along the trail.

Clad only in summer shorts and blouse, with bare legs, Marion and Louis—with Clyde Matheson, a former British Columbian Policeman, and his daughter Sheila—immediately pressed Jennifer to lead them back to the spot where she had last seen Suzanne. Struggling the mile uphill to the area, Matheson could see the anxiety straining deeply within Marion Duckitt.

"Don't worry," he told her. "She'll be around. Don't worry!"

Sweating, scratched, and short of breath, they reached the spot where Jennifer indicated she had last seen Suzanne. Searching the area, they found the tiger-striped swimming shorts that Suzanne had been given on her birthday, only ten days before. There was no sign of the youngster.

Sensing the danger and the inadequacy of the five of them in the area, ex-constable Matheson turned to Louis and Marion Duckitt with a decision.

"Look, she'll be around here," he said. "What we need is people for a search. We'll go down to the lake and get a group together."

The five of them returned to the lake. Almost immediately, more than a hundred of the lakeshore residents, many still in their bathing suits, volunteered to climb to the area of the attack and search for the little girl. Louis Duckitt was with his wife, Marion, in the advance group that headed up the mountain.

Once at the site where they had found the swimming trunks, the searchers went to work. This time the men found blood and a torn blouse. They asked the Duckitts to stay where they were.

The Duckitts' young son, Phillip, hearing the searchers, came up with some other boys. They were wondering about all the people in the area. They had not seen any bears, nor had they heard anything. They hadn't seen Suzanne either.

The groups had spread out and gone ahead uphill. One of the women volunteers, Mary Gellattly, saw the bear first. It was near a tree, partly obscured behind some bushes. One of the men, upon approaching the bear, saw that it was guarding Suzanne's body.

They prevailed upon the Duckitts to leave. Their daughter was obviously dead. Shocked, and futilely uncomprehending, they stumbled down the mountain.

Marion's voice, as she spoke now in the family room, was low and calm. "We never saw Suzanne again. They wouldn't let us go to her. Clyde Matheson identified her body for us."

I couldn't help glancing at silent Louis Duckitt. There was in me a very deep sense of compassion and realization. Had it not been for my own wife, Thelma, reaching into the crib in front of a black bear's jaws, that animal would likely have killed our own daughter, Pamela. He and his wife had lost a daughter. Ours is now the mother of our only grandson.

Good Friday. Dear God, I hope you heal this couple's suffering!

It was a bad moment. I broke in with a ramble about how I had a bear come after me during the previous hunting season, how it had come right around in a 300-yard circle, and out of the bush from behind where I had been sitting. I had not killed it, but was tempted and just fired over its head.

Louis Duckitt said, "I'd have killed it!"

God knows. In his position, I would have too.

I stared at the wall above him.

"Are you a hunter, Lou?"

"Well, not now," he replied. "I just fish. I used to like hunting, but I sold my .303-caliber Parker-Hale rifle to our son, Phillip. He's an avid hunter. He has all sorts of hunting equipment, and belongs to the hunting and fishing club. I used to pistol shoot, when I belonged to the Capilano Rod and Gun Club in West Vancouver."

The statement struck a familiar chord between us. I told him that I was a charter member of that club and still held one of their initial bonds, issued in order to get the organization on its feet. We talked about the club briefly. As we conversed, I heard the conversation between my wife and Marion Duckitt. I looked at my watch. It was getting late. Marion Duckitt saw me look at the dial.

"Oh, I'm sorry! We didn't ask you to have tea or coffee. I'll get some—right now." She started to get up.

I persuaded her not to do so. The afternoon shadows were lengthening, and we had a 40-mile drive to get home. It was too much to ask of her. We arose to leave. Marion Duckitt left the room while Louis and I, for a moment, talked casually about gardening.

Seconds later, Marion reentered the room with a hinged group of three photos of Suzanne. They were beautifully set in polished wooden frames, the portraits hand-colored. She held the photographs out to me. I took them almost reluctantly.

Suzanne Duckitt was a radiantly beautiful child: She had lovely, frank, wide-set eyes, a perky nose, a sort of cupid's-bow mouth, and a cascade of long curls framing her beauty. Tears welled up in my eyes, a constriction in my throat. Even our own daughter, Pamela, always an acknowledged beauty, as child and woman, was not so pretty. The child seemed to look at me as if she knew me. It was what everyone said about Suzanne.

We traveled home almost in silence. There wasn't much to say, except how deeply we felt for the family. Perhaps it was worse for my wife. I'd been a cop, knew all too well the numb feeling of defeat people have when confronted with an untimely death. As a reporter, I had also known the pangs one feels when an interviewee relates his personal tragedy. Strangely, it seemed to me, there was a desire in most people to talk of their tragedy. Perhaps it is a release. At least, the medical profession prescribes it as such. It *does* take some of the burden off the interviewer to know that. Still, I can't help being angry at inquisitive reporters who ask devastating questions of distressed people during sensitive moments.

That evening at home, I went back to the unfeeling sources in my files. The reporting of the tragedy had been fairly accurate. The Indian youngster, mentioned as having shot the bear several times without killing it, was the son of the Duckill's landlord, Joe Lawrence, whom I believed to be the Indian who years previously had assisted me in finding the right fishing spots.

The bear had remained on guard over the mauled form of Suzanne. When one of the men who had joined in the second search had approached it, the animal came after him and drove him up a tree. Then the bear returned to guard the body. A single shot by Gordon Hogue of Edmonton, Alberta, fired from a .303 rifle, hit the animal in the spine and killed it instantly. It had dragged the child 300 yards from where the searchers had picked up her torn clothing.

Aftermaths are much the same in all such emotion-wrought tragedies. Personal opinions and hindsight move in on the facts.

As quoted from the files of the *Vancouver Sun*, August 9, 1967:

An 11-man posse [was] led by Faye Price of the Vernon Fish and Game Club's search and rescue team, which arrived on the scene after the bear had been shot.

Price said several dozen people were milling around the hillside after the alarm was raised.

"It's a miracle there weren't several people mauled or killed," he said.

Price suggested that garbage scattered on the hillside—a popular picnic area—may have attracted the bear.

Vernon Conservation Officer, Alan Frisby, said he had been in the area 17 years and had never before heard of an attack of this type.

He said he could offer no reason why the four-year-old male black bear had attacked the child.

Frisby said the animal was young and in good health, and there were no cubs in the area to his knowledge.

"There was an inch of fat on its rump, its claws and teeth were good, and there were no old bullet marks," he said.

"Bears have attacked sheep and cows in the area, but I've never heard of anything like this in the 17 years I've been here."

Frisby said the bear was about five feet tall.

RCMP said an inquiry will be held by coroner J. A. G. Illington.

Dr. Ian McTaggart Cowan, dean of graduate studies at University of B.C. and recognized as one of North America's leading zoologists, said today he can offer no explanation for the attack.

"I have never heard of an unprovoked attack by a healthy male black in wilderness conditions," he said.

"I have heard of people being clawed by semi-tame black bears in parks or by females with cubs, but never a case like this.

"I am desperately sorry for this little girl's parents."

Dr. McTaggart Cowan said an attack could have been expected had the bear been a grizzly.

"Grizzlies will attack without any provocation at all, and there are numerous instances of this," he said.

On August 10, the follow-up of that same Vancouver, B.C., daily brought more facts and opinions about the case:

GIRL'S KILLER BRANDED ODDBALL BEAR

A black bear's predatory instinct to pursue its prey probably triggered the savage attack which killed a 10-year-old girl, a wildlife expert said Wednesday.

Susan Duckitt of Haney was mauled to death by a black bear Tuesday at Whiteman's Creek, a popular resort and picnic area on the west side of Okanagan Lake.

A companion, Jennifer McHugh, 9, of North Vancouver, escaped to tell how the girls had fled screaming after meeting the bear on a hillside.

"It was normal for the girls to run away when they saw the bear, but this could have stimulated the attack," said Dr. James Hatter, director of B. C. fish and wildlife branch.

"Any predator animal which is accustomed to pursuing its prey is stimulated by the prey running away."

Hatter described the 250-pound animal which killed the girl as "a criminal among the bear population," whose behavior was extremely abnormal.

"This was very much an individual bear—an oddball bear—and it didn't behave in the manner of any other black bear I've heard of," he said.

Hatter added that bears are noted for poor eyesight and the screams of the girls may have resembled the sounds of an animal which the bear had once hunted.

He said the bear will be examined by his department for evidence of rabies, but chances of the bear having had the disease are remote.

Al West, the branch's regional supervisor for the Lower Mainland, said he has personally hunted and killed 126 bears, many of which had entered settled areas on the North Shore.

"A lot of these wild animals are totally unpredictable. They are individuals like people and you never know which is going to be the bad one," he said.

"Most black bears are not killers, but when one learns to kill livestock it won't stop until you kill it."

West said bears can become dangerous if they lose their fear of man and no longer regard him as a threat.

He said 31 bears were killed in one season two years ago on the North Shore, "and these were only the ones we had to take out."

Vernon coroner J. A. G. Illington said indications are that the girl killed Tuesday was rendered unconscious by a blow which broke her neck in the bear's first attack.

Illington said he will conduct an inquiry, but no inquest will be held.

There is an awesome finality to the word of a coroner. You mentally fight to move back the time and space to a beginning which would turn out in some happy way.

Snatches of conversation with Louis and Marion Duckitt came back to me.

Marion had been speaking: "I don't know why Suzanne put the two dogs in the cabin and locked them there. I had told her not to take old Cindy, because the veterinarian had said she had a bad heart and should not be allowed strenuous exercise. We were giving her doses of medicine regularly.

"She could have taken King. He wasn't much of a dog anyway, but he might have helped. He died a year later, from eating rubber balls.

"Perhaps if they'd had the dogs with them . . ."

I recalled how Louis Duckitt had been staring solemnly at the floor. He got up and left the room. I listened absently to my wife and Marion Duckitt talking. He came back and took his seat quietly. Asking questions always bothers me in such cases. I took a deep breath.

"Had there been any signs of bears in the vicinity, previous to the attack?"

"Yes, there had been reports of bears dumping over garbage cans. That is pretty commonplace in outlying summer camps. I guess you get used to hearing it."

A little while later, Louis said, "You know, when we came back the next year, we came in late at night. My daughter Gayle wanted to go to the bathroom. I got a flashlight out of the car and took her down the path to the outhouse."

Marion Duckitt broke in.

"Gayle has never liked going out to the privy at night in camp. Suzanne wasn't at all afraid. Even when Phillip, her brother, didn't want to go down into the darkness of the basement, she would say, 'I'll go with you.' She didn't seem to know fear of such things."

Louis Duckitt nodded his head.

"When I came back up from the privy, there was a surprise. Right beside the door of the car, out of which we'd just climbed, was a pile of steaming hot bear dung. The bear had been there during that minute I'd been down the trail—and none of us saw a sign of it!"

Marion Duckitt nodded. "It was still steaming! It had been that close to us right on our property."

I shook my head in disbelief. It was a belly-tingling revelation. Lou Duckitt nodded his head again.

"Yes, just seconds away. I reported the incident to the game department and they made an investigation. But no one ever saw the bear. We're very careful up there now. We'll be going up in May. Perhaps you will come up then. Marion said you have visited several of the sites."

"Sure, Lou. I'd like to come up and see you then."

My hand rested on the last news item about Suzanne Duckitt. It was also from the *Vancouver Sun,* August 12, 1967.

DEAD GIRL PRAISED

Friends and relatives paid their last respects today to a shy little girl with long brown hair and a smile for everyone.

A brief memorial service for 10-year-old Suzanne Duckitt was held at West Vancouver United Church.

The girl was mauled to death Tuesday by a black bear at an Okanagan Lake picnic area near Vernon.

Her companion, nine-year-old Jennifer McHugh, of 787 Donegal Place, North Vancouver, escaped the bear.

Rev. Tom Oliver told the 60 people at the service that Suzanne was a radiant child.

"Some of you would speak of her adventurous spirit and others of her friendliness," said the minister. "She was a radiant child who loved and had the capability of love in her."

On June 23, 1979, with my vehicle parked near the edge of Okanagan Lake, along which I had fished so successfully in 1950, I could barely believe my eyes. The cottage by the hill was gone. On the flatlands where the farmlands had been was a road leading to dozens of ranch-style and summer homes. This modern community on leased Indian lands was Joe Lawrence's development. Largest among the homes was Joe Lawrence's.

Before climbing the hill behind the residential area, I stopped and talked with Joe Lawrence. It turned out he wasn't the man I had met nearly thirty years before.

He shook his head when I asked.

"No, not me. That sounds just like my dad. He was a good guy. He's dead now. So, you're writing a book about bears. I could tell you lots of stories about bears. One friend of mine in

Keremeos . . ." He turned to his wife, "What's his name—who got mauled by the grizzly?"

His wife responded easily: "You mean Joe Bone? He got attacked by a grizzly. Or Sylvester MacLean. He was attacked by a black bear."

"I meant Joe Bone," said Joe Lawrence. "That's him. You should see him, mister. He's in Keremeos reserve."

Two more of the hidden statistics were coming to light, another pair of the injured to talk with. I asked the Lawrences about the death of Suzanne Duckitt. Mrs. Lawrence remembered all the details quite clearly.

She said, "Suzanne was a nice girl. It's too bad." She turned toward the hillside above the cottage lands. "It happened just up on top of that hill—over there. Just too bad!"

After a few more words about the tragedy, they told me that the Duckitts were expected back on the next weekend. I would miss them. Half an hour later I came down from the hot, sun-baked bluffs where the tragic incident had happened. It really wasn't any place in which to expect a bear. I could even hear the distantly muted voices from the beachfront below— right from the fateful summit.

10

The Off-limits
Campsite

"Their camp couldn't be seen from the area of the board-walk. I think it was right here that they had their camp." My guide was pointing to a flatter area among the rock-bound Alpine coniferous trees.

It had been seven years since twenty-five-year-old Harry Eugene Walker paid with his life for defying Yellowstone Park's regulations. He had camped with his companion, twenty-four-year-old Phillip Howard Bradberry, near the boiling waters of Riverside Geyser and the cold, tumultuous stream called the Firehole River. The man speaking to me was Chester Cantrell, Park Ranger, Old Faithful Ranger Station, twenty-five-year veteran of the National Park Service.

It was the third such site to which we had climbed on the bluffs that arise from the white deposition of minerals spouted from thermal springs and geysers which had formed the plains in the wide valley of the Old Faithful geyser. Any one of the

150

three sites could have been the choice of visitors if they wished to be hidden from the scrutiny of rangers or other personnel. The tiny, rocky bluff, upon which we stood at the instant of Ranger Chet Cantrell's statement, was the most logical of such locations for the campsite—all within 30 to 50 feet of each other. This site had a moderate slope, fairly clear walkway to and from the supervised area, quite close enough that a trip to the river for water for use in the campsite would not be arduous, yet also located in a position in which the movements of a person camped in that locality might not arouse suspicion and would be unlikely to be noted by anyone.

I walked around the perimeters of the three sites. In each usable camping position were the bedding areas common to all such mountainous forest bluffs between Mexico and Alaska. Such areas have been the site of 90 percent of my sightings of animals during more than sixty years of hunting. In fact, while covering hundreds of miles on foot, I have sought out such locations, approaching them from below, on the level, and from above. In such beds of compacted earth spread with coniferous needles, twigs, dried moss, and grasses, I have seen buck and doe deer of all subspecies, as well as mountain sheep; while in a 100-yard circumference, I've seen blue, willow or spruce grouse, lynx, marten, squirrels, in fact almost any type of wildlife. I have not seen any type of bear bed down in such a spot, but I have seen them within 100 to 400 yards. The only place in which I have seen bears bed down during the day is in meadows such as those by the stream to which the young men would go for their water supply. From studying the contour maps of the Old Faithful section of Yellowstone Park, I'd expect it would be a crossover point for any ranging animal to choose in its movement through that country.

Winds in Yellowstone are thermal and variable, almost vagrant, just as they are on most mountaintops. The smell of food being cooked will carry at least a mile—some people say three miles. At such distances a grizzly—which is noted for its powers of scenting—could easily pick up such an odor and home in on it. Bears do home in on odor or scent, even in their wildest state. If you have difficulty in believing that, try cooking a stew of hoary marmot in a valley where grizzlies roam free. The odor of bacon is not much different from such a dish. To picture that idea, you might think of it as cooking in the woods on any camping trip, or by remembering the aromatic scent of bacon wafting out over a lake and interfering with the complacency of your fishing.

All this must be contemplated in regard to the death of Harry Walker. His campsite showed signs of cooking and had food residue about it. The pair had been there for at least two days, and it was known grizzly country.

Yet as I looked out from this most logically chosen site, I could see (as could illegal campers) several people strolling leisurely along the geyser boardwalk. A glance from another opening between the trees showed a man and a girl, and to the southeast a group of fifty or more people were waiting for the spouting of Grand Geyser. Only 300 yards separated Warden Chester Cantrell and me from the crowds of humanity to which we become accustomed in any park.

I felt quite secure as I undid my pack, took out my camera loaded with black-and-white film, and photographed through the trees; then repeated the act with the color film camera. Ranger Cantrell's walkie-talkie buzzed him from headquarters. He casually replied to the office. I also photographed the forest behind the campsite. The screening began at a distance of only 15 to 20 feet. Any animal, up to one as big as a moose, would be hidden, and the campers would not know it was there.

The location was an ideal site for surprise confrontation or a sudden ambush.

Harry Walker and Phillip Bradberry were not experienced in the habits of big game animals. It is quite unlikely that they would have known there was even a million-to-one chance that their camp might be raided by a bear. They'd more likely be worried about possible discovery of such an unauthorized camp by the rangers.

During the seven years since the tragedy, the forest had reclaimed its floor: The flora had regrown and the carpet of needles and deciduous growth had been renewed. I searched for the scar of a campfire. Charcoal has a long endurance, ashes even greater life if left in the spot where they subside after burning. Nothing of the camp remained that indicated human habitation—only the oval-ball scats of elk and the well-worn trails that animal passage have used since the glaciers melted.

An odd thought struck me. I recalled that just after entering the highway system into Montana from Alberta, I had seen little white crosses placed on the sides of the road to denote highway deaths. Most often there was one small white cross, occasionally two, and in one case five. Even if all the people killed by bears in Yellowstone Park were added up since the turn of the century, they wouldn't equal that one set of five crosses.

Ranger Cantrell was looking around the site. He returned to the adjacent ones we had visited. He shook his head.

"I didn't come into the site to pick up the body," he said, "but I did visit this spot. There was camp litter around it, which is known to attract bears. It was described by other rangers who did the investigations as a 'dirty' camp, the likes of which would not be tolerated in the authorized camping spots."

I asked him a few more questions about the incident itself. We retraced our steps across the small, shale-covered, iron-and-sulfur-stained plains formed by the eruptions of the many geysers. Near a bubbling pool called Beauty, I stood on the weather-whitened planks of the boardwalk, staring back at the shady location of the tragic campsite we'd just visited. A line of mixed coniferous trees stood like an erect blind, blocking out all view of the area beyond them. The land contour to the waters of the Firehole River was easily climbed. It was obvious that anyone could carry a bucket or pitcher of water up there without spilling it, yet not reveal the location of a small back-packing tent.

As we walked along the boardwalk, people buttonholed Cantrell. His twenty-five years of polite service showed in his easy answers even to naive questions.

"Yes, ma'am. It's boiling. Water boils at 199 degrees Fahrenheit here. The temperature in the pools is about 204 degrees. Yes, sir, it *is* boiling."

On our way in, along the boardwalk, past Castle Geyser, and several clear, bubbling pools, I had asked him the same question and received the same answer. I had been fascinated by the clear, bubbling water. For some reason, even with nearby Castle Geyser spouting a 20-foot fountain of steaming water, I had thought of the bubbling in these side pools as partly gaseous or carbonic. There was no sensation of standing next to a cauldron, as there is inside a building. The gusty breezes seemed to be warmed with strong bright sunlight, nothing more.

I think I said, "You could easily fall into one of those things if you got off the boardwalk."

Chet looked at me thoughtfully for a moment.

"Yes. Years ago, we didn't have the fence rails on the walks. And the platforms went even closer to the pools. A family from New York, I believe it was, had a couple of children with them. One of the boys, about five years old—so park visitors who witnessed it said—took a run across the space between them. Then he pulled up his legs and cannonballed right into this one. He was gone from sight in seconds. We collected only fragments of his body, and whole garments, using nets, as they came to the surface."

My stomach balled up in a knot.

"My God! Boiled alive!"

Cantrell nodded his head at the exclamation.

"His father sued the park service. He said he wasn't interested in money—he just wanted to increase the safety of the system of viewing the pools by visitors. The distances of approach were increased, and the fencing was increased.

"Bears are only some of the problems in parks," said Cantrell. "A man was killed not far from here by a bison. He wanted an action photograph of the animal."

A short time later, during our walk back to the parking area where I had left my pickup camper we passed a majestic buffalo standing in the meadow. It bent its massive head occasionally, grazing on the lush spring grasses. I stopped for a moment, admiring the enormous proportions of this North American bovine species.

"I heard that the man who was killed by the buffalo went up really close and prodded it," I said.

Cantrell nodded his head thoughtfully: "In fact, witnesses said he kicked it, to make it get up. It went for him, knocked him down, and gored him to death. I was on that investigation. A horn penetrated the liver and killed the man almost instantly."

The conversation with Cantrell had been enlightening. He holds a doctorate in psychology and is associated with the educational system in California. His efforts and answers had filled in the on-the-site data.

Back at my camper, I sorted out the news file and notes I'd taken on the killing of Harry Walker by the grizzly bear.

The Province, June 26, 1972

CAMPER KILLED

Yellowstone National Park, Wyo. (UP)—An Alabama man camping with a friend was attacked and killed before dawn Sunday near Old Faithful geyser by a bear apparently raiding a food cache.

The Province, June 27, 1972

KILLER GRIZZLY WAS "INVITED" INTO CAMPSITE

United Press International

Yellowstone National Park, Wyo.—Phillip Bradberry, of Oxford, Ala., who may be charged with violating park rules, Monday described how a bear chased him and attacked and killed his companion near Old Faithful geyser.

Harry Walker, 25, of Anniston, Ala., was mauled to death Sunday when he and Bradberry returned to their campsite and surprised a bear eating their food.

"Harry, my friend, heard it first," said Bradberry, "and when he shined his flashlight on it (the bear), it was right on top of us."

The bear knocked Walker down and chased Bradberry. Then the animal returned to Walker and mauled him fatally, Bradberry said.

"I dived and rolled," said Bradberry, describing how he got away from the bear's initial rush. Bradberry said he stopped running for a few minutes and called out to Walker: "Has the bear left?"

Bradberry said he heard Walker scream: "Help me, Crow, help me."

Bradberry, nicknamed "Crow," scrambled down a steep incline going in circles for some time before he finally found a bridge in the darkness which crosses several geysers.

Winded and partially in shock, he collapsed after reaching Old Faithful Inn.

A park ranger and two other men began an immediate search for Walker, but decided not to go too far into the woods in the darkness. Four and a half hours later they found Walker's badly mauled body in a campsite in an off-limits area.

Vernon Hennesay, assistant park superintendent, said the men not only camped in a prohibited site, but had a dirty camp. Off-limits camping areas are those within a mile of a developed area such as the Old Faithful geyser.

Jim Brady, district park ranger who led a team of six men that finally killed a suspect grizzly, Monday said, "They invited the bear into their camp by leaving their food on the ground."

Hennesay said park rules prohibited leaving food accessible to bears. He added the park service could conceivably charge Bradberry with violating park rules.

The two had hitchhiked from Alabama to the park and had somehow entered without seeing any park literature about bears, according to Bradberry.

Bradberry's account of the killing of his chum was authenticated quite clearly in these items from the archives of the *Bozeman Chronicle* and the *Great Falls Tribune,* dated June 27 and a few days later.

'KILLER' BEAR SHOT AT YELLOWSTONE

Yellowstone National Park (AP)—The remains of a 400-pound female grizzly bear thought to be the one that killed a camper in Yellowstone National Park Sunday have been sent to the University of Montana at Bozeman for analysis.

Asst. Park Supt. Bob Haraden said the bear was caught in a snare trap baited with meat Monday near the unauthorized campsite where 25-year-old Harry Walker of Anniston, Ala., was mauled to death.

Haraden said the bear was shot and the tests will determine whether it had eaten human flesh.

He said Walker's body was "badly mangled and there were indications the bear had eaten portions of the body."

Walker and 25-year-old Phillip Bradberry of Oxford, Ala., hitchhiked into the Old Faithful geyser area Friday and set up camp in the unauthorized area about a half-mile from the geyser.

Bradberry told how he and Walker were returning to the camp early Sunday and discovered the bear raiding their food supply. Bradberry managed to escape and went to the Old Faithful Inn where he reported the attack to park rangers.

It took rangers four hours to find Walker's body because of the early morning darkness and the rough terrain.

Haraden said only two bears had been spotted near Old Faithful this spring, although there are an estimated 250 grizzlies and 500 black bears in the park.

Walker was the fourth person to have been killed by a bear in the history of the 100-year-old park. The last nonfatal bear attack in the scenic park was reported in the summer of 1970.

AUTOPSY PERFORMED ON KILLER GRIZZLY

Yellowstone National Park, Wyo. (AP)—Yellowstone National Park officials said Tuesday an autopsy report from Montana State University indicated human hair was found on the claws of a 400-pound grizzly bear killed in the park Monday.

The bear was caught in a snare and shot by rangers when it returned to the site where a camper was mauled to death Sunday morning.

Assistant Park Supt. Vern Hennessy said they also found other items in the digestive tract to indicate the bear had been at the camp before. He said they found aluminum foil and other scrap material from the campsite.

Hennessey said the findings, coupled with the fact that the bear was trapped at the campsite, gave park rangers conclusive evidence that they killed the right animal.

As is the case in some attacks by bears upon park visitors, the aftermath of Harry Eugene Walker's killing ended up in an expensive court battle. This is illustrated by the item from the files of Associated Press, which appeared in the *Vancouver Sun* of February 25, 1975.

BEAR DEATH
$87,417 AWARDED

Los Angeles (AP)—A judge awarded $87,417 Monday to the parents and sister of Harry Walker, 25, of Anniston, Alabama, killed by a grizzly bear in Yellowstone National Park June 26, 1972.

The damages—less than a fifth of the $500,000 sought—were awarded when Judge Andrew Hawk ruled the park service was negligent on several counts.

The judge said officers should have warned that garbage dumps had recently been closed and that bears might attempt to get into the picnic area to feed.

The judge said the bear involved in the attack had been moved out of the area and should have been moved even farther away.

Then two years later, in the *Bozeman* (Montana) *Chronicle,* dated June 21, 1977:

SUPREME COURT WON'T HEAR GRIZZLY BEAR CASE

Washington (AP)—The Supreme Court has refused to hear the case of a young Alabama man killed by a grizzly bear in Yellowstone National Park.

Surviving relatives of Harry Eugene Walker had asked the court to rule that negligence by park employes led to Walker's death and that the park service should have to pay damages under the Federal Tort Claims Act.

The 9th U.S. Circuit Court of Appeals had overturned a trial court's award of $87,417 to Walker's parents and sisters, ruling that the details of Walker's death were not covered by the federal law entitling individuals to collect damages from the government and that Walker had contributed to the negligence.

The Supreme Court, without comment, on Monday let stand the appeals court's judgment.

Walker, 25, and a friend had hitchhiked to Yellowstone from their Anniston, Alabama, homes in 1972.

The two young men had set up a campsite in an unauthorized area near the Old Faithful geyser, and on the night of June 24 Walker was attacked by a grizzly at the campsite.

In their suit, Walker's surviving relatives charged that the park had endangered all campers at Yellowstone by closing down backcountry open-pit garbage dumps, sending the grizzly into tourist areas in search of food.

During a conversation, one of the Yellowstone Park wardens told me that the Walker lawsuit ended in defeat for the relatives of the victim. Such actions against governments would appear to be a no-contest match wherever they are instigated.

While still fresh from interviews with people who have been devastatingly injured by park-protected bears and other people attacked by bears in the wilds, I find that my sense of compassion is with the victims.

As I write this, I recall a talk I had with a young hiker-camper the night before my interview with Cantrell.

I met Sigmund Letner at a campsite in Yellowstone Park. He had come over to North America in late May 1979 from Luxembourg. He was, at that meeting, a pink-tanned twenty-year-old university student on an adventure few of us would undertake. He was walking and hitchhiking about America's outdoors, his worldly possessions in a knapsack on his back.

I met him during my third circuit of driving throughout the road system of the busy campsite. His nylon tent was off to one side in the land area adjacent to a parking spot that could accommodate a vehicle. I was getting desperate for a location for the night, so I stopped just in front of the parking spot. Sigmund was sitting at the campsite table with a book before him, facing sideways to the roadway.

"Are you occupying this site?" I asked.

"You can use it," he stated quietly, with a trace of German accent.

"Don't you have a vehicle—one to come in here?"

"No, you can use it. I camp—only," he said with a smile.

"Many thanks. There aren't any other spaces I can find."

After moving my vehicle into the open space, I went about getting my dinner and then washed up. Next I sorted my notes from the day, redefining some of the poorly written ones, recording remembered statements. Occasionally, when I looked out, Sigmund was also doing a camping chore. He prepared a dinner from dried packaged foods over a small alcohol stove, drank a boiled-water beverage, tidied up his tent, and stuffed his viands into containers. Then he began a surprising activity.

He dragged in a 15-foot tree trunk, studded with sturdy branches which had been cut off at a six-inch length from the trunk. This rough "ladder" he placed against the trunk of a taller pine, lodging the device in the first high branches available to hold it. This accomplished, he climbed the studded pole to the higher section of the pine trunk. There he tied a thong about the top of his rudimentary ladder to hold it to the trunk. From his shoulder he took the end of a coil of quarter-inch rope and tied a knot unfamiliar to me, but which secured one end of the rope to the tall pine's trunk. He then unwrapped the thong which was holding the "ladder," and descended gingerly to the ground.

Once at the base, he dropped the coil of rope, then pulled the other end of the rope through a loop in his knapsack. I expected to see Sigmund haul his cache up the pine. Instead, he carried the makeshift ladder-pole to another tall pine about 20 feet distant, and proceeded up it with his rope coiled, but unwinding from his shoulder as he ascended. Again at the 15-foot height, he fixed the thong of rope to the tree trunk binding the ladder, then arranged a slip-loop through which he passed the coiled rope. With this accomplished, he dropped the coil to the foot of the tree before descending.

I was fascinated by this activity as I watched without comment from my camper. I was fairly familiar with various types of caches contrived in trees during big-game hunting, and most of these caches, incidentally, were broken into by some animal—often blamed on wolverines.

Later, in the near darkness, I saw Sigmund haul his packsack up to a 13- to 14-foot height above the ground, well above the reach of a bear and obviously safe for the night. This was all accomplished as a routine for him. His only sign of impatience was the odd swipe at a mosquito.

"Would you," I called out from the door of my camper, "like a cup of coffee or tea before you settle down?"

"I'm sorry. I didn't understand," he answered politely.

"Would you like a cup of coffee—or tea?"

"Thank you very much. I would like it."

He was a pleasant surprise in a youngster, a distinct reminder that our North American freedoms had allowed some of the courtesy and good manners of the Old World to dissipate with our attitude of how-to-make-friends-and-influence-your-own-future. He chose coffee and was delighted with a plate of refrigerated cheese and cold cuts, followed by a second cup and crisp sugar cookies.

My curiosity eventually got around to his elevated cache. He stated that it was a park rule to have all of one's foodstuffs in a cache, that no scraps were to be left around camp, nothing edible in the tent. He had learned the cache method while camping in other parks. I complimented him on his observance of regulations.

"You say you have visited several parks—camped out in each one. Have you experienced any trouble with bears?"

He nodded quickly.

"Yes. I have done. One bear came into my camp while in Sequoia National Park—when I was first camping out."

The answer was a complete surprise.

"That is interesting. I'm writing a book about bear attacks upon humans. In fact, the work I was doing while you were putting up your cache was research for that book."

He lifted his eyebrows politely. While he had been eating, I had been asking him of his origins, his schooling, his journey across America on foot, without informing him of my own quest or occupation. He was pleased and pleasantly naive.

"You are a famous book writer—I never met one before," he said. He seemed impressed. When I nodded and said I was *just a writer,* he asked, "You are writing of *bears?*"

"Yes, attacks and killings by bears here in North America."

"There are many of them?"

"Quite a few—over a long period—say thirty years, which I am tracing. But actually, when compared by numbers to almost any other tragic incident—very few of them. Would you like to tell me what happened to you in Sequoia National Park?"

"You will put it in the book . . . ?"

"That might be. Why don't you tell me about it?"

He looked a trifle embarrassed, colored a bit beneath his tan.

"It wasn't much. The bear tried to get my food. It was on the bottom of my tent. The animal came in the night while I was at another camp."

My curiosity was aroused.

"Was it a grizzly or a black bear? Do you know?"

He looked embarrassed, unsure of English translation.

"It was a *bear*. I didn't see it very well, because it was dark. I came to the tent, and it was there. I took fire sticks out of the campfire, and hit it. It went away."

"You hit it with a burning piece of wood?"

"Yes, I didn't quite well know what it was . . ."

My incredulity must have shown on my face; Sigmund became more embarrassed and apologetic.

"I was surprised," he went on. "I did not wish to lose my food."

"You were lucky, Sigmund! Very lucky! It could have killed you."

He was nodding his head in agreement.

"They told me that—later. I didn't know."

I showed him copies of a couple of my earlier published books, the traveling file, cartons of notes on bear attacks, the case histories. I discussed some of the incidents and suggested that he stick with the larger official campsites, such as the one in which we were. He nodded in agreement. His brush with a bear in the night had occurred in Sequoia National Park during the first two weeks of his travels. Since then, he had used the method, earlier described, to cache his food overnight. He left shortly thereafter, to bed down on a foam pad on the ground sheet in his tent. I had invited him in for early morning coffee—I would be leaving about 7:30 A.M.

At 7:45 A.M. there was still no movement from his tent. I had been up for an hour, and had a long stretch of mileage to cover in the day's planned itinerary. I left without seeing Sigmund Letner again. It kept running through my mind that if Harry Walker and Phillip Bradberry had been as knowledgeable and well prepared, Harry Walker might still be alive.

11

I Look Behind
Every Tree Now

She is slight, bright, and blonde, twenty-one years of age, now doing environmental studies at the University of Utah, toward a degree that she hopes will get her into either the National Park Service or the Forest Service. Her name is Marianna Young. In 1978, a grizzly sow picked her up in its teeth, threw her up against a tree, and mauled her terribly.

While visiting the administration office at Mammoth, in Yellowstone National Park, Dale Nuss answered my questions about Marianna Young in a matter-of-fact manner. Nuss is a supervisory ranger with a couple of years left before retirement. He clearly recalled the case when shown the clipping below:

The Province, June 15, 1978

BEAR ATTACK

Yellowstone Park, Wyo.—Rangers temporarily closed the park's rugged backcountry to campers Wednesday following a nearly fatal attack on a young woman hiker by a mother bear with three cubs. Mary Anna [sic] Young, 21, of Jackson, who was attacked while hiking in the Heart Lake area of the park, was found by other hikers and given emergency treatment. She was then flown to [the] hospital in Salt Lake City where she underwent five hours of surgery.

Nuss fingered the clipping, looked up at me.

"How can I help you, Mr. Cramond?"

"I'd like to get in touch with her to do an interview for a book I'm writing."

He shook his head, thoughtfully.

"I don't have her present address. But, I do know that she is studying at the University of Utah. You could write her in care of the university. Perhaps I can tell you something else you'd like to know?"

It was a typical "parks" approach—cautious, protective of the privacy of the victim, noncommittal.

"Well, did you have anything to do with the actual investigation? On the spot?"

He shook his head before replying.

"No," he said. "That was done by rangers Jones, Grant, and McDowell."

"Were they on the spot?"

"Yes. They attended to her following the attack."

"I'd like to talk to them, any one of them. Do you have any objection to that?"

"No. You could contact Janie McDowell, sub-district ranger at the South Entrance. She was with Marianna on the scene."

I noted the name and address in the file.

"Okay. After I've been in and visited the site of the killing of Harry Walker, I will interview Ranger McDowell. Tell me, did you—as an active ranger—ever have a grizzly come after you—unprovoked?"

He stared at me for a moment, then broke into a grin.

"Well—yes! A sow with two cubs came after me."

"I'd like to hear about it."

He nodded, the grin slowly subsiding from his face.

"I was riding a bicycle up to visit some parks service buildings," he began. "Suddenly this sow grizzly with two cubs just burst out of the timber and came directly at me on the road. It was so sudden that I jumped off my bicycle and held it in front of me. She stopped about fifteen feet away and raised a fuss, bellowing and squealing and blowing the way they do. She made a couple of feints. I thought of falling flat and pulling the bicycle over me as some sort of protection. But, just as suddenly, she turned and went off into the bush."

He stopped and picked up a pencil and sheet of paper. I asked if that was all. He shook his head and drew a double-line road, then indicated a stand of timber and some squares for building sites.

"It was a long way back to any other shelter. I decided to go on to the service building." He drew a mark from the timber to the road, intersecting it at the scene of the first attack, then a second and a third line of rushes from the grizzly. "I just got a few yards, and she came out at me again. Right here." He indicated on the drawing. "She repeated the performance, rushing up to within a few feet of me and raising a fuss. Again, I was wondering if my bike could protect me if she decided to charge. Suddenly she turned and went back to her cubs. I noticed that she was a very small, lean bear . . . but . . ." He grinned at the recollection, "they all look *big* at a time like that."

His description of the squealing and bellowing aroused such a memory in my own past that my belly muscles had tightened.

"She was bluffing you?"

"Yes, and did a good job of it."

We both laughed as he continued.

"Well, she came at me once more as I kept heading for the service buildings. I repeated the act of getting behind my bicycle. Then, just like that, she took off with her cubs."

The story was a familiar one. The twist can go either way: attack, mauling, and death—or sudden departure. I noted that fact, adding a query: "Dale, you said 'small.' Was she a precocious yearling, bred before her second year?"

He shook his head emphatically: "No. That is what we all

thought—that she might just have been highly protective of her cubs. But she later proved to be twenty-one years old and 126 pounds."

"My gosh. You said 126 pounds—not 226!"

He nodded. "She was old, very old for cubs," he continued. "Her teeth were gone, rotten and worn out. She was in poor condition for coping with cubs. I guess she didn't really want any part of me."

I picked up the file on Marianna Young.

"What happened in the Young case?"

Nuss stared over my shoulder at the wall behind me. He nodded to an array of colored cards, about 12 by 14 inches square, with printed bear warnings on each one.

"She walked right past a couple of those signs. She also was hiking alone, which is against park regulations. She passed another hiking group and then ran into a sow grizzly with two cubs. The sow immediately took after her, knocked her down, and gave her a very bad mauling. She was lying face down when the hiking party caught up with her, and her back was badly torn. In fact, the doctor told me her muscle structure was so badly torn away that he could have inserted his hand almost from waist to shoulder. But she healed well. I'm told she's back, walking in the park this year. Lots of courage."

"You don't know where she can be located now?"

He got up and called to his secretary outside the office, asking her for the information. The girl brought in a file. After a moment of looking through it, he shook his head.

"Why don't you see Ranger Janie McDowell, at South Gate? She can fill in the details—perhaps take you up the trail to where it happened."

We talked for a while about bear problems in parks. He took me out into the yard and showed me a new welded-aluminum combined bear trap and helicopter transport unit, his own design. He explained that it traveled very well when in flight and that it was equipped with an electrical release mechanism which could be operated from inside the cab of the pickup truck. I inquired about that, and he grinned.

"We transport bears back into the mountains occasionally," he said. "When the bear is released, the truck is usually moving away at up to fifteen or twenty miles an hour. The bear usually goes out in the opposite direction. One big boar that I was releasing went out backwards, however, which put him in the same line of travel as the truck. He came right after the truck. He caught up twice, and once got hold of the spare tire on the side rack. He practically got back into the truck before the driver was able to accelerate and shake him loose. No one likes that type of experience. If the door of the trap is lifted by electronics, no one has to be out on the back."

His explanation was another case of the unseen dramas handled by parks personnel. We parted moments later, with mutual good wishes.

When I drove to South Gate the following day, I found that Janie McDowell just happened to be on duty. I had driven from the Old Faithful site of Harry Walker's death down to the Heart Lake Trail, just eight miles farther along the highway. At the Heart Lake Trail entrance, where the cars of other visitors were parked, I saw a large three-by-four-foot sign painted with explicit instructions not to enter without a parks permit, to be wary of bears, and not to go up the trail unaccompanied. It was placed so that visitors could not miss it if they were headed for Heart Lake. This was the trail up which Marianna Young had gone ahead, alone. During my earlier discussion on the phone with Ranger McDowell, she had informed me that she couldn't possibly get away from her supervisory duties and go up the trail with me that day.

I walked the short distance along the trail to the registration sign, looking over the terrain. It consisted of fairly dense mountain-plateau timber with pine needles and underbrush on a loam-covered floor, not really the type of terrain in which one would normally expect to see a bear. It seemed more like deer, elk, or moose territory. I figured that the bear country was probably farther in. I got into the Jeep and drove the rest of the way to the multi-gate entrance at the south end of the park.

As I walked to the registration gate, a pretty young woman with brown eyes and a pleasant smile greeted me from beneath her ranger's Stetson. She asked if she could be of any assistance.

"I'm Mike Cramond, and I'm looking for Janie McDowell."

"Oh, yes, I was expecting you. I'm Jane McDowell. The other ranger is coming on duty in just a couple of minutes."

It was a surprise. One doesn't expect a young slip of a girl to be a sub-district ranger. Times change by the time you reach sixty-six years of age, I guess. I said I'd wait in my camper and make her a cup of tea. I put the kettle on and dug out Marianna Young's file. Shortly thereafter, Janie McDowell came in and sat down at the other end of the table. I told her she looked very much like my own daughter—but younger—who had almost ended up as part of the diet of a black bear. I remarked that she was very young to be an executive warden.

"I'm twenty-nine, Mr. Cramond," she responded. "What can I tell you about Marianna Young?"

"You were here at the time of the attack. Did you go in?"

"Yes, Ranger Gary Grant was in there first. We followed with the medical gear and a Stoke's litter. Gary had been attending to her. She was very quiet, and most of the bleeding had stopped. I was afraid she was slipping away. Her breathing seemed very faint. But when I said, 'If you hear me, open your eyes,' she did! Almost instantly, with lovely blue eyes. It was a relief. I was worried."

"Do you know how the attack occurred?"

"The other rangers did most of that investigation," Ranger McDowell said. "She had apparently gone ahead of a party of some twenty-five organized hikers, just pushing on up the trail alone. When they came up some five minutes later, she was lying about fifteen feet off the trail. I guess they scared the bears off. She said there were either two or three cubs with the sow grizzly. It came right after her—almost immediately, it appears."

Other sources had informed me that the girl was photographing the bear. I asked McDowell about that.

"Did you find her camera?"

"No, I didn't," she replied. "I don't think I saw it. I was interested in getting her to medical aid as soon as possible. They found her glasses about fifteen feet from her. She was an avid hiker."

"I hear that she is once again hiking in the woods."

"Yes, I'm told that, too. I visited her in the hospital. She made a very good recovery, and was anxious to get back to work in the parks."

I interrupted her.

"Janie, I was talking with some of the concessionaire supervisors at Old Faithful about the Young attack. They tell me she is now working not too far from here. Do you know where Signal Mountain Lodge is?"

Ranger McDowell looked at me for a long moment without much expression.

"Yes, it's just beyond Jackson Lake Junction, Mr. Cramond."

My hope was to reassure her.

"Well, I think she's there. Anyway, I don't want to bother her. I just want to leave a note and ask if she can stand being interviewed. With the incident this fresh, she may be sensitive. It's important to my research that I get the facts of the case quite straight. Each interview turns up a new fact, or a fact that fits into previous cases. Perhaps you can describe the exact terrain. I went in on the path a little way—just typical timber. Was there any other factor you could describe?"

She looked out the camper's open doorway.

"Yes, there are two small meadows just before the rise of the ridge where she was attacked."

It was part of what was missing. I broke in: "Meadows? Then a rise in land—with timber?"

"Yes. Why?"

"Well, Janie. Bears seem to frequent meadows when they have cubs. And the rising land beside the meadows is a typical sort of outlook for any game that wants to rest after browsing or grazing. It's a more probable spot for a bear than just timber. It fits in better with what I've discovered so far."

We talked pleasantly for half an hour. She acknowledged that a friend of the deceased Harry Walker, a girl employee of the park's concessions, had been a Parks Service witness for the government when the suit had been laid against that department. That bit of information also fitted into the jigsaw puzzle. Most of the bear incidents seemed to have in common the fact that the victim was either actively involved with the park government services or was connected with the concessionaires or businesses conducted within the parks.

I said so.

Janie nodded her head thoughtfully.

"That *is* interesting," she said. "Do you have any conclusions?"

"Well, it appears that the employees' familiarity with the proximity of bears might dull their fear of them."

Shortly thereafter, I drove to Signal Mountain Lodge and asked where I could find Marianna Young. I was told that she was off duty. Apparently, she had just left to visit the area from which I had driven. Nettled, I left a note. It was strange how often I just missed someone key to my inquiries—and usually shortly after I had left word that my destination was in their direction. Coincidental? My cop senses suggested otherwise.

A week later, after a trip to New Mexico had cleared my other commitments, I walked into Signal Mountain Lodge, unannounced, and asked the restaurant supervisor if Marianna Young was in. She nodded at a girl who was at that instant approaching the cash desk. I spoke to her.

"Hello, I'm Mike Cramond—the writer who left you a note last week."

"Oh, hello, Mr. Cramond. Yes, I got it."

So! This slightly built, lithe young blonde was Marianna. She was perky, unscarred, bright-eyed, and friendly. Damn the grizzly that would attack her. I realized I was staring at her. My eyes were unconsciously searching for signs, and obviously showing surprise that none were evident. She was waiting for my response.

"Do you mind talking to me, Marianna?"

"Not a bit," she replied. "I'd be happy to—but it will have to be either tonight—after work—or in the morning."

"Tonight? What time?"

"I'm through here about eleven-thirty. Is that okay?"

"I'll be here," I said.

That night, we met in one of the coffeeshop booths.

"You're certainly not marked, Marianna," I noted, opening the interview.

"I am—on my body—and here." She extended her left arm, where a not-too-noticeable scar crossed under her bicep. "She bit me on the legs and thighs too."

I was, for some old-fashioned reason, embarrassed. I interjected, "You're back hiking again, I hear."

She smiled enthusiastically. "Oh, yes. I like the outdoors very much," she replied.

"Not afraid?"

"Oh yes, I am! I look behind every tree now."

I nodded in full agreement.

"It's a hell of an experience to go through, and you are taking it very well," I remarked. "It's a strange thing, Marianna. I've interviewed more than twenty people who have gone through bear attacks. All of you appear much superior to normal people, aware and well adjusted, not embittered—just bigger than most others."

She looked down shyly, at what she felt was a compliment. "Thank you. I . . . " her voice trailed off.

"Marianna, I've interviewed a couple of other people about the general details of your attack. Tell me, why did you push on ahead of all the other hikers?"

She eyed me, a bit surprised by the directness.

"Well, I just didn't want to be behind a group of twenty-seven guided people, behind a crowd to which I didn't belong. I wanted to be ahead of them, to go my own way."

I looked at her frank young face, open and honest. "How long after passing them did you meet the grizzly?" I asked.

"Oh, about five minutes or less. I saw it about 100 feet away, with the two or three cubs. I've never been sure how many cubs."

"Did you try to photograph them?"

"Yes."

"Were you using a telephoto lens?"

"No, it was just an Instamatic. They say there was nothing on the film."

"Did the grizzly hear the camera, then come?"

"Yes, it just suddenly started after me. I tried to run, and I screamed. It got to me right away. I don't remember much except that it was a terrifying and gruesome experience. The bear *was* biting me and tossing me around. It threw me up against a tree. I guess that was what broke seven of my ribs."

I interjected, "You mean like a cat with a mouse."

"That would describe it—I couldn't do anything," she continued. "It just tossed me around, biting me. I guess I lay there, and it went away. Then the hikers came up."

"Was there much pain during the attack?"

"No, not pain. There was just an awful feeling of tearing flesh —I was conscious all the time."

I remarked, "Janie McDowell said you were very calm and quiet."

"Did she? I thought I was telling everybody to shut up. I thought I was noisy."

She looked embarrassed, to think she had been brash. I reassured her that others said she was very calm and composed. (In the hospital for two months, she underwent skin graftings and plastic surgery numerous times.) I said, "Tell me. Have you had much experience with the wilds?"

"Not really," she said. "I was born in Ohio. Not much time in the wilds at all back there."

"What about here, in the parks? Had you ever encountered bears previously?"

She stopped for a moment and asked if I meant in the wild, while hiking. She nodded when I responded, "Just anywhere."

"Yes, twice. The first time was here in Yellowstone in 1974, with two young black bears. And, in 1977 in Grand Tetons, I was part of a group that was close to a black bear near a trail going to Amphitheater Lake. There were seven or eight people. We were all watching it."

"How close?"

"Oh, I'd guess about fifteen feet away. There were people around. It didn't seem to be bothered."

It was almost the answer that I had expected. I didn't say anything to Marianna about my thoughts.

"Have you been back on the Heart Lake Trail?"

She smiled almost bashfully.

"Yes, I went back there with my mother and father and a bunch of others—I guess to see where it had happened."

We talked about her schooling. She said she would be attending the University of Utah in the fall. She hoped to finish her degree (at the time in environmental studies, later in geography) then find work in the Park Service or perhaps in the Forestry Service.

I wish I were a supervisor in one of those areas. Believe me, that spunky young lady wouldn't get a chance to apply in any other department but mine.

12

He Loved Bears;
They Were His Life

When Wilfred Etherington successfully terminated his first career as a pharmacist in Edmonton, Alberta, Canada, he went back to college and took a degree in zoology. He had always loved animals, both domestic and wild. At nearly fifty years of age, with his new diploma still fresh, he applied to the Canadian Wildlife Service for a job that involved studying bears.

A Canadian Wildlife Service senior biologist, Laszlo Retfalvi, hired him. When Etherington's application had first been received, his age and possible lack of rugged physique were considered marks against his being hired in such a physically demanding job as muscling around the inert hulks of tranquilized grizzly bears in the field.

According to Retfalvi, however, "There was never any doubt after our first interview. He was most sincere and dedicated to outdoor biology. In our program we studied problem bears in National Parks. Tranquilizing and marking captured

174

animals were part of the duties. I personally had a very great respect for Wilf. He really loved bears. They became his whole life."

I looked at the slightly built man sitting opposite me in my Jeep. When I had phoned Retfalvi and asked him for an interview, he had almost immediately said that he might not be the one to discuss the situation with, that he was emotionally involved and felt a sense of guilt because he was the one who had hired the late Wilfred Etherington. He now expressed that opinion once again.

My reaction was a sense of reasoning compassion.

"Hell, Mr. Retfalvi, that is misplaced guilt. You can't feel guilty for doing something that you thought was good for Etherington and good for the Wildlife Service. You made a wise decision, and it's not your fault that Wilfred Etherington died in the course of his duty—a duty that you have just said became his whole new life."

Retfalvi's face relaxed somewhat after those words. I urged him to tell me about Etherington's work as a member of the CWS.

"Wilf did a terrific job," he said. "We worked together for two years studying many animals. He was conscientious, cheerful, and very efficient. His wife was also very supportive and interested in his new career. You see, they had raised and educated two daughters—one a physician, the other a lawyer. This new field was, to some extent, taking him back to his beginnings. He had two brothers who were farmers. One of them was killed just two years ago, coincidentally, by a horse. It seems strange. Both of them loved animals."

Retfalvi was pensive for a moment. I asked him what their research work held, as an end result.

"Well, we primarily were studying problem parks bears and their association with people."

"You mean only problem bears? You didn't tranquilize bears that were roving free, but not creating problems?"

Retfalvi was most emphatic.

"No," he stated. "The only bears that we worked with were problem bears. Our main objective was to save bears. Parks have their problems, caused by high public visitation to them.

Garbage at campgrounds and at disposal sites attract bears. The presence of bears in heavy visitor-use areas poses a threat to both human life and property. To reduce the threat, park officials customarily trapped such bears and moved them to distant parts of the park. Most translocated bears, however, returned to heavy visitor-use areas, and if judged to be troublesome ended up destroyed. Our program was aimed at determining the causes and effects of this situation with a goal of reducing the mortality of parks bears. Our program was dovetailed into the parks bear management program, and it consisted, in part, of tranquilizing, handling and marking of captured bears. After release we followed the bears' movements and studied their habits."

The statement challenged some of my earlier conclusions, and I said so: "My own interpretation, from what I have seen on television, read, or heard, was that experimental bears were singled out in chosen areas, then trapped, tranquilized, or whatever, weighed, biologically examined, marked or outfitted with radio-equipped collars, and then released to wander their way around. I thought they were not problem bears—but that they might have become so after the scientific examinations, handlings, and markings."

Retfalvi's response was immediate and definite: "No, that was certainly *not* the case in our study. The only manner in which we came by a bear was if the parks had trouble with it. Bears having a bad record in human relationships were, as a final resort, usually killed—destroyed, if you prefer the word. Our studies attempted to find ways to reduce bear-human conflict, without having to destroy bears. Bears in parks usually have access to garbage dumps, or at least garbage containers. They are omniverous, like man, and anything that man uses as food is acceptable to them. They eat roots, wild fruits, vegetables, fish, and flesh. When humans make food or scraps available, bears easily learn to use it. They are intelligent animals. It is an easy source of sustenance to them, and they change their habits to accommodate the patterns provided for in the parks. They eat garbage and become conditioned to the practice."

The statement was made as a scientific fact, derived from extended studies in parks. I pointed out that "garbage," as we term it, is a different product in our magnificently affluent society than it might be elsewhere in the world. In some countries, people comb the garbage heaps or repositories for cast-off tidbits, while we of temperate North America throw away or waste more food during a week than some families of have-not nations have to eat for two weeks. Our "garbage" is often merely unspoiled food for which we have no more need. It is little wonder that bears find it inviting.

Retfalvi gave me a long look.

"Yes, I think you have said it clearly," he said. "We studied the bears' habits on the garbage dumps. A black bear, upon approaching a dump, would put its cubs up a tree, in a safe place, then go in gingerly and feed. A sow grizzly would make a charge, or charges, into an area containing food, displace the other bears around a specific area, then take her young in with her. She would perhaps pull out a plastic bag of garbage and take it to the cubs to feed them. This may have some relationship to the attacks in sleeping bags—the smell of humans that they associate with food—garbage containers—the sleeping bag with a human in it."

The scientist's logic applied to dozens of items that I had come across during my own readings and research into attacks and deaths. Frankly, it was a shock to realize that such a factor had not been obvious to me. I pointed this out to Retfalvi and asked if he had any specific cases.

"Yes," he replied. "There was a sow that had been causing problems and had been tranquilized twice previously. She attacked two men in sleeping bags. You may have that incident in your files—it was at Baker Lake. The bear left her cubs by the water, where they stayed quite silent. She then went to the area where the men were sleeping in their bags. She grabbed at one bag and tried to pull it down. Without uttering a sound, the man in it pulled it back. She repeated her act three times while he pulled the bag up again noiselessly. He finally kicked out at her, and she bit him in the heel. They all made a fuss and she finally ran away."

I nodded. "Yes, I do have that item. What happened to the animal in that instance?"

He looked sadly perturbed by his recollections as he went

on. "As I told you, I am biased toward bears. We were asked to locate the bears, and I asked Wilf to assist in the search. A sow bear and three yearling cubs were shot. Wilf was almost in tears upon his return. I felt the same way."

It isn't the type of story anyone enjoys hearing. I pointed out that if the sow had had two previous tranquilizings and a history of trouble, it was a logical decision by any management group. The same logic would apply to the cubs, which had also fed in garbage dumps and would have been imprinted, or conditioned, to that pattern of feeding.

In fact, what else could be done?

Retfalvi shook his head. He was as aware of this reasoning as I. I asked him about the use of tranquilizers. What were his findings? Were there any new discoveries in the use of them?

"There is a new drug, sernylan, that has a lesser probability of mortality and detrimental aftereffects, both on the bear and possibly on its human associations," he told me.

My curiosity was piqued by the suggestion of mortality: "Mortality among drugged bears? Is it high?"

He shook his head emphatically. "We didn't have such a case in our small program. It might run to 10 percent, in early attempts to drug bears, particularly if the animals were misjudged as to weight. In earlier attempts Anectine was used, a drug having much less tolerance. There is the problem of estimating muscle tissue to fat. A very large-appearing bear may carry a lot of fat. The effects of the drug are in relation to the muscle tissues, not the fat; thus, total weight is not the only factor. We took the utmost care to handle ours, using the lesser dosage that might be estimated."

"Is there any particular drug that is best?" I asked.

He nodded thoughtfully. "I'm more impressed with sernylan. It actually puts the animal to sleep. You may have noticed that the animal's eyes remain open under some tranquilizers."

"Yes, I remember that was a most definite focal point of cameras that had filmed such animals. I've seen that factor on several captures and releases on television."

He nodded and continued: "Well, animals put under by

anectine are fully conscious of the human activity and of being handled."

I asked, "Tell me, would such an apparently conscious, but paralyzed animal retain the memory of that handling?"

His answer was revealing: "The drug actually blocks the electrical connection at the nerve endings, which paralyzes the muscles. The animals are inert, but conscious. You will notice that as they regain conscious control, the front sections will revive first, then the middle sections, then the hind section after the animal's head is up."

I interjected a question: "Do you consider the bear's recognition of humans being about—handling them—to be a factor in their losing fear, or causing attacks as an aftermath?"

He stared at me for a moment. It wasn't a question that I enjoyed asking a scientist who was being understanding and cooperative in his revelations. He turned away and glanced up the street before answering.

"It may affect the behavior of some animals. But I don't believe that tranquilizing has triggered any attacks. There isn't any such evidence," he said. "Bears become used to human scent as soon as they enter the areas frequented by humans. They feed in garbage dumps on scraps left or even handed to them by humans. Any natural intolerance of mankind is diminished by any association that the animal has with people. Bears are a dominant animal, particularly the grizzlies. They progressively lose their respect for, or fear of, human kind with any association."

My mind went back to another official in another government service. I had asked him about tranquilizing, and his answer had been less negative. Investigations of particular cases had shown no signs of ear-tagging or other scientific markings. (Note: Even when tags that have been put in both ears of drugged and examined bears are removed or lost, the ear will retain a small, apparent scar.) I said so and mentioned that there had been a sensitivity in departmental quarters to the suggestion that drugging may cause human attacks. I asked him about the drug called sernylan.

"It is my preference, but it is difficult to get. It is one of the items on a restricted list, one that may be addictive to humans. We got only very controlled portions of it, and had to account for every bit of it that we received. It was a good precaution. As I said, the animal goes into a deep sleep when under it. There appear to be no aftereffects either. Unfortunately, our program was meagerly funded and using a helicopter at $450 an hour made waiting around too expensive. We didn't get many chances to watch a bear fully recover from the drugs. We did, regularly, take a fixed-wing aircraft out to check, but it was not nearly as effective as a helicopter for such observations."

His words were revealing some of the problems not fully understood or comprehended by most of us. Details about such cases are frequently not available to the public, either. Facts can often be omitted from brief news items, for instance. Or data in some case histories might not be volunteered, either for departmental convenience or because they were not considered pertinent to public announcements of the incidents.

I referred Retfalvi to the departmental letters that follow.

Environment	Environnement	WLU 200 Bears
Canada	Canada	Grizzly Incidents
Environmental	Gestion	
Management	de l'environnement	Edmonton, Alberta
		May 8, 1979

CANADIAN WILDLIFE SERVICE

Mr. Mike Cramond
4875 The Dale
West Vancouver, B.C.
V7W 1K2

Dear Mr. Cramond:

I would like to acknowledge your letter requesting information regarding the grizzly bear related death of Mr. Wilf Etherington. Unfortunately, because of possible legal implications, the information on file is of a confidential nature.

We would, however, refer you to Mr. Laszlo Retfalvi, Canadian Wildlife Service, Vancouver, who was Mr. Etherington's supervisor at the time of the accident. Mr. Retfalvi may be able to supply you with many of the details that you are interested in. . . .

Sincerely yours,

M. R. Robertson
Regional Director

| Indian and | Affaires indiennes |
| Northern Affairs | et du Nord |

Calgary, Alberta
April 5, 1979

Mr. Mike Cramond
4875 The Dale
West Vancouver, British Columbia
V7W 1K2   C 9810—133—3

Dear Mr. Cramond:

I have your letter dated March 28, 1979 for reply. You requested additional information regarding Mr. W. Etherington in that his death occurred while actively engaged in grizzly research work as an employee of the Canadian Wildlife Service. I will give you as clear a picture of the circumstances as I can.

On September 23, 1973 a fairly large male grizzly was trapped at Baker Creek Bungalows in Banff. This bear was held and maintained until September 25, because poor weather and availability of aircraft prevented flying the animal for release in a remote area until that time.

Prior to this date it was agreed that when the opportunity occurred, Mr. Etherington would work together with a photographer, Mr. W. Schmalz, on a bear release. Mr. Schmalz was under contract to produce a bear film (Bear and Man— currently available through the National Film Board) for Parks Canada. Because of the combined weight of the bear, pilot, two passengers and necessary fuel, the aircraft was loaded close to the maximum thus making it impossible to carry additional passengers. Mr. Etherington's principal interest at that time was to observe the reaction of the bear coming out of a tranquilizing drug which it is necessary to administer in order to immobilize the animal for helicopter-sling transport. Mr. Schmalz of course wished to get whatever film he could, possibly to be used in the Bear and Man film. The bear in question proved to be a fine specimen for either person's interest, being a fully mature, fairly large male weighing over 500 pounds. (Whenever feasible, bears are weighed and measured when under the drug. This one weighed 527 pounds at that time.)

The work in relocating the bear began with the administration by Mr. Etherington of two different drugs at 12:41 p.m. The bear was down and out at 1:25 p.m. It was transported then by helicopter to a very remote area near the north east boundary of Banff park, north of Lake Louise. Because it was a large dominant male it was released in an area not used previously for release, to avoid if possible, conflict with other bears. The release was made at approximately 2:20 p.m. The aircraft landed approximately 200 yards from the released bear and the pilot shut down to await Mr. Etherington and Mr. Schmalz. Schmalz and Etherington left the aircraft by some distance to locations where they felt they could best observe and film the bear as it recovered from the drug.

Both Etherington and Schmalz continued to observe and film the bear until about 5:30 p.m. as it gradually recovered from the effects of the drug. At this time both persons were within 100 feet of the now almost fully recovered bear when it charged them. Both men retreated, soon separating, the charging bear following Etherington who was overtaken and fatally mauled. In spite of efforts by Schmalz to drive off the bear, it was not until the pilot of the helicopter made passes at the animal at low altitude that it was driven some distance away. It was very quickly ascertained that the victim was beyond help, having sustained massive head, face and neck injuries.

It is often difficult and perhaps redundant in cases such as this, to form conclusions. Obviously, had the participants exercised greater prudence, the accident could have been prevented. Unlike most such incidents all participants were aware of the hazards involved. In the coroners words, "the cause of death was an error in judgement in not taking proper safety precautions with a live grizzly bear in the area."

I trust the foregoing will provide the detail you require on this particular incident.

Yours sincerely,

W. C. Turnbull
Director
Western Region
Parks Canada

For several minutes Laszlo Retfalvi studied the detailed letter of April 5, 1979, from W. C. Turnbull, director, Western Region, Parks Canada, whose cooperation in my own research had been excellent, if cautious. Retfalvi would occasionally shake or nod his head and then go on.

"That's a fair account from a person who was not actually participating in the actual incident and investigation. Actually there was much more detail than is given here," he said more to himself than to me.

His finger was at the sentence, "Mr. Etherington's principal interest at that time was to observe the reaction of the bear coming out of a tranquilizing drug . . ." Then he hesitated again, at the middle of the fourth paragraph, and shook his head as if in some denial. When Retfalvi had read the letter, I showed him the news accounts that follow:

The Vancouver Sun, Wednesday, September 26, 1973

BANFF PARK GRIZZLY KILLS MAN

Lake Louise, Alta. (CP)—A grizzly bear, thought to be sedated, attacked and killed a biologist Tuesday, in a wilderness area 35 miles north of here.

Wilfred Arthur Etherington, 51, of Edmonton, was killed when the adult grizzly charged him shortly after being released from a trap, Tom Ross, operations supervisor of Banff National Park, said today.

Bill Schmalz of Wilderness Scenigraphic (Films) Ltd. of Vancouver, escaped injury when the tranquilized bear apparently regained its senses and surprised the men as they approached to film it.

The bear had been transported by helicopter to the area from another part of the park, and the two men were filming the event for an educational film on the park's bear management program.

"It was just a normal situation. The bear was released and moved away from the aircraft. Mr. Etherington and Mr. Schmalz got near the bear, filming to within 50 to 100 feet. Then the bear began to approach them.

"I assume the bear must have recovered more quickly than they anticipated and then charged. Etherington was the first person it reached."

Ross said the bear has been shot to protect the public and the Banff park warden service is continuing its investigation into the incident.

It is believed to be the first death as a result of a bear attack in the park's history.

(Note: The same release is in the *Province*, September 27, 1973.)

Retfalvi nodded his head when I asked him if the case history was comparatively accurate in its details.

"My contention with these documents which you have presented to me is not that they are inaccurate to any great degree, but that they miss important details in the case."

I noted that my own dealings with government people had shown me that most personnel are reluctant to reveal either their own attitudes, or all of the facts about any inquiry run by their departments. A full twenty-two years of dealing with bureaucracies had continuously revealed, to me, a competitiveness, or even jealousy, among sections of government agencies: attitudes that interfered with their own work; fears of releasing interdepartmental information, because of the possibility of rebuke, or just plain nit-picking from associates. The don't-get-your-tail-in-the-gate principle runs through all government agencies, mainly because of the smallness of some officials, and certainly not for want of an excellent general staff. Those nit-pickers, whose hindsight is always phenomenal, are the main reason why civil service organizations have a reputation for being costly bureaucracies. Because much of my former environmental-impact work required release of government information, I found that political pressure, requested from friends in the parliaments or legislatures, inevitably forced out the facts. My own reputation for keeping my sources absolutely confidential also helped unveil most facts. I had expressed these opinions to Laszlo Retfalvi at the outset of our interview.

"Had the bear, the grizzly that killed Etherington, a record of being tranquilized?" I asked Retfalvi.

His answer was frank and immediate: "Yes. The bear was a large dominant male. It had been handled in 1972 after it had broken into an unoccupied building containing food. We measured it and took its weight at 550 pounds. I questioned its stated weight of 527. It should have been heavier."

"You tranquilized it that first time?"

"Yes. This was the second time it had been trapped. In fact, the Parks Branch was cooperating in the production of *Bear and Man*—I suppose you saw that recent film on television a couple of weeks ago, by the National Film Board?—No? Well, it had some of the footage taken at the time Wilf Etherington was killed."

He paused. "As I was Wilf's supervisor, I had to go into the case quite intensively—apart from the fact that I felt very much responsible for the tragedy."

His lack of detachment was an evident qualification of both the truth and accuracy of his recollections. He had been deeply affected by the death of his friend and associate. I waited for his next statement.

"The bear had been held for longer than it normally would have been," he said, "in order to cooperate with National Film Board in their documentary. Not an ideal situation, but I guess logical under the circumstances. It had been held in a steel cage during that period. Unauthorized people had visited it— not a desirable situation, as the bear had charged the bars during such visits and had broken its canines and cut and bruised its jaws and head by smashing against the cage."

I broke in, "Would you consider that its mood could have

been caused by that exposure—possibly making it resentful and aggressive?"

He paused without affirming by word or nod, as if reflecting deeply upon the whole incident. I remembered witnessing the charges of several newly caged animals against the unyielding sides of a crib, or steel bars, and my empathy for such animals during captivity is strong. The enormous power of a grizzly is brought up short, and with resultant woundings. This one, no doubt, had been given a heightened desire for retaliation.

Retfalvi continued in his explanation: "Wilf didn't have to go along with them. He had been offered the opportunity to accompany the party. Actually his work with the studies required of that bear had been completed. Perhaps he was motivated by the opportunity to closely study a bear as it came out of the drug. You see, Mr. Cramond, we had a small budget for our studies, as I have told you. In this case, they were making a film documentary in cooperation with other departments, and the budget was more extensive. Wilf's scientific interest was probably inspired by the opportunity to watch the animal regain its strength—and Wilf was a very helpful person. I'm also sure that he wished to assist the photographer concerned. Actually, he was more cooperative than I felt necessary."

Retfalvi was looking at the letter lying on the file in the front seat of the Jeep.

"Wilf and I had breakfast together that morning in Banff," he continued. "He said he was going over to Lake Louise to tranquilize a bear caught two days earlier, and that was still in the trap. He planned to be back by lunch. When he didn't show, I left a note for him to call me when he got back, as I had to return to Edmonton. That evening, shortly after arriving home, the RCMP [Royal Canadian Mounted Police] called with the sad news that Wilf had been killed."

He shook his head at the recollection and continued: "I checked quite thoroughly into what had actually happened. Wilf had given the bear a less than normal dosage in order to shorten the process of recovery, so that Schmalz could photograph a fully mobile bear. In spite of the small dose, the bear stayed immobilized much longer than expected. We—Wilf and I—never took guns with us. We felt we would be protecting ourselves in such a case, and not the bears. Our purpose was to save bears, not to destroy them. Therefore we planned our activities in such a manner as not to put ourselves in situations with bears where guns were necessary. And, in handling a score of them, it is possible that Wilf may have lost some of his fear of them."

"Having a gun in the proximity of bears does give the bearer of the arm a false sense of security, and could likely result in a less cautious behavior that in turn could invite an attack by the bear. Few would not use a handy gun for self defense if attacked by a bear."

I agreed that a lack of respect was apparent in some of the documentaries, that the men seen handling the creatures had either exhibited much more courage, or less appreciation of the potential danger than seemed normal. Was this the case in Etherington's tragedy?

Retfalvi thought about that. "Well," he said, "my own inquiry into the situation showed more facts than you have accumulated. After the helicopter pilot set the sling down in the chosen spot, he flew Wilf and Schmalz to a spot a few hundred feet away, where they set up their cameras. The pilot then flew back to the bear and hovered over it, to see if it would react. He set down then flew out to the Banff Jasper highway in order to make radio contact with headquarters. When he returned, the bear was showing some sign of recovery. Its hindquarters were still under paralysis. The pilot took off and hovered over it again. This time the animal reacted by attempting to rise and bat at the hovering craft. In the meantime, Schmalz and Wilf had moved in closer. Wilf, incidentally, was using a "Super 8" camera on his own and made some recordings of the animal's behavior on a small tape recorder that he had borrowed from Schmalz, having left his own behind. The animal was recovering quickly, and was on its feet, moving to a small spring to quench its thirst. The film that was exposed—it wasn't included in the documentary shown on television—showed the bear looking right into the lens. It was definitely aware of the two men photographing it. It seems they were just too close."

Retfalvi shook his head almost angrily. "They wanted dramatic pictures. Photographers always want dramatic pictures.

The bear then began to come toward the camera. As it became apparent that the animal was going to charge, both men ran in the same direction, away from it. Wilf turned after about fifteen feet, and the grizzly went right after him. It got him after Wilf apparently stumbled on loose rocks. Schmalz yelled and tried to distract it. The pilot, who saw this from a distance, ran back to his helicopter and took off and buzzed the animal, but it had apparently killed Wilf instantly; his head was badly mutilated. They finally drove it off, but it was too late to save Wilf. They tried to pull his body into the helicopter, but the bear was too aggressive. Finally they flew back to parks headquarters and got a ranger with a rifle. The animal was destroyed."

The story was nearly complete. It differed, not in accuracy as much as in detail, from departmental versions.

But what had been revealed from Retfalvi's account was the human side of the incident. I thought of the rangers and conservation officers that I knew, men who courageously walk in on the aftermath of tragedy and who have to take care of the blood and guts of the bear attacks. Fully cognizant of the dangers, such men go in and calmly dispose of an animal that has shown its ability to destroy, maim, and, on occasion, eat human flesh. Whether they are scientists in search of knowledge or officers who must protect the public from overly aggressive animals, these men perform duties that few are courageous enough to face.

It really doesn't matter if so-called blame is placed anywhere. There is no real blame. Mistakes are sometimes made in such cases because all of the facts are not evident. If they had always been evident, the tragedies would have been averted.

What does matter is that the injury or loss is taken into account, and that steps are taken to avoid repetition. Also, those who are the recipients of loss and injury should be compensated so that they do not suffer needlessly further.

Wilf Etherington loved bears. He gave his life in an effort to help you and me understand the species, that we may live in greater harmony with them. That is all that really matters.

13

My First Bear Attack

The black bear that attacked me gave me the biggest surprise I've ever had in my life. The animal came soundlessly, with no growl or warning of any kind. I didn't even know it was there until it was within 20 feet of me—in full charge.

If I hadn't been holding a rifle in my hands at that instant, the chances are that my case would have been one of those in the files now before me, and that someone else would have been writing about it.

Facing a charging bear, even with a loaded rifle in your hands, is a helluva shock. During my sixty years of living in bear country (which I still do), as a hunter and outdoor writer-photographer, I have learned to expect a sudden attack from *any* bear. It doesn't matter whether you deliberately or unwittingly provoke the animal, whether you're unaware of its presence, or whether you're attempting to avoid it—a bear can be expected to attack anything or anyone, at any time.

Don't listen to anyone who tells you otherwise.

It also doesn't matter whether it is a polar bear, which is generally considered to be the most likely to attack; a grizzly, which is known to be extremely courageous and frequently belligerent; or an ordinary black bear, which is erroneously, even foolishly, touted as nonbelligerent.

Two black bears that I wasn't even aware of nearly got to me and could have killed me if they had not been shot. Two grizzlies that I wounded came at me the moment they ascertained my location. That kind of retaliation is to be expected. The former type of attack isn't.

An attack by any wounded bear cannot be classified as an attack by a "killer bear." Yet even by omitting such attacks, statistics show that more people have been killed by black bears than by grizzlies. The only qualification to that fact is that black bears are more numerous and widespread in their habitat.

In an article originally entitled "Unpredictable Ursus," published in the November 1944 issue of *Outdoor Life* as "Never Trust a Bear," I related the story of a black bear attacking me without provocation. Until the autumn before that article was published, I would never have believed that a black bear would attack anyone from ambush, and particularly that one would attack one of two fully grown men who were sitting only a few hundred feet from a well-traveled road.

At the time, I had been living in or near bush country for most of my thirty-one years. I was an experienced hunter, having killed dozens of game animals, and had on several occasions fished streams while a black bear was on the opposite bank.

I didn't take liberties with bears. In fact, I always avoided them if I encountered them on my side of a stream, valley, lake, or road. I had found that a loud yell usually made a bear lift its head, perhaps shake it from side to side or wag its body at the shoulders for a moment or two and then move off into the surrounding growth, not to return. Some bears simply took off at a dead run the moment they discovered that a human was nearby. These, of course, were bears encountered in wild country. Some raised their hackles at the shoulders in a show of aggressive bravado or fear, but they nevertheless turned away. It was never my hunting practice to kill a black bear either. This was simply because I have always hunted for meat and personally have no liking for black bear on the table— despite its many excellent qualities as a viand.

The surprise attack occurred near Campbell River, British Columbia. My hunting partners, Jerry and Frank, and I were residents of the then-small fishing and logging outpost settlement, which at that time was the terminus of Vancouver Island's highway. I was a constable with the famed old B.C. Provincial Police (the first legally constituted territorial police force in North America, antedating both the Royal Canadian Mounted Police and the Texas Rangers), and had just been assigned to the area that summer.

I think it was Frank who arranged the deer hunt. He wanted a buck, and knew of a good deer concentration near the confluence of the Quinsam River and the larger, world-famous Campbell River. The area lent itself to a cooperative or drive hunt, a kind of hunting I had done only once before, and which I don't particularly enjoy. Frank parked the car on the road edge not more than a mile from the center of town, near the point where he had on several occasions seen black-tailed deer.

When we got out of the car, we drew straws for the positions we would assume in the drive. My draw was the short stem, leaving me last choice. That turned out to be the course that went through the alder-crowded deltas along the river. Frank drew the middle section, which placed him halfway up the ridge of the valley, and Jerry took the highest section, in fairly clear country along the summit of the hill. Jerry's area would be the natural exit for any deer that we drove out of the delta. It also afforded the greatest chance for taking a buck. After a minor tactical discussion, Frank and Jerry left for their locations. While I waited for them to get into position for the drive, I loaded my small .32–20-caliber pump-action rifle. It was, I knew, a less than high-power rifle, but it performed well for me in the past, and I had confidence in it.

As I looked at the closely spaced alder growth in the delta, and then at the couple of hundred yards to the adjacent ridge summit, I hoped that a buck might come into view. This type of hunting required close-range shooting—not more than 75 yards and more likely 25 to 50 yards. It would probably demand a quick snap shot on a rapidly departing buck. It could give me a chance to prove my little rifle, which was extremely light and well-suited to hunting in the often-tangled jungles left by logging in much of the coastal range.

A few minutes later, as I made my way down to the river's edge, I was impressed by the profusion of salmon carcasses strewn along the banks—some carried up into the pockets between salmonberry and salal bushes, others stacked in the mud and on the small gravel beaches of the stream. Varying stages of decay and consumption were evident in most of the salmon. Some of those that were more recently killed had only a single bite taken out of the fat stomach section. Others were partially torn apart by mink, otter, herons, and sea gulls. Some remains were shredded by the forest rodents, while still earlier remains were hollowed out by maggots.

In between this evidence of many feasts were the patterns and etchings of tiny and large feet, their impressions cut sharply into the mud of the delta: the spidery, three-pronged imprints of herons, bald eagles, or crows; the webbed, shallow indentations of sea gulls; small, pugged and tiny-nailed footprints of mink; larger, longer ones of raccoons; the definite round pugs of an otter; an occasional manlike footprint of a black bear; and, what I was more interested in, the enormous abundance of sharply cut pockets made by cloven-hooved coastal blacktailed deer. There was no doubt about the large number of deer using the delta. The area was practically trampled with small imprints of fawns, larger ones of their doe parents, and occasionally the deeply imposed, larger marks left by a buck searching for a mate in anticipation of the upcoming rutting season.

I noticed at least four buck tracks during the first few hundred yards. This kept me doing my part, which was to bark like a dog, stamp my logging shoes against fallen debris, rustle the bushes, break fallen branches, and make noises intended to move nearby animals into flight. I did in fact put up five deer almost immediately: a doe with two yearling fawns that stood uncertainly before running, and two single does that slipped silently into the surrounding growth at an angle to my approach.

Once or twice while stopping, looking, and listening for any animals that might be moving ahead of me, I heard Frank a couple of hundred feet ahead of me on the hillside. Once I heard the sound of voices as Jerry and Frank called out where they were in relation to the drive. They knew my position by the continuous uproar I was putting up.

To be honest, neither my enthusiasm nor my hunting instinct was aroused. From the does and fawns I saw in retreat, I thought it unlikely that I'd get an opportunity to down a buck. Bucks are much more wary than does and fawns when a man is nearby—and particularly when that man is an obviously noisy one apparently accompanied by a dog.

My commotion did cause another doe, close at hand, to jump from where it was lying and run up the steepening hillside. Shortly thereafter, I heard what could have been the faster, heavier pounding of a buck. I yelled a warning to Frank. Seconds later he shouted back that he had seen the deer—a good buck—but that it had run away so quickly that he couldn't get off a good shot. I continued along the narrowing delta.

About 400 yards from my starting point, the hillside closed in on the side of the river into a sheer embankment that had been created by glacial silts collecting against a protruding rock bluff. The brush, ferns, salal, and second-growth conifers grew so thickly on the steep incline that further passage along the river was impossible. Fortunately, I soon found a game trail that tunneled under the growth and headed upward, toward the top of the bluff. It was a type of trail with which I'd first become familiar while hunting and following traplines on streams and rivers as a youth. For want of a better name, we called them bear trails. These were different from deer trails, which were about double their height and somewhat less clearly defined, but which offered passage through thicker rain-forest underbrush.

There is no doubt that bears, otters, raccoons, and perhaps cougars or wolves followed the so-called bear trails, finding them a means of navigating through heavily grown sections such as the one I was entering. As I crawled on my knees over the next 15 or 20 feet, I could smell the fishy stench that emanated from the well-worn and almost slick floor of the passage. The branches that were pushed aside by my thrusting shoulders were leafless, worn smooth on their undersides by the trail's fairly constant use.

It was with a sigh of physical relief that I broke out into the open about 30 feet higher on the edge of the bluff. It was a particularly inviting spot, not only because of the scramble up the bank, but also because it was on a southern exposure that allowed the afternoon sun to shine upon the enclosure. The rock formation of the bluff was close to the surface and created an opening covered with dry moss ringed with second-growth hemlock saplings that grew so thickly that even a strong logger would have trouble pushing his way through.

The odor of fish was even stronger than what I'd encountered in the tunneled undergrowth. I glanced about the 30-foot clearing and saw the dried remains of several salmon carcasses and skeletons. The reason for their presence occurred to me immediately. Some of the skeletal head remains and backbones were large enough to have come from salmon that weighed 10 to 20 pounds at the time they were transported. It was unlikely that they had been carried there by an eagle, a raccoon, or even an otter; more probably, those big salmon had been carried there by a bear, or bears. Those impressions were only fleeting thoughts at the time. Their meaning was to become clearer shortly thereafter.

When I discovered the denning area, I decided to find a comfortable open spot and sit down, there to roll a cigarette and enjoy a smoke. In order to get into the stronger sunlight and sit on a rock hummock that afforded me a spot to stretch my legs, I strode to the end farthest from the tunneled approach.

To the west of me, not more than 50 feet away, I heard the progress Frank was making through the bushes, which had also become denser at his level. I yelled to him, asking if he had seen anything.

"Just a couple of more does and fawns," he said.

I suggested that he come in where I was and enjoy a smoke.

"Hell!" he replied. "How did you get where you are? It's so damn thick here I have to push my way!"

I had previously noted another break in the thickly grown hemlock at the top edge of the tiny clearing. This tunneled passage led up the continuing steep slope of the hillside.

"Go uphill, a bit ahead of you!" I said. "Then you should see a sort of tunnel that leads right into here. It's right on the edge of the bluff. And it is open, once you get in."

For a few more minutes, only the sounds of Frank's cussing and slow progress were audible. He eventually pushed into view, crouched in a stooped-over position. Unable to locate my point of access into the enclosure, he shook his head.

"How in hell d'you get in?" he asked.

"Down there!" I pointed to the dark opening at the other end, and then inquired, "Did you see anything other than the buck and doe?"

"No. Lots of sign, though," he said.

Frank sat down just above me, his back against the thick growth of hemlock and low brush. He rolled a smoke from my proffered packet of tobacco. The air temperature was comfortable, the sun striking us directly. Frank wasn't too impressed.

"Christ, it stinks in here!" he said. "Look at those old fish carcasses lying around!"

"Yeah, it stinks all right," I answered. "But it's open."

I reached toward a splintered hemlock sapling at my side. It had been bitten off at about the belly height of a bear. I picked a flimsy tuft of frizzy, black and gray-yellow belly hair from its sharp stump.

I said, "Some old biddy of a bear has been bringing salmon up here, to eat at her leisure. See?"

I extended the tuft of hair for Frank to examine.

"She's been rubbing her belly on that bitten-off hemlock butt."

Frank nodded with some small interest, not particularly impressed.

At my heel I noticed, for the first time, a rounded bear scat, dried out from the time of its deposition, probably during the spring months. Picking it up, I broke it open. In the inner section, I found the small, undigested darts of the hoof of a baby fawn. I pointed them out to Frank, holding the broken scat faces toward him.

"That damn bear ate a deer!" he said.

"Yeah. They take the odd fawn," I nodded.

"Let's get outa here," urged Frank. "It looks as if that bear denned up in here—with all those salmon carcasses lying around. That bear eats meat, and that's what *I* am. Let's go!"

I laughed and said, "Heck, Frank, a black bear would never hurt you!"

The last thought on my mind was that a black bear might be anywhere near us. Down on the riverbank feeding, yes. Here, after all that noise, never!

Just at that moment there was the sound of a shot, perhaps a couple of hundred yards away, in the direction Jerry would have taken. We both listened for a second shot.

"Sounds like Jerry got a shot," Frank said. "Only a single. He's a good shot. Probably got it. Let's go help him."

I grinned lazily and replied, "Give him a chance to gut it. We'll have to pack it out anyway—if he got it."

It was hunting buddies' logic. Frank recognized it and relaxed with a grin against the wall of brush. Suddenly he sat bolt upright.

It was the look on his face that alerted me. He didn't say a word.

Out of the corner of my eye I just caught movement at the end of the tunnel through which I had just crawled. The sight that faced me when I turned to look was stupefying. Not more than 20 feet from me was a black bear. She was in full charge. Loam and fallen fir needles were spurting from her flying feet like buckshot. Her beady red eyes were fastened on me with anger.

As I rose to one knee, my stomach turned to jelly.

Frank jumped to his feet and turned to run, striking the wall of interwoven hemlock. The bear was within 10 feet and moving like an express train before I yelled, "Shoot! Don't run! Shoot!"

My little .32-20 Remington pump felt like a bent hatpin. Frank had a .303 British Winchester, which could knock that bear off her feet at that distance.

Without aim, shooting from the hip, I pulled the trigger. The bullet caught the bear in the forepaw, and she rose up bellowing and shaking it so viciously that it threw blood on my shirt and pants. Like some black volcano, she was reared on her hind legs. I pumped a second shot into her shoulder as she stood up. It knocked a tuft of hair out. The third, unaimed bullet hit her in the rib cage as she almost somersaulted in a turn away.

In an instant the sow was charging toward the tunnel from which she had just erupted. The gun didn't ever reach my shoulder, so quick was my fearful reaction. The fourth and fifth bullets hit her, one knocking a chunk of meat and hide out of her rear quarters just as she reentered the tunnel.

A deafening crash from just behind me thundered into my eardrums as Frank's big .303 exploded the charge of a bullet. He was standing now, facing the outlet, a completely distraught expression on his face. I nodded toward the opening.

"I know I hit her four times!" I panted. "Look at the blood on those bushes! Maybe she won't go far."

His face held the look of a man caught off guard.

"I think I hit her too," he stated somewhat lamely.

We waited for a few minutes listening for sounds, perhaps of a thrashing bear. None came. I reloaded the rifle with all the shells in my pocket and started into the tunnel. The pursuit didn't bother me too much, because I was reassured by the efficient action of the little gun. If the bear came into the tunnel again, every bullet would hit her right in the face, enough to stop her charge.

We located her trail immediately outside the opening. Arterial blood had spurted from her wounds, as much as four feet up the trunks of the alders as she rushed away. Patches of it had spilled onto the brown leaves on the ground, yet she had traveled an unbelievable distance in so short a time.

Almost a mile on the blood trail brought us right back to within a few yards of the tunnel entrance. That bear had five slugs in her, which had drained most of her blood as she made her efforts to return to the den. We didn't find any sign of cubs, which her teats indicated she might have been feeding earlier in the year.

We did find Jerry on top of the ridge, however. He had a nice two-point buck, which he was packing out. He looked inquisitively at me.

"What happened to you?" he asked. "You've got blood on you."

"A goddamn bear came after me," I said.

"You're kidding!" He shook his head and looked at Frank, who nodded.

Jerry inclined his head toward the road. "Let's get to hell out of here!" he said.

We didn't go back for the bear carcass. My police work, which often consumed twenty-four hours a day, kept me away in the outer district for at least a week. Frank, whose small business was open six days a week, had no desire to return. Jerry, who had his buck, couldn't have cared less.

I look back with some concern and curiosity about that bear incident.

Why did that sow bear attack?

For at least thirty minutes there had been the loud sounds of my barking and scuffling on the delta from which she had come. There had also been the occasional shouting and talking of all three of us. All that commotion would normally have been quite sufficient to move a bear away from the scene.

However, I had entered what could be considered a denning location. Evidence pointing that way included the multiple remains of feeding, the dried-up old scat from the previous spring, the numerous salmon carcasses in varying stages of decay, and the bitten-off hemlock sapling with the belly hair caught on it. There was no evidence of that sow's having cubs, although her teats could have indicated a set that spring, but obviously past suckling. If there were any cubs, we didn't see them, either before or after the incident.

Then, there had been Jerry's single shot from quite nearby.

If the sow had cubs anywhere in the vicinity, the gunshot may have triggered some impulse in her to rush to her den. Though no cubs were in evidence, they might have been killed by a hunter earlier in the season. Such an experience might be a reason for panicking her into action.

That is all pure speculation based on the common belief that the bear species is protective of its cubs, however. And even that belief, to some degree, is fallacious. Rather than attacking to protect her cubs, a sow will usually drive them up a tree. In fact, she will leave them up a tree in order to forage for food. And, she *can* be moved off by determined men or other predators, particularly dogs or wolves. That isn't a pattern you can depend on when cubs are seen treed, but it is known to happen frequently.

This particular bear was in full charge from the instant I first saw it. I never did ask Frank if the bear was charging when he first saw it.

It was coming directly at me, with full intent.

Some things never fade from the memory. The downthrust head, the dirt flying off the paws, the ruby red eyes, the snarling lips with exposed white teeth, all left an indelible imprint that I've recalled many times. The actual physical evidence of her blood on my hunting shirt and pants, which I left unwashed for two years in order to preserve and display as evidence, attested to the reality of the attack.

That incident, however, still did not convince me of the dangers of black bears. I continued to treat them with the casualness bred by having spent all my life in their habitat. As much as fifteen years later, I fed Yellowstone Park's wild bears by hand. One of them was a sow with three cubs.

In the face of the facts, that act, my friends, was downright stupid.

14

Stay Still and a Grizzly Won't Hurt You?

"My husband put his gun on me. He didn't know what I was. My boots were full up with blood."

It was Mattie Jack, grandmother, member of the Alkatcho Indian band, at the Anahim Indian Reserve in British Columbia, speaking quite casually about her attack and burial at the whim of a grizzly bear. She spoke in a soft, native style of English. A pretty woman of age forty-five, she handed her daughter's newborn baby over to the girl as she came into the room from the outside.

"How old is your grandchild, Mattie?" I asked, for want of something to say after her shocking statement.

"He's one month," she replied.

"Our latest grandchild is four months; she's my son's first daughter."

"You got a boy?"

"Yes. Our daughter and son-in-law have a three-year-old son. He's a real boy, and I enjoy him."

She looked out the window as some of the men members of the band passed by, talking noisily and enjoying the aftermath of the funeral which she had also just attended.

It had been a long, seventeen-year search for Mattie—and she had turned up right under my nose, quite coincidentally.

Five days previously, at Pine Valley British Columbia, just north of Williams Lake, Jack Mackill—my long-time friend who is now a retired district conservation officer—and I had been laughing and talking of the good times we had had as member officers of associated prevention forces. He had been a conservation officer (game warden) in several different sections of the province, knew most of the guides and outfitters, their Indian assistant guides, and most of what went on in outlying areas. I mentioned that when I was in the back country of Anahim Lake seventeen to twenty years previously, I had heard of a woman who was buried by a grizzly bear, but so far had been unable to find her. Jack nodded and said he had heard of that attack.

"I think she's a member of the Alkatcho Indian Band," he told me. "She may still be at the reserve. You're going out that way. Why don't you ask D'Arcy Christiensen, at his store out there, about her. I'm almost sure he would know where she is. He buys furs."

I wrote down the name and information. Actually, I had been trying for months to get to Connie King, ex-hockey great, for the details on his own attack by a grizzly. Connie was a friend and teammate of two friends of mine, ex-hockey stars Clint Smith and Neil Colville. They had given me some of the details on Connie's attack while at the seasonal "Canuck" hockey games, which we all regularly attend. But Connie lived a long horse-ride back in the bush and was not expected to come out. I consequently traveled the 300-mile blacktop and dirt road all the way to the seaport town of Bella Coola, on a deep fjord of the Pacific Coast.

At Bella Coola, I asked Conservation Officer Tony Karop if he had heard of an Indian woman being buried by a grizzly bear. He said he had, but that he didn't know her name. But D'Arcy Christiensen or Chester Dorsey, old-timers at Anahim Lake, should know her. Try them on the way home, he suggested. He also mentioned an unusual bacterial infection that resulted from being mauled by bears (the bacteria were common to all bears). He told me that Dr. Barg, at the local hospital, had isolated a bear-attack victim named Fred Sholtes during his hospitalization, as the bacteria were airborne. That bit of information was new to me. I went to see Dr. Barg at the tiny local hospital near the waterfront of the village. Barg looked at me quizzically when I asked him about the nature of the infectious airborne bacteria, but he told me the name and the antibiotics that controlled it. He replied, "We isolated Mr. Sholtes because of the serious nature of his injury."

Sensing from his tone that the isolation was not solely for contaminatory reasons, I dropped the subject and asked if he knew of an Indian woman who was buried by a bear. "Yes, it was before my time here," he replied. "But I examined her at the hospital once, when she was a patient here. I asked her about her injuries, and she told me they were from a grizzly attack. I think she is in the Indian village at Anahim Lake."

He paused and got up, "I may have her name in my files."

A few minutes later he returned, shaking his head. "I thought I had her name, but I can't seem to find it. It may have been Catooch. I think she still lives up at Anahim."

He told me about some of the rescue action pertaining to the Fred Sholtes grizzly attack. The patient had been a healthy man who, although he had the usual aftermath of infection from grizzly bites, had recovered very well. Dr. Barg was interrupted by the arrival of a youngster whom he greeted warmly. I thanked him and left.

The "buried Indian woman" search was progressing. That evening I slept in the camper in an officially abandoned public campsite, close to the scene of another grizzly attack. Earlier in the evening, one of the Bella Coola housewives had asked me if that particular campsite was where I was staying. When I said yes, she pursed her lips and asked, "See any grizzlies in there?"

"No. Just youngsters in cars. A couple of hotrods came through."

"Yes, they use that place," she said, nodding.

That evening the journey to the wooden outhouse, using a dim flashlight in the dark, was more than your average jumpy trip. As I finally latched the camper door for the night, I had to grin at myself. The following morning, the early May sunlight was pouring through the cracks around the blinds. A robin chirped continuously from the nearby willows. I had had a very deep sleep, in the total silence of the wilds. If there had been fifty grizzlies around, I'd not have known of it.

As I rolled up the blind on the kitchenette side of the camper, I was surprised to find an Anna's hummingbird fanning its wings before its image in the glass. When I opened the rear door, it came around and hovered in the open space. In the wilds this was a surprising display; the bird was entirely unafraid of my presence in the doorway, a sight to which we are accustomed at the three feeders surrounding our honeysuckle-rimmed back porch. I forgot about grizzlies and looked out on the beauty of the newly greening, sylvan forest. It had quickly crept back to reclaim the campsite with alders and grasses.

Maybe I would find the Indian woman later in the day, at Anahim Lake. Or maybe Connie King had answered my note telling him that I would be back on Thursday, and maybe I would find him too.

At the post office at Anahim Lake, five hours and 100 miles of rough mountain highway climbing later (five miles of the road were actually hanging over a precipice, and it would have been impossible for two vehicles to pass except at treacherous turn-outs), I asked the post mistress if Connie had been in. She said he had and was expected again that day, to vote in the provincial elections. Didn't he phone me? No? Too bad. The woman did tell me that D'Arcy Christiensen's general store was on the bend of the road through the village.

At the rustic trading post, a young man was serving two Indian customers with the same patience I had had fifty years earlier, when serving them in our country store. The man was about thirty, and he used some Indian phrases while talking to them. This was my man, a "bush raised" person for sure. He eventually looked up at me.

"Can I help you?" he asked.

"Yes, please. I'm Mike Cramond, a writer, and I'm looking for an Indian woman who was attacked by a grizzly bear. Tony Karup, down at Bella Coola, said you might know her. I've . . ."

"Sure, I know her. Mattie Jack. She lives over on the reserve here."

"Well, I'm writing a book on bear attacks. She was buried by a grizzly, I think."

"Yes she was. Down at Mud Lake ranch. You're writing a book about bear attacks?"

"Yes, I've been researching it for about five years. Mattie— did you say, Jack?—she is the only person I'd heard of as having been buried alive by a grizzly."

One of the Indian customers interjected something to D'Arcy. Three more of them had come into the store, and I felt them eyeing me curiously. Christiensen said, "He's writing a book about bear attacks."

"Good country for it—out here," someone said.

There was some quiet laughter.

D'Arcy volunteered a personal revelation.

"A couple of other guys and I held down a grizzly cub and tried to get the old sow to come out of the bushes after it. She wouldn't come, though."

He was grinning a bit at the memory.

"What rifles did you have?" I asked.

"Not enough, really. I had a 6.5 Mannlicker, and my partner had a .22 high-power."

"You're damn lucky she didn't come," I said. "Those guns are too small to stop a grizzly quickly."

He looked straight at me, with a slight grin.

"Yeah, we were young guys, feelin' our oats. I know they were too small caliber—now. Say, I'll take you over to Mattie's."

"Okay. I'll be parked in the gray Jeep and Alaskan camper, over by the post office. I'm waiting for Connie King."

"Connie comin' in to see you?" D'Arcy asked.

"Maybe. I hope so," I said.

King's manner of answering letters was a trifle lackadaisical. He enjoyed the isolation of his ranch out in the bush and wasn't in any hurry to get a road out to it.

A couple of hours later, while I was typing out my handwritten notes on the two grizzly attacks down in Bella Coola Valley, D'Arcy Christiensen came to the camper door.

"I'll take you over to Mattie's now," he offered.

I was just dropping my folding-type camper down on its air jacks when D'Arcy said, "Here's Connie now."

I looked out at the small grove of conifers 20 feet from my camper. A spare man, very upright in posture, was tying a bay saddle horse to one of the worn tree trunks. Connie King still looked like an athlete. "You talk to him, Mike," D'Arcy said. "We can see Mattie anytime."

And he was gone.

Connie and I talked of hockey and grizzlies and black bears and mutual friends for five hours. I cooked him dinner while we discussed our experiences. He was a very quiet man, lucid in slightly bush-oriented accents. Sure, he knew Mattie Jack well. Having arrived in the area in 1937, Connie met Mattie Jack and her husband John soon after. Was I going to talk to her? Well, she had quite a story to tell.

It was too late to talk with Mattie that evening. I went over and talked with D'Arcy Christiensen, between bouts of election results coming in on his flickering color television screen. He'd take me to Mattie's in the morning, he said. He'd also tell me about the grizzly cubs and the sow and about some other bears he'd tangled with while ranching and trapping.

When I got to his store the following morning, he was already busy with a number of Indians who were purchasing items. After a short wait, I asked, "Can I go over there myself? And not bother you? Will she talk to me?"

"Sure, why not? She lives in that pink house between the trees," he said, pointing out the window of his store at a small bungalow about two blocks away.

"She won't mind?"

"No. She speaks good English."

I drove along the winding dirt road to the row of houses fronting the road through the village of the Indian reservation. When I reached the dirt yard of the neat little home, three mongrel dogs yapped at me, their tails between their legs. I patted them as they followed at my heels, sniffing.

A young woman answered the door, and I asked for Mattie. "She's not in," said the woman.

"I want to talk to her—about a grizzly attack."

"She's not in. She's gone."

The young woman's attitude shocked me. She obviously didn't wish to talk.

"I'd like to see her," I said. "Will she be back by five o'clock?"

"I guess—maybe. She just went down the road to work. She's wearin' blue pants, a purple jacket and—oh, *There* she is! Coming out of that house over there, with that other woman."

"Many thanks," I replied.

I drove along the dirt road after the two women. As I approached, they stopped and looked at me curiously. I hailed them.

"I'm a writer," I told them. "Name's Mike Cramond. Is one of you Mattie Jack?"

The prettier of the women replied, "I am."

"You're going to work at the hotel. May I drive you there? I want to talk to you—about the bear attack—when you aren't busy."

"Sure," she replied.

Both women got into the front seat and began talking to each other in a combination of English and Indian. They giggled when I drove them past the hotel without seeing it.

"You missed the hotel. It's back there," said Mattie Jack, apologetically. "I thought you knew where it was."

She and the other woman then got out of the cab. I couldn't tell if Mattie wanted to talk.

"Do you want to talk to me about your attack by a grizzly, Mattie?"

"Sure, but I have to work now," she said. "Mebbe I'm through about three o'clock. You could come to the house."

"Okay. I'll go fishing until then. I'll bring you some trout."

"Okay," she said.

She closed the car door and walked away with her companion without looking back. It was coming back to me too slowly. One shouldn't expect much conversation from new acquaintances made among Indians. They want to size you up, let you talk. Perhaps they also had had bitter experiences with white men. *Damn,* I thought. *I'd better bring her some trout!* Otherwise she might think I was a big yahoo white man. I drove to Little Anahim Lake, about two miles down the Bella Coola Road.

The whole surface of the lake seemed to be rippling with trout rises.

Well, I wasn't doing so well with Indian women, but it looked like I'd make out pretty well with these mystery trout of the Anahim Lake-Dean River system.

I had discovered these trout nearly twenty years before. I had taken six of them in gutted condition to the biologists of the Provincial Game Department, the Federal Fisheries Branch, and the Fishery Research Center at the University of British Columbia. None of the icthyologists could properly identify them. Some said they were cutthroat trout; others said rainbow trout. Some were noncommittal, and said they were hybrids.

I'd argued that no hybridization could have taken place by way of hatchery plantings, not in the lakes I'd taken them from. "I checked to see if there had been plantings *before* I brought them in to you people," I said.

That next spring had seen me back for another supply—this time twenty-four fish in pairs of the same size, fingerlings to five-pounders. There was no intergrading of species. All phases had the red splash typical of the cutthroat, the pink lateral line of the rainbow, pink to red fins, and spots typical of the cutthroat. One ichthyologist expressed the possibility that they were the single species from which both rainbows and cutthroats had sprung, while another said that they were related to *mices*, the Asiatic continental trout of the Pacific Coast. But no one could come up with a positive identification. When I told them I'd taken such trout in Alaska in 1927, they were quite interested. Then, some time later, following a big game hunt in the Cassiar Plateau, far up in northern British Columbia, I brought them more of the same trout from the head-waters of the Stikine River. They were surprised and still unable to identify them.

Why all this effort on my part?

I had noticed that these trout inhabited lakes that had warmer summer temperatures than the southern B.C. lakes and that the waters must be frozen nearly to their bottoms in the below-zero winters. I thought such a strain or subspecies might be a good hatchery fish. The biologists agreed, but did nothing. I saw the specimens once more, years later, all yellowed in their jars of preservative at the University of British Columbia. No one had proved them out. Two of the biologists had become doctors of ichthyology during the interim. One said he was "studying them." When he wrote a book entitled *Canadian Fishes* in concert with another doctor, however, he didn't identify the cutthroat-rainbow mystery trout at all.

I thought about them as I set up my two fly rods, one with a wet line and the other with a dry line. I'd bet that Mattie Jack could identify the trout if I caught some for her. Perhaps she would then be more receptive to an interview.

I pushed my aluminum punt boat out onto the small lake, knowing I had just three hours to catch a couple of trout for lunch, cook them, and then go out and catch some fresh ones for Mattie. Naturally, the fish didn't cooperate. I noted that the dark amber water was more shallow than I'd expected, and set out the dry line with a gold-banded chironomid nymph, tied by Jack Shaw of Kamloops, on the light leader. That fly had been deadly during the past weekend at lakes in the south Cariboo.

After 100 feet of trolling, the fly took a two-pounder that put up an excellent fight. I had to land it without a net, but I managed. Then I set the line out for the duration of the row back to shore—about 200 yards. I hooked a one-pounder of similar fighting ability that jumped all over the lake before I reached the beach. It also came into the boat.

One for Mattie—at least. This had to be the fly pattern. I was sure of that—perhaps. Anyway, a mystery trout sautéed in butter! Wonder if they were really as red of flesh and as sweet tasting as I'd remembered them?

Half an hour later, I discovered that even half of the fat two-pounder I cooked for lunch had more than filled me up. The trout were still rising, even more steadily, as I pushed the boat off the beach. I was back an hour later, reloading my camper with gear, boat, and six more (a limit) trout. All but one was taken on the floater line and chironomid nymph. Mattie, I hoped, would be impressed. At least she wouldn't think me to be just a boastful white man!

Half an hour later, at 3:00 P.M. I was at the door of her pink cottage. Another Indian girl came to the knock. I nodded politely.

"Hello. Is Mattie Jack in? I had an appointment with her at three o'clock," I stated. "She said she would be here."

"She's not here."

"Can you tell me where she is?"

The girl looked at me for some time before answering, "She's gone to the funeral."

"But—she—Oh, hell! I brought her some trout. I'll get them out of the Jeep."

I went back to the truck, took the trout from the cooler, hooked them onto a willow twig stringer, and returned to the door where the girl still waited. I was also feeling quite foolish.

She took the trout calmly.

"Thanks," she said.

"When will Mattie be back?" I asked.

"I don't know."

"Will you tell her I'll come back at four or five o'clock?"

"Okay." She closed the door behind her.

At Christiensen's store, I asked if Mattie might be celebrating at the big Indian funeral. D'Arcy looked up, amused at the question. He knew that I realized Indians sometimes had three days of celebration in remembrance of a beloved departed.

He shook his head. "No, I don't think Mattie will celebrate too much," he said. "She's a quiet woman. Go back later. She'll be there."

At 4:00 P.M., I was again at Mattie's doorstep. The pleasant, barely audible voice came from inside.

"Come in." Then, louder, "Come in!"

I pushed the door open and stepped into the neat living

room. Mattie Jack was sitting in an easy chair. She looked up at me pleasantly.

"Sit down," she said.

I was surprised at the several crucifixes and paintings of Christ on the walls.

"Mattie, do you mind talking to me about the bear attacking you?" I asked. "Does it bother you to tell about it?"

"No. It was a long time ago. It doesn't bother me."

She remained quiet, eyeing me. I explained my mission.

"I heard about the incident about eighteen or twenty years ago," I said, "when I was up here fishing. But I could never get hold of you. Jack MacKill, the game warden at Williams Lake, told me you were here. And D'Arcy Christiensen too. I hope you don't mind my coming."

"I don't mind," she replied. "I tell lots of people about it."

"Were you born out here?"

"I was born in the reserve here. This is my band, the Alkatcho, Ulkatcho Band."

"You must have been a young girl when it happened," I remarked.

"No, I wasn't. It was in 1963—mebbe fifteen years ago."

I scrutinized her more closely than I normally would have. She showed no facial scars, as did all of the men I'd interviewed thus far. In fact, she was quite pretty, in a mature way, a well-kept woman—not like a grandmother at all.

"Mattie, you don't show any signs of the bear mauling," I said.

"He bit me all behind the head and all over the body, near here," she replied.

She indicated her right breast and underarm area.

"And all over this leg. I had over two hundred stitches in me."

"How did it happen? I heard that you were gathering wood."

"No, I was lookin' for horses. My husband John and I were camped out in a shack on the Mud Lake ranch, about fourteen miles out. John was putting in fence posts for the ranch.

"The horses strayed one evening," she continued. "He went one way to look for them, and I went the other way, uphill.

"I came to a brushy, wet area that was too dense for my saddle horse. So I tied him up and walked toward the hillside. I got about a mile away from him. Then I saw the grizzly bear and the two cubs about two hundred feet away.

"It was getting toward dusk, and I remembered what the old-timers say: 'Stay still and a grizzly bear won't hurt you.' They had said that to me many times.

"I stood still, and the bear came toward me. It walked around behind me, stood up, and bit me in the neck. I didn't move or cry out. I remembered what the old-timers said: 'Stay still. Don't move. Grizzly will go away.'

"The bear threw me down on the ground and started biting at my neck. Then it bit me behind the shoulder and all over the leg. It shook me. I guess I went unconscious. I don't remember anything until I woke up.

"When I came to, I was all covered over in dirt and mud. Right under it. Covered right up.

"I thought about God. 'He'll save me,' I thought. My grandmother was a Catholic. She told me that! I was bleeding and dirt all over me. My clothes were torn."

I looked at her quietly composed face.

"It was a terrible experience, Mattie. Did your husband come and find you?"

"No, I walked back to the horse and he was there," she said. She paused. "He didn't know *what* I was. He put his gun on me. It was nearly dark. My boots were full up with blood."

I sat silently, wondering what to ask next, feeling inadequate to express myself. Her daughter came and sat, holding her baby, in another chair. She didn't say anything. I finally broke the silence: "It's funny, Mattie. I could never seem to find you. I heard about the attack, but it wasn't in the newspapers."

"It was in *Outdoor Life* book," she said. "Dinah French, of Williams Lake newspaper, wrote the story. D'Arcy Christiensen has my book with the story."

This was a total surprise.

"You mean *Outdoor Life* magazine had the story?" I was perplexed. Occasionally my issues, which for years came to the news office, were apt to disappear before I got them. I had both read and written for *Outdoor Life* since I was a young hunter.

Admittedly, I didn't read every issue. This was obviously one I had missed. But, why hadn't it been in the newspapers? She didn't know, and continued with her story.

"They got me to Mud Lake. They said a plane couldn't land on that lake. The lake was too small. But Dick Poet, a pilot from here, got a plane down on it and flew me out to Nimpo Lake. I was in the hospital all summer. Then I went back for treatment for four years."

"Did anyone ever get the grizzly bear? Did they hunt for it?" I asked.

She looked pensive, just sitting quietly for a moment.

"One hunter got a big sow grizzly there that fall. It was a big one. I think maybe it was the one. That plane pilot was killed later. He was a nice guy—a good pilot."

Yes, Dick Poet was a good pilot, a bold one who put mercy before his own safety.

That evening I talked with local garage owner, Wayne Escott, also a flyer. He had worked with Dick. His friend had crashed when his motor cut out while taking off in ice and snow.

Wayne also talked about his father, Del Escott, my friend.

Thirty-three years previously, I had taken Del north for his first trip into the country beyond the Chilcotin—the Omineca —on a combined moose hunt and business venture. Del had liked the country, and eventually left the coast to settle at Anahim. Wayne remembered a coyote skin that had been around the house when he was a kid. His father had told him I had shot the animal—which had a very beautiful coat—and had given it to him. It was true. His dad has passed on now. He, too, was a nice guy.

It's funny. Mattie Jack had been living right among my friends, almost under my nose, all these years—and I just hadn't asked the right questions. I sent her a jade cross, similar to the one she had admired exposed by my own open-neck shirt, and promised her a copy of this book. She said, "Thanks for the trout!"

15

He Was Tough at Hockey, Too!

"When the grizzly was chewin' on my arm and I was protec-
tin' my face from a bite, I remember thinking, 'I can take this.'
It was when he got to my face that it hurt!"

Connie King, one of the past's hockey greats, was sitting
opposite me in my camper, just outside the post office and
store at Anahim Lake. He was eating a supper of hamburger
and onions, beans, and mixed canned vegetables, which I had
prepared while we talked about his fight with a grizzly bear.
A couple of hours earlier, he had tied his saddle and packhorse
to a tree just beside my Jeep. I had seen him dismount with a
quick easy motion, despite having spent four hours in the saddle while riding out from his backcountry ranch.

His bearing was impressive: a not-too-tall, slender man with
the well-rounded upper chest common to strong men and
athletes. He stood upright and square, bent easily to loosen the
horse's cinch, then began unbuttoning his worn hand-tooled

213

leather chaps. When I went up to him, he turned a quietly placid face toward me. I had expected the slight shock that usually comes with the first sight of a grizzly-mauled face, but there wasn't any. His face was round, healthy, and slightly scarred, with one eye closed as if in a blink. He grinned an even, white-toothed smile at my greeting.

"Connie, I'm Mike Cramond. I wrote you a couple of months back."

"Hi, Mike. Yeah, I got your letter. Figured the roads and weather wcrc too bad for you to come out for a while yet."

"They tell me you're a lousy correspondent, anyway," I said, grinning. "I am too. Did you get my message the other day, when I came through?"

Nodding his head, he replied. "Yeah, I did. Had to come in to vote, and figured I might see you."

He undid the other hitch on his chaps, revealing the blue denim, well-weathered, horseback-shiny pants. Around his neck was a creamy yellow handkerchief commonly worn by bush cowboys. His hat was a bush- and branch-worn, wide-brimmed Stetson rolled tight to the crown, a really sun-bleached and useful hat that had probably held drinking water and oats in the course of its uses. He wore warm, quilted underwear visible beneath his bleached-denim outer jacket. He was clean-shaven, with that amazingly youthful skin color of a healthy, land-using man.

I guess he noted my studious appraisal. He said, "You know Clint Smith and Neil Colville . . . you said so in your letter. I played against the Clint."

"Yeah, we've talked about you at the Canuck games. They tell me you were *some* hockey player. How about coming into the camper for a cup of coffee?"

"I'd like that. Haven't had anything since breakfast."

We sat in the sunlit dinette of the camper, with me asking the questions.

Connie King was born in Provost, Alberta, in 1910, not too far from where I was born. He eventually moved to Saskatoon to attend school. There he played tournament baseball during the summers until he was seventeen years of age, and hockey during the winters. The latter endeavors led him to being signed as a center in the old Philadelphia Minor League. After scoring 20 goals in his second year, he was traded to the existing Boston team in the early 1930s. That club paid him the handsome sum of $2,200 a year, until it went broke; at which time he went to the newly formed New York American Club. The next year he was back at the original Philadelphia club, where he scored 30 goals in a 40-game season. A good reference point for that achievement can be had by considering that today's superstars, whose schedules contain 80 games, score about 60 goals in a season.

During that decade his hockey career took him to teams at Detroit, Oakland, Spokane, Seattle and Tulsa, after resisting offers from the famed Patrick brothers of hockey. Other travels during that period brought him to the summer of 1937, when he ventured into the Anahim Lake district, his present homeland. There he worked as a cowhand for pioneer, Andy Christiensen.

King went on to be the hockey league's leading scorer in 1940. As he talked about it, he grinned about being sent out to check hockey great, Charlie Connacher, during a Toronto Maple Leaf game against Detroit, in which Connacher wasn't able to score.

In 1941, with his fonder memories of that Cariboo country, and his pro hockey career in decline, he took his second wife and their children back there and settled lands in nearby Bella Coola Valley. He became a rancher at age 44, after he concluded that ranching was the life that best suited him.

As he sat placidly before me, I said, "Connie, they tell me, here, that you can still skate backwards faster than most can forward! Do you miss hockey?"

"I sure enjoyed it," was his reply, "but, you get too old to play in a league."

He was silent for a moment. I filled his coffee mug once more.

"Have you had many experiences with bears, besides the attack?"

He nodded with a grin. "Sure. I was with my three kids—two were on horses—down near Stewie, in Bella Coola Valley. I was driving my Jeep up the narrow road, with my small daughter and our collie beside me. That darn dog jumped out of the car and ran down to the creek bed where there were five grizzlies—two big ones and three small ones. The collie yapped at them and then bit one of the grizzlies right on the heel. Well, that big grizzly came right up over the cutbank after him, up in front of the Jeep. I was afraid for the kids on the horses just ahead on the trail, so I got out and yelled and waved my hat. The grizzly took right off, and I sure was glad. The kids came back on their horses while I was scolding our dog. Afterwards, my little girl said to me 'Daddy, I didn't see the bear.' She was disappointed!"

He grinned, and continued: "Before that dog attack, my neighbor, Jim Holt, had a bear get him down while he was walking his two small dogs near his place. His gun jammed as he went to load a shell, and the bear bowled him over. The two dogs were yapping and biting on the bear's behind while the bear was chewin' on Jim's leg.

"Jim finally managed to get a shell into his gun and kill the bear. He later told me, 'My leg didn't bleed much. It looked just like hamburger, though.'

"One day he came over to my place and killed three grizzlies that had turned up there. He didn't like bears after that mauling."

"He must have been a tough man," I remarked.

"Yeah, he sure was!" He paused. "Say, when you get back to town, would you tell Neil Colville to get in touch with me? He has a place up here, and I'd like to see him."

"Yes, I will. I'll phone him when I get back. Any other bear incidents?"

He looked at me calmly. "Oh, yeah," he said. "You can't ranch in this country without coming up against bears. I run my cattle down near a place called the Precipice. There's lots of wild onions down there, and the grizzly bears like them. I had a part-Airedale dog, and he went ahead of me one day while I was on horseback. He ran right in among five grizzlies and started fighting with all of them. And he kept looking back at me as if he wanted me to join in with him! I didn't want to get tangled up with them, so I took off and went up a sidehill. He came along later."

"Airedales were bred to fight bears, I believe," I acknowledged.

"Yeah, I've heard that. Another time I was with my second wife and three kids. We had just bought a milk cow from Furvale and were bringing it back to the ranch at the Precipice. It was gettin' dark, and we decided to make camp. My wife was takin' the saddle horse up to the meadow in the old orchard when she said, "Is that deer or bears?" I looked toward the old apple trees and saw an old grizzly bear sow with three cubs about seventy-five yards away. She came up to about thirty feet, but we yelled and she went away."

I apologized for not having any dessert to top off the supper he had just eaten and then offered Connie some toast and grape jelly. He said that was fine. I put the toaster on the propane gas flame while he talked about another memory.

"About twelve years ago, I ran out of hay when it was eight below. Irene and I were near the top of the Bella Coola Hill when she looked down and said, 'There's some cattle down in that valley.' I got off my horse and walked around the cattle. There was a black one right in the center, and mine are mostly black cattle. I moved toward it figuring I'd move it back to my herd, and then saw it was a black bear, right among the cattle. I was gonna chase it when I saw she had three cubs, two of them right up a nearby tree. One little guy was at the base of the tree, standing on his hind legs, with one paw against the tree trunk. He looked so funny, just staring at me like he was going to talk. I just circled the cattle.

"When I went back up and told Irene, she said, 'Yeah! I found her! She came right up here and chased me and the dog. I went up a tree!' "

He paused reflectively. "Another time a grizzly killed one of my steers. It was about a two-year-old silvertip. I saw it, but couldn't get a shot at it. It was near the cabin, so I cut a swath out of the trees to get a clear shot, then wired the steer's carcass to a couple of trees.

"The game warden came out with two new dogs that the government buys for them. That was a funny trip. He lost his dogs, even though I'd told him to be careful about letting them run loose. Then his horse fell down in the creek, and he filled his boots up with water. He never got a line on the grizzly, and it never came back."

He sat silently for a moment, as if thinking of the past. I asked him if he would like to tell me about the grizzly attack. Before the interview, I'd read Tony Eberts' news story about the incident, to see if it was correctly described. I took the clipping out of the file and, after explaining that Tony and I had worked together on the same newspaper for twenty-odd years, read the item to Connie.

May 7, 1968—*The Province*

MAULED RANCHER WAS BEAR FOR PUNISHMENT

By Tony Eberts

If there was a touch of pride in the bandage-muffled voice of the man in the hospital bed, it was because he had been mauled by a 500-pound grizzly bear, but never stopped fighting.

Connie King, 58-year-old Anahim Lake rancher, in "satisfactory" condition in Vancouver General Hospital Monday night, told his astounding story of a stand-up battle with a raging mother grizzly on Saturday—and the equally astounding tale of how he finally walked away from it.

"I never passed out, and I never got knocked off my feet," said King—one eye missing, his mangled nose stitched up the middle, the unbandaged part of his face swollen and still bloody, dozens of deep cuts on his arms, legs, and body.

By wagon, jeep and aircraft, the leather-tough cattle rancher was brought to Vancouver for specialized treatment of injuries that would have killed many a younger man.

This is his story:

"I was out to check over feed on the winter range. There was a lot of snow on the ground, so I didn't even think about bears. Figured they'd be still holed up for the winter.

"About a mile from the house, I heard what sounded like a calf bawling. I headed over there, and next thing there was a mother bear—a silvertip grizzly. She was about 150 feet away. She had a cub, maybe two.

"She came for me like lightning. I tried to get up a small poplar tree, but I couldn't make it, so I headed for a big spruce.

The grizzly got to me just as I reached it. It didn't take her long to cover that 150 feet.

"I turned and kicked her in the face, but she got her teeth into my boot and ripped it off. When she came for my head, I got my arm in her mouth [he held up a heavily bandaged forearm] and she chewed that up pretty good, too.

"She got to my face and ripped it up some [this was when he lost one eye], but I never went down. I didn't think I had much chance, but you just keep fighting.

"I stayed by the tree, standing there kicking at her and sticking my arm in her mouth to protect my head. It all took only about a minute and then she went away. I don't know why. Maybe one of her cubs hollered.

"It was pretty cold, a bit below freezing, and most all my clothes were torn off. One foot was bare, and that was the worst, with snow and ice on the ground. I started home. I had to lie down a few times before I could make it.

"I knew I had to get there before I passed out. I must have looked an awful sight when I got there—all blood and no clothes."

Why did the bear attack?

"Well, a mother grizzly is always dangerous. There was a piece of moose hide there that they'd been chewing on. I guess they were mighty hungry. Not much feed this time of year."

Had he had run-ins with grizzlies before?

"Sure, but they never caught me before. I either scared 'em off, shot 'em, or got away myself."

Will he be back ranching when he's well enough?

"Oh, yes. Don't know much else. Anyway, the gods must be with me if I survived this.

"But she was only a small grizzly, you know. Wouldn't have gone more than 500 pounds—600 at the outside."

Sister Cecilia Cormier, a nurse at the Anahim Lake Roman Catholic mission, said King's sister-in-law, Minnie Sulin, was at the ranch cabin when he staggered into it, and she was able to stop the worst of the bleeding.

"A neighboring rancher, George Reid, was notified and got King out with a horse and wagon to where a jeep could pick him up," said Sister Cormier. "When they got him here, I was surprised that he was still conscious after all the blood he'd lost.

"He was badly mauled, so I telephoned the doctor at Bella Coola and we decided to send him there."

Anahim resident Wayne Escott drove King in the mission's jeep to the coast community, 90 miles by rough and snowy gravel road. The trip took about three hours. Escott said King remained conscious most of the time and never complained.

On Sunday, he was flown to Vancouver for surgery in General Hospital.

King was well known as a player in the Pacific Coast Hockey League, where he won the 1937–38 season scoring title with the Spokane team. He also played for Seattle before taking up ranching, and one of his Vancouver friends is former hockey great, Fred "Cyclone" Taylor.

Connie listened to the news story in silence. When I was finished, he acknowledged, "That's just about as it happened."

I was pleased. The writer of the article had a good reputation. I said so, then asked how Connie happened to be walking at the time of the attack. He asked me for a piece of paper and a pencil. He said he would draw me a map, as I wasn't going to go out there.

After handing him the paper and ballpoint pen, I said, "Connie, I once had a grizzly come after my dog during the night. It ran him right under my bed, and I thought it was an earthquake! It was out at Pelican Lake."

He looked up with interest. "That's only a couple of miles from my place," he said.

I grinned. "I know. That's why I told you about it. It was about a year after the bear got Mattie Jack. I guess I was luckier than I thought."

"Yeah, I guess so." His hand was outlining a stream, the location of his cabin, a beaver dam, a line of trees beside the meadow, and a long finger of brush that reached out into the meadow.

His finger pointed to the beaver dam in the stream: "I crossed here at the beaver dam, wearing rubber boots. It's about a quarter of a mile from the cabin. Then I walked up across the meadow. It was early May, but there was still snow on the ground. I walked up to the rising land where the pines are and went along the higher ground to where this finger of brush comes well out into the meadow.

"Just past that, I heard what sounded like a calf bawling. It was about a mile from the house. It may have been a grizzly cub making the noise. I don't know. I went down toward the meadow to find out what it was, and there was the grizzly, with her cubs, chewing on an old piece of moose hide. It was a surprise to find them out that early in the year. I didn't think they would be out, with snow still on the ground, and I wasn't packin' my rifle.

"The next thing I knew, the sow came for me.

"I first tried to climb a poplar tree, but it was too slippery and I couldn't make it. Then I went to a big spruce tree and got up a couple of branches, but she got me by the foot as quick as lightning. She tore my boot off and shook it, then came back at me. I stuck up my arm, and she bit that.

"I didn't want her to get at my head, which she was trying for. I kept putting my arm up, and she kept biting it. I remember saying to myself, 'I can take this!' It didn't seem to hurt that much. I just kept on my feet, fighting her off. She grabbed my leg then, and chewed. Suddenly she let go and made a grab for my face—got me under the cheek and eye and ripped. That hurt! She kept biting at me, and I kept fending her off. Then she just went away and left me. The whole thing couldn't have taken more than a minute. I couldn't believe the blood from my face and head. I headed for camp—walked all the way, but fell down a couple of times."

He stopped for a moment, as if thinking about it. I asked him if he had lost consciousness at any time, as others had.

"No. I remember crossing the creek and being very cold. When I got to the cabin, I was an awful sight for the two women. I told Minnie Sulin, the sister of the Indian girl who stays with me, to jump on a horse and go to the neighbors' house. While she was gone, I wrapped a towel around my head and lay down. Got my girl to put hot compresses on me until they came. Then I got into the wagon and rode it out into town."

I was amazed at the calm doggedness of the ex-hockey player.

"Didn't you ever pass out, Connie?"

"No. I was conscious right up until they got me to the hospital in Vancouver. The nurse there gave me something to make me sleep. They went to work on me right away. It was a bad wound in the face that took away my eye. The doctor told me he could see my brain through it."

"Jesus! And you stayed conscious through *that!*"

"Well, there was no use passing out, I guess."

"You had a hell of a good surgeon. You aren't that badly scarred, Connie. He made a real job of it."

He shrugged appreciatively. "Yeah, he made a new nose for me out of part of my arm. That was a tough time. My arm was tied up to my face during the grafting of the chunk in there."

I noticed that the sun had gone yellow on the western horizon.

"Connie, would you like to stay overnight in the camper? Lots of room."

"No thanks, Mike," he replied. "I've got to get back to the ranch tonight."

We went over to where his horse was tied to the tree. He removed the leather chaps from the saddle horn, buckled them on, patted his dog, and swung easily into the saddle. It was difficult to believe that the man was sixty-nine years of age. He looked and acted twenty years younger, still a pro.

Later, while I was talking to Wayne Escott at the local garage, he told me that he had driven Connie King down to Bella Coola. He said he couldn't believe that the man was still on his feet, torn up as he was that day, a blood-soaked towel wrapped around his head. He had remained conscious and talking through the bandages.

"That man is sure as hell tough!" he said. "And I mean tough, both inside and out!"

A lot of hockey players knew that too. He wasn't a dirty player or a fighter, but he hit hard and took what came. In fact, he was so tough that a grizzly couldn't get him onto his back. It had to walk away from him, and leave him still on his feet.

16

If Bears Played by Predictable Rules

"Bears are ten times as powerful and twice as quick as men. By the time you have thought of what actions to take, the bear has already reached for your move."

The six-foot, handsome, muscular man who was speaking was Ted Watchuk, age twenty-seven, an experienced field geologist who stayed on his feet to fight a bear after yelling to attract it away from his companion geologist, Neil Le Noble. The two of them had been road surveying deep in the northern bushlands.

The fact that Ted Watchuk had stayed on his feet to fight off a bear had specific relevance to my research. Connie King had also accomplished that feat during his battle with a grizzly sow in British Columbia's Chilcotin wilderness. The bears that attacked both King and Watchuk were sows with cubs, and both had been encountered accidentally. Both men survived, and both are again active in the wilds. Neither is bitter or vindictive toward bears.

The main difference between the two attacks was that Watchuk's bear did not get to his head—an apparent target of all grizzlies.

My correspondence with Ted had begun a couple of months before my talk with him. It had been difficult for us to arrange an interview because of our divergent paths, and we once missed as a result of a deficient phone line. In the meantime, he wrote me a thoughtful letter:

April 17, 79

Dear Mike Cramond:

Just recently received your letter (Mar. 27) and thought a quick reply was in order. There's no problem with me as far as reviewing the "incident." I'm quite open about it, but writing the complete history would be quite a chore and no doubt I would miss some of the salient points that you are after. However, I shall try to summarize as much as possible in this letter and leave the major portion of it for an interview. I will tentatively be in Vancouver May 17 to 21 and would probably be available during that time, if it's convenient for you. If I am in Vancouver, I'll give you a call then, and we can take it from there. I shall now try to summarize what I think you want.

The bear (a tree-climbing grizzly—a point I will not argue) went after Neil first, far up into a tree. I'm not much of a tree climber at the best of times and all I managed was a willow which took me about 6 feet off the ground. When the bear left Neil and came over to my tree, it got up on its hind legs, which brought it up to my boot level. I solidly planted my boot into her nose, and she backed down—only to come up a second time, and quickly grab onto my boot and remove me from my perch. I landed on the ground, but as was the case through the entire attack, she never mauled me while I was down. All my actions were instinctive, none were a form of rational thought. Whatever I did was an intrinsic part of my nature. No decisions or actions were made on the basis of thought.

The fight from that point involved trying to position a small willow between myself and the bear. She would lunge and swat at me while I was kicking and hitting her, interlaced with a solid stream of obscenities. She did manage to knock me away from this stance a few times, but it was always to return to the same form of combat. By this means, and that bear's benevolent fighting nature, I managed (or at least she did) to limit my injuries to all 4 limbs. The fight ended when she tore a large portion of my calf muscles out, looked at me and walked away. I'm not here today, relatively unscathed, due to any intelligent defense, but rather solely due to that bear walking away.

As far as lying down and playing dead: I would strongly recommend it when a bear has you down and continues to maul. But, as a general rule, no. If bears "played" by predictable rules, then there could be rules made to avoid, or come out unscathed from an attack. But, they don't have any rules and so it's impossible to make rules for human response. If a person wants to "play dead," there's no guarantee that the bear won't remove the "play" part out of it.

Sincerely,

(Signed) Ted Watchuk

On June 3, after on-the-spot interviews with rangers at Glacier National Park, Canada, and with the owner of the Northlander Hotel, where Malcolm and Barbara Aspeslet (see Chapter 6) worked when they suffered their grizzly attack, I drove into Calgary late in the afternoon. Ted Watchuk answered the telephone at his home.

"Look, Mike," he said. "It would be easier for me to drive over and meet you than it would to try to give you instructions on how to get here. I'll be there in half an hour."

When he got out of his new Volvo sedan, I was quite surprised. He was tall and athletic, and his face was unmarked. I invited him into the traveling home and office of my compact Alaskan camper, where his file lay on the table. He shook his head at a cup of coffee and said he had just finished supper.

"Sorry about missing you at the Coast, Mike. I tried to contact you ten times over the weekend. Your phone was either busy, or there was no answer."

"Too bad, Ted. We would have liked you to stay, as our guest. Maybe next time?"

He smiled appreciatively. "I wouldn't want to put you out. I have friends there who usually put me up. I guess you'd like to discuss the bear attack."

"Well, your letter was very explicit. But, actually, I'm more interested in background. There often are important items left out, which might create a better understanding of the actual happenings. I tried to get Le Noble, but he's in Bogotá and hasn't answered."

"He may not want to talk about it. He has suffered a bit of an emotional upset, I guess."

"That's understandable. Does it bother you to discuss it?"

He shook his head and grinned. "Not really," he said. "At first, I was stunned about it. Then I had a session of verbal diarrhea. Wanted to talk to everyone about it. Bored the hell out of everybody, I guess. That happened when I was in the hospital."

I laughed at his forthrightness and asked, "Has any publication had your story, Ted?"

He nodded with a grin: "Yes. While I was in the hospital, wanting to talk to everyone, a reporter from Boston phoned and said he would like my story. I asked him, 'How much?' and he offered me fifty dollars. I thought, 'Why not? I'm telling everybody for nothing anyway!' "

I was laughing with him, amused by the newsman's fifty-dollar bid.

"By the time he paid for his phone call and sold his story, he wouldn't come out with much of a profit anyway, Ted," I remarked. "In the news business, we don't pay for stories—in a newspaper that is. If we can't get the story from the participant, then we go to the witnesses and officials—we have to go to them for certification anyway. Magazines are different. A personal version from the participant has that first-person element, which is one-on-one with the reader. It has more impact than a third-person item. In news, you are a statistic. In person, the reader can relate and judge, come to conclusions. It's one of the reasons I wanted to interview you: I get to see you and come to conclusions, verify facts. Often a news item is not fully correct as to detail. It's shortened for space and brevity and leaves out many of the details."

He was listening thoughtfully. "I guess you'd like me to start at the beginning, then," he said.

"Yes, if you don't mind."

"Okay. We were marking out a new road. Neil Le Noble would walk 100 feet ahead with the chain. Then I would catch up with him, we would ribbon the spot, and he would go ahead again. Neil suddenly stopped and pointed, and yelled, 'Look out! A bear is coming!' I looked up and saw it was coming our way."

I stopped Watchuk for a moment: "How far away was it, Ted?"

"I'd say about 100 feet."

I pointed out the camper window to a park area nearby.

"Would it be about those first hedges?" I asked.

He studied the indicated hedges and shook his head. "No. About at the higher line of bushes from where we are. The tree that Neil went up was about at the distance of that far telephone pole."

I interjected once more: "Ted, it's 200 feet to that first line of bushes—and more like 150 feet to the telephone pole. Pardon me if I correct you, but knowing the exact distance gives me a better perspective for ascertaining the territorial boundaries a bear might consider to be its safe point, or which area it might defend. That bear probably came 200 feet to get at Le Noble and then another 150 to 175 to get at you—a total of 350 to 400 feet. That, to me, means that a sow will probably come farther to defend its cubs than some would think."

He nodded and didn't contest the distance estimates.

"Well, Neil went up a pine tree with a trunk about—this round." He indicated a circle with his arms, which would enclose a 15- to 20-inch diameter. "Neil doesn't know how he got up it. The bear was coming at him, and there weren't any branches for about the first fifteen feet! I'm not much of a tree climber either. The best I could find was a small willow that took me about six feet above the ground. I thought that would be enough for a grizzly."

I stopped him and referred to a news article: "In this item, Gerald Paull, the fish and wildlife officer, says he thinks it was a *black* bear. What do you think of that?"

Ted Watchuk shook his head. "I'm no expert on bears, Mike, but I think it was a grizzly."

"What color was it?"

"It was brown."

"You saw the cubs. What color were they?"

"My recollection is that they were brown too."

"Did you notice any yellowing or gray on the bear?" I asked.

"I can't remember any."

"Did you see any white patch at its throat, that you can recall?"

Again he shook his head. "No, not that I noticed, or remember."

He was looking at me, preoccupied, trying to recall. I pointed out that black bears—the brown-colored ones included—have a white patch under their throat. He couldn't recall any such marking.

I explained my question in relation to the cubs: "Ted, the brown or henna hue of the black bear is a color mutation—like a red-haired person. There is an absence of pigmentation. If the cubs were brown, that would probably indicate they were grizzlies; if they were black, they were probably black bears. Even in the brown phase of black bear, the cubs are often black—some sort of a dominant gene carryover, I guess. It's hard to say, really. You say the sow went up the tree after Neil."

He nodded thoughtfully. "She certainly did!" he said. "Just like a lineman humping up a pole on his spurs; grabbing with her front feet, pushing up with her back. Neil had got up about forty feet, and she went right up after him. He kicked at her, and she got hold of his foot. He started yelling and screaming in pain. I began yelling and screaming to distract her. Then she slid down his tree and ran over to mine. She stopped about ten feet away, then came right after me and reached up. I kicked her a good one in the snout, and she backed off about ten feet. I think I saw the two cubs run over to Neil's tree. She reached up again with her head, and as I was only about six feet off the ground, she was able to grab my foot and pull me out of the tree. When I was on the ground, though, she never touched me. When I got up, I tried to put the tree between us. She got my arms as I punched at her. These . . ."

He lifted his two well-muscled, bronzed arms and showed me 12- to 14-inch scars that extended to his hands. The claw marks were about half an inch wide, and there were teeth marks in the muscling. The tip of one finger was missing, but the hands were otherwise unmarked. The surgery and the healing had left little disturbance of normal contour. He pointed to his thigh.

"She got a big chunk out of here, too."

Beneath the cloth of his pantleg was an indentation that was quite noticeable. He lifted his pantleg to reveal a badly torn, but similarly well-healed calf.

"After she got my thigh and tore out a chunk, I was still on my feet, but I was sure I was going to die. It was a funny thing, though. When she knocked me down, she didn't attack me. When I got up, she'd come in again, and I'd fight her off with my arms. After she tore the chunks out of my thigh and calf, she backed off. I was still standing there, but she just backed off. I guess she figured she had taught me my lesson. She just collected her cubs and left."

He was looking out the window into the park.

"You know, when she tore out the section of my calf, I thought I was already gone. I don't know why she turned away. After a while Neil came down from his tree and came over."

He stopped his narration, and looked at me.

"You know, all I experienced was a deep feeling of elation. I said to Neil, 'Well, shall we go on with the job?' He could see I was torn all to hell, and he thought I was out of my mind. I was so relieved to be alive that I was trying to be funny. He didn't understand.

"We went back toward the truck. Neil couldn't help me because the brush was too thick and the terrain too tough. He was hurt, too. It took us about forty-five minutes to walk the half-mile to the truck and drive to camp, then another forty-five minutes on the chopper they sent, then about the same to get to the hospital. I was in the hospital for about six weeks. They did a lot of sewing and stitching and adjusting muscles. There was some minor infection, but I survived."

My admiration for him, and for his attitude, had to be expressed.

"You yelled when the bear was biting at Neil, and actually brought it over to *you!*"

"Yes. What else? He was in pain and being attacked. I thought I could distract it."

"That was a brave act, Ted."

"What else could I do?" he said, shrugging.

"Did anyone ever suggest giving you a medal?"

He nodded nonchalantly: "They gave me the Carnegie Bronze and the Workmen's Compensation Bronze Medal."

It was a surprise. I had not seen any such press releases. "You deserved better than the bronze," I said.

He shrugged again. "I wasn't looking for any medals."

It is sometimes difficult to express what you think, man to man. I just shook my head.

"Are you an outdoorsman, hunter, and fisherman?"

"Not really. Social pressures at school, when I was a kid here on the prairie, made me go out duck hunting a few times. I didn't like killing things, so I just quit after I'd seen a few of the ducks I'd killed."

"How about contact sports. Did you play them?"

"No. I wasn't any athlete."

"You look like one," I said. "What do you weigh now? It says here that you lost about ten pounds of flesh during the attack."

"I was about 187 pounds at the time of the attack. The doctors estimated that I lost 10 pounds. I'm about 185 now."

"How do you feel about bears?"

"Oh, I don't feel vindictive, if that's what you mean. That bear thought she was defending her cubs."

"What about going back into the bush, Ted?"

He grinned broadly, looking slightly abashed.

"I bought a 44-caliber Magnum handgun and went back by myself to site of the incident. I just had to go, I guess. Something to prove. It's funny what comes into your mind. I looked around, and it was just a section of ordinary bush and trees. I thought, 'Huh! No monuments or anything! Nothing is changed. Just the same as it was before we came.'"

He was looking sheepish, forthright. I was laughing. Somehow I knew just what he meant. The scenes of the dramas in our lives always appear dull and unmarked by incidents that affect us so deeply. Revisiting the scene is always a disappointment.

"We do expect something, Ted," I said. "We never know what, but it is always a shock to find that there isn't a shining brass plaque there. Who the hell cares? It's life, I guess."

He was smiling, and I asked him if he had any advice about going into bear country. His handsome young face grew serious.

"Mostly, I'd say don't go into the deep backcountry without a companion, someone to help in case of an attack. Workman's Compensation is now requiring pairs of men to work together in such areas. A lot of geologists work alone, and I don't think they should."

My next questions were purposeful: "What about trauma? Have you any emotional aftereffects?"

He answered with an immediate smile: "No, not too much. I got over that by talking to everybody who would listen in the hospital. I accept it."

He stopped for a moment, then went on: "Oh, yes! About a year ago, while I was driving through Jasper Park, I saw a bunch of cars stopped along the highway. There were about thirty people out of their vehicles and milling about a bear—feeding it, taking pictures and so on. I wanted to stop. But I couldn't trust myself. I might have been emotional. I just drove on to the park gate and informed the ranger there. People just don't seem to understand, Mike."

"No, Ted, they don't seem to understand. I was one of them —even after two bad incidents with bears."

"Would you do it now?" he asked.

I shook my head emphatically. "Hell no! Bears don't know where food leaves off and your arm begins. They'll gladly eat both."

He nodded in agreement. I looked at his scarred arm leaning on the table and said, "Ted, you said bears were strong. You fought one off."

"No, Mike. I fought it. *It left me.* I'd say my actions were just about as effective as sticking your hand into a car or truck's fan to try to stop the motor—if you want a simile."

"That's a good simile, Ted. Best I've ever heard."

That, ladies and gentlemen, was a smart, lucid, and experienced young man—who called a bear off his companion
and fought it with his bare hands. Maybe, like me, you've
learned something. It came out in the newspapers in the following manner:

From the *Vancouver Sun*, June 13, 1975

'LUCKY' MAN LOSES 10 LBS TO ANGRY BEAR

By Doug Rushton

"You could hear her coming up after you, snorting like a
steam engine."

That's what Neil Le Noble, 23, of Richmond, says now—but
last Friday in dense bush 25 miles west of the Bennett dam, he
was climbing a tree for his life, with a raging bear clawing at his
heels.

And, while Le Noble was scrambling 60 feet up a tree, his
companion, Ted Watchuk, 23, of Calgary, was standing on the
ground screaming and yelling, trying to distract the angry she-
bear.

"I did a little too well," Watchuk said Thursday in an interview from a Prince George hospital.

Watchuk was subsequently mauled by the bear, losing an
estimated eight to ten pounds of flesh in the process. Le Noble
suffered a badly injured foot, and he is recovering at home
today.

The two geologists were marking out a road route for a mining company when Le Noble said he thought he heard a bear.
A few seconds later, "I looked down the road and she was about
30 feet away, coming at me," Le Noble said.

"She came after me first," he said. "I went up a tree and she
came up after me. I was about 20 feet up when she got me. She
just clawed my foot and I kept going up the tree."

Le Noble didn't stop climbing until he had gone 60 feet up
the tree. "I don't know how he did it," Watchuk said. "Neil just
shot up a tree. He should be in a circus."

Le Noble said he, too, is wondering just how he managed to
climb the tree since the first 10 to 12 feet of it had no branches.
"How does a guy climb a tree without any branches on the
bottom?" he said.

He answered his own question: "I just kind of leaped at it and started climbing. That bear moved terrifyingly fast. It's unbelievable how fast they can move."

Watchuk said the bear chased Le Noble 20 feet up the tree before it noticed him and came down after him "like a freight train."

But Watchuk wasn't so lucky in his choice of a climbing tree. He scrambled up a 10-foot-high one. "It was not a very good insurance tree," he said wryly.

"At first the bear ran past the tree, then turned around and looked at me," he said.

"Then the bear charged over to my tree and started to bite my foot. I gave her a boot on the face and she didn't like that so she knocked me out of the tree.

"Once she grabbed me, I figured it was all over."

Le Noble described the fight this way: "He (Watchuk) kept trying to get away from her. She just literally tore him apart."

Watchuk said that for most of the battle he was standing, "except for the occasional knockdown.

"My first thought was: 'Can this bear really be going for us?' I managed to grab a pretty big stick, but that was just a toothpick to the bear," he said.

Le Noble said that, during the fight, Watchuk was constantly yelling at the bear and at one point shouted, "This is it, Neil. I think it's all over for me."

"How in hell he did it I don't know," Le Noble said. "The doctor told me later that he had lost eight to ten pounds of flesh."

Le Noble said it was all over in no more than ten minutes. The bear just stopped, he said, and after it had ended, Watchuk was still standing.

"Ted never passed out. He was standing there saying, 'I've got to find my glasses,'" he said.

Watchuk said he still isn't sure why the bear decided to stop mauling him. "I guess I put up enough of a struggle that I was becoming more of a nuisance than a threat," he said.

"I definitely don't hold a grudge against that bear. I can't really blame that bear."

Watchuk said he saw a couple of cubs. Le Noble said he guesses that the cubs had begun to wander off and the mother wanted to rejoin them.

The two men had marked about 2,000 feet of road into the

bush off a gravel road where their truck was parked. Le Noble said they walked back to the road, drove the two miles to the mining camp, and called a helicopter to take them to the hospital.

Gerald Paull, fish and wildlife branch protection officer for the region, said Thursday that it is still not clear if the animal was a black bear or a grizzly, even though both Le Noble and Watchuk think it was a grizzly.

"But I want to stress that in no way is this bear considered a man-killer or anything," Paull said. "It was just an isolated incident."

From the *Vancouver Sun*, June 12, 1975

BEAR MAULS ROAD WORKER

Sun Staff Reporter

Prince George—A man is still in the hospital after being severely mauled by a bear about 80 miles north of here Friday.

Ted Watchuk, 23, lost a finger and received severe injuries to both arms and legs during the mauling, but was reported in satisfactory condition today.

Neil Le Noble, 23, was treated for a badly bitten foot and has been released.

Gerald Paull, fish and wildlife branch protection officer for the region, said Wednesday that the men were working in a wilderness area marking out road routes for a mining company when the bear appeared.

Both men fled for nearby trees when they saw the bear, Paull said.

Le Noble climbed nearly 70 feet up a tree in an effort to avoid the bear, but the bear followed him and bit his foot, said Paull.

The bear then came down and started to leave the area, but saw Watchuk, who had climbed a smaller tree.

The bear started pulling at Watchuk, but was kicked down. The bear then made a second attack, pulled Watchuk out of the 11-foot tree and mauled him, Paull said.

Paull said he thinks it was a black bear.

17

What About Polar Bears?

Polar bears, as a subspecies, are isolated from other North American subspecies by the nature of their habitat. The remoteness of their range, which includes regularly traveled outposts such as Churchill, Inuvik, and Yellowknife (on the North American continent), relegates my research into polar bear attacks to just one chapter. Actual interviews with polar bear victims, or with officials concerned with the cases, were simply impossible to obtain in many cases.

One interview I *was* able to conduct was with Dr. C. J. Jonkel, Professor of Research, School of Forestry, the University of Montana in Missoula. A Ph.D. and widely recognized authority on bears, Dr. Jonkel provided me with a number of facts about the polar bear species.

A down-to-earth, medium-built man whose desk is piled high with scientific papers, Dr. Charles Jonkel is a very busy man. When interviewing him in his office, I found him to be accommodating and informative. He was able to supply me with the names, phone numbers, and addresses of five necessary and informative men who could further my research. I would say that his published works are probably the most authoritative in the polar bear field.

From one of his own scientific papers, entitled "Some Comments on Polar Bear Management" (*Biological Conservation*, Vol. 2, No. 2, January 1970, Elsevier Publishing Company Ltd., England), the following assertions reveal a high degree of experience in the field:

". . . the Eskimo has always killed the Polar Bear for food, dog feed, and clothing. In recent years interaction between Man and Polar Bears has increased as the numbers of people, and possibly the numbers of bears, have increased in certain areas. On 1 October 1966 a sub-adult male Polar Bear attacked a 12-year-old boy near Fort Churchill, Manitoba, and on 2 November, 1967, a different sub-adult male attacked two Cree Indians with the Dené Village Indian settlement about two miles (3.2 km) SSW of Churchill. Then on 17 November 1968 a third sub-adult male attacked and killed a 19-year-old Eskimo boy just outside Fort Churchill. These three bears were all killed by Royal Canadian Mounted Police officers.

Polar bears are protected in Manitoba, and up to 20 can be seen in or around Churchill in a single autumn day, but no other serious encounters have been reported. Some bears become a considerable nuisance, however, and four near Fort Churchill and three at an oil exploration camp at the mouth of the Kaskattama River near the Manitoba-Ontario border . . . were killed by hunters or workers during the autumns of 1967 and 1968 respectively. They were all considered dangerous by the persons involved.

Harrington (1964) found in a review of the literature that there are few documented cases of deliberate attack on Man by Polar Bears. Pederson (1956) cites two instances, though the circumstances were not investigated thoroughly. Seldom does an opportunity arise whereby one can make an adequate investigation, but the 1966 attack on the boy near Fort Churchill provided such a chance. During the autopsy (of the animal) I found that the bear had been wounded with firearms earlier in the year, and also again on the same day of the attack. The earlier wound had driven a canine tooth into the nasal passage, blinding at least one eye. This discovery was not made until the skull was cleaned in the laboratory. The fresh wounds were inflicted by 22-calibre slugs, which lodged in the abdomen and hind legs. The attack by the bear, therefore, could hardly be considered unprovoked, though a police report filed shortly after the attack referred to it as an unprovoked attack.

The attack on the two Indians in 1967 [Author's note: See item that follows: *Vancouver Sun,* Vancouver, B.C., Nov. 20, 1967, "Across Canada, Bear Mauls Two."] was also found to be provoked, though evidence was less conclusive than in the 1966 case. This bear had been captured and ear-tagged 10 days earlier as part of a long-term research project on Polar Bears. He had a discoloured coat and garbage in his scats when captured, and was in exceptionally good physical condition. As a bear of similar appearance had frequented Fort Churchill for about two months prior to this capture, I concluded he was that bear. If the assumption was correct, the attack on the two Indians could hardly be considered unprovoked, as during the two months this bear had been stoned, photographed, fed and chased with dogs and snowmobiles, until he had little fear of men.

The bear that attacked and killed an Eskimo in 1968 [Author's note: See item that follows: Canadian Press, Nov. 18, 1968, "Polar Bear Kills Student in Group."] just outside Fort Churchill had given no previous indication of being dangerous. The boy and several companions saw tracks of two bears bypassing the settlement along the Hudsons Bay coast. They decided to track the bears through the snow, and one boy simply approached too closely when he came to where the bear was bedded in a protected area. An autopsy (on the animal) disclosed that the bear had garbage in its stomach, no physical anomalies. This tragic accident ending in death of both boy and the bear might easily have been avoided through greater forbearance by Man.

More Problems Are Pending

In the Churchill area, and in places such as Eskimo Point, oil drilling camps, and weather stations, it will only be a matter of time before other serious encounters between Man and Polar Bears occur. Because personnel changes are frequent, many of the people visiting or residing in these areas are new each year. This association of Bears that are familiar with humans, and of people who are unfamiliar with Bears, presents a continually dangerous situation, and the residents of these settlements are already not inclined to be patient with the Bears. The problem originates locally when bears are lured by garbage near the settlements or work camps.

At Fort Churchill the garbage dump is less than one mile (1.6 km) from the apartment dwellings and the immediate Churchill dump is actually within the townsite. Dozens of people, at one time, can be found parked in cars or walking among the feeding Bears. Bears wander at will between the buildings, or among dogs and children. The Bears are often completely surrounded by people taking photographs, feeding them scraps of food, or teasing them. Obviously, certain Bears in such situations will react aggressively, just as the Grizzlies have done in National Parks when fed in the vicinity of public camp areas (Glacier National Park, 1967).

In addition, with Polar Bears so common, certain humans have reacted viciously towards the Bears. At least three Polar Bears were shot illegally by vandals and abandoned in the Churchill and Fort Churchill dumps in the fall of 1967 (Fig. 4) and there were indications that three Bears were killed needlessly on the Kaskattama River (Fig. 1), though a full investigation was not made. In the autumn of 1968, one bear was shot by goose hunters on Cape Churchill for no known reason (Fig. 5) while a female and a cub and a sub-adult female were shot and abandoned in the Churchill dump.

Polar Bears are apparently not looked upon by these people as the Great White Bear of the North, but rather as creatures akin to rats. Should the present trend continue, this view of Polar Bears will prevail as it has in regard to the Black and Grizzly Bears in some southern regions.

It would be difficult to find a more authentic transcript than the foregoing by Dr. Charles Jonkel. Few such scientifically verified reports are available to a researcher. More often than not, they are "buried" in interdepartment memos or reports that are often not available to the public. They occasionally surface in rather obscure journals having extremely limited circulation, and much of the terminology and data are difficult for the layman to understand. Such regrettable circumstances withhold from the public material that could actively change attitudes about bears. The news clippings that follow should help shed light on the least-known subspecies, the polar bear.

Nov. 20, 1967

ACROSS CANADA
BEAR MAULS TWO

Churchill, Man. (CP)—A polar bear was shot and killed in an Indian village three miles east of here as it was dragging off one of two persons it had mauled, it was reported Saturday.

Adolphe Thorassie, 28, was attacked while he was walking home in the village 600 miles north of Winnipeg on Nov. 7.

The commotion of the attack drew Adele Nagle out of her home. The bear caught her and began dragging her off when Alex Sandberry rushed from his house with a gun and shot the 350-pound bear in the head.

Nov. 20, 1967

POLAR BEAR SHOT AFTER MAULING TWO

Churchill, Man. (CP)—A polar bear was shot and killed in an Indian village three miles east of here as it was dragging off one of the two persons it had attacked and mauled, it was reported at the weekend.

Adolphe Thorassie, 28, was attacked while he was walking home in the village 600 miles north of Winnipeg.

Thorassie was surprised by the bear and severely mauled and bitten before he was able to get loose and run to the nearby home of Alex Sandberry.

The commotion drew Adele Nagle out of her home. The bear caught her and began dragging her off when Sandberry rushed from his house with a shotgun and killed the 350-pound animal.

Both the injured were taken to hospital. Mrs. Nagle has since been released.

Polar bears, common in the area at this time of year, usually leave once the Hudson Bay freezes over.

Nov. 18, 1968

Polar Bear Kills Student In Group

Churchill, Man. (CP)—A polar bear attacked and killed an Eskimo student Sunday as his horrified schoolmates looked on helplessly.

Paulosie Meeko, 19, of Great Whale River, Que., died less than two hours after the attack which occurred at midday in this sub-Arctic community of 2,500. The youth's throat was slashed.

The bear was shot by police 20 minutes later.

Another bear was chased away by police. It scattered children returning home from Sunday school as it made its escape.

S. H. Uhrich, an official of the National Research Council base, which is near the attack site, said there is an unusually large number of bears around Churchill this year because of the late freeze-up, which has kept them off Hudson Bay.

"They keep congregating in town and at the dump. I saw a dozen at noon Sunday at the dump," he said.

"They kept walking between the cars—there were about thirty people out taking pictures."

Uhrich said there are at least two dozen bears in the area—twice as many as usual. Many are females with twin cubs.

A week ago, two polar bears were killed and another wounded when they were ambushed illegally at the local garbage dump. The wounded bear was tracked down by police and shot.

Nov. 19, 1968

Polar Bears Kill Youth, Terrorize Pair In Home

Churchill, Man. (CP)—Polar bears killed a youth and terrorized an adult couple in separate incidents near this sub-Arctic port.

Paulosie Meeko, 19, of Great Whale River, Que., died after a bear slashed his neck in Fort Churchill, 10 miles east of here.

Douglas Ritchie, local government district administrator, and his wife were trapped in their cabin 11 miles south of here by a bear that broke through a plate glass window.

S. H. Uhrich of the National Research Council at Fort

Churchill, 610 miles north of Winnipeg, says there are about two dozen bears, many females with cubs, in the area. Late freeze-up has kept them off Hudsons Bay and resulted in the unusually high concentration.

"They keep congregating in camp and at the dump," he says. "The RCMP have been chasing them out of camp."

Meeko, a student at a vocational school for Arctic children, apparently was following the bear with two companions, when it attacked him.

RCMP constable Jim Madrigga responded to the companions' cry for help.

He killed the bear.

Uhrich said another bear was chased away from the post office in Fort Churchill, a community of 2,500, by police. As it escaped, it scattered children returning from a nearby church.

Ritchie said he got up in the morning to let his dog out and was met by a bear as he opened the door. He outstared the bear, but it returned later and crashed through a window.

Mr. and Mrs. Ritchie fought the bear with brooms and bottles until police arrived and frightened it off with several shots.

Aug. 22, 1969

ARM TORN OFF

Montreal (UP)—A nine-year-old boy is reported in good condition in hospital here after a polar bear tore off his right arm as he tried to feed the animal in the Granby Zoo.

Doctors at the Ste. Justine Children's Hospital said no attempt was made to graft the arm back on because of the condition of the severed limb.

Nov. 18, 1969

POLICE KILL POLAR BEAR AS BOY HURT

Churchill, Man. (CP)—RCMP killed a 400-pound polar bear after it swiped at a seven-year-old boy returning from Sunday school in this Hudson Bay town.

Nanook, the Eskimo word for the big white bears, is making his annual migration through the town, feeding on garbage and occasionally molesting residents.

RCMP say they are using a new system for polar bear control this year. Officers are tagging the bears when possible.

"If the tagged polar bear continues to come into the populated area, an attempt is made to trap it," an RCMP sergeant said. "If that is unsuccessful, then it is destroyed."

The captured bears are sent on a one-way trip to the Assiniboine Zoo in Winnipeg. One bear has been sent to the zoo this year.

Police say the bear population near the town is "heaviest" this month as the animals await the freezing over of Hudson Bay. Then they will continue their northern migration.

The boy injured Sunday, Bradley Whyte, was not seriously hurt, police said. An Eskimo boy was killed by a bear last year.

Vancouver Sun, Aug. 9, 1972

Oil Worker Killed By Polar Bear

Yellowknife, N.W.T. (CP)—A Calgary oil worker has apparently been killed by a polar bear on Devon Island in the high Arctic, RCMP said today.

The body of Franciscus Alphonsus Maria Yland, 34, was brought here for an autopsy.

RCMP said Yland, a Dutch national employed by Foothills Catering Ltd. for City Services Oil Co., both of Calgary, was found with his rifle and apparently had been hunting on Grimmell Peninsula at Bear Bay on the island.

They said he was killed about 1:30 P.M. Monday, but there were no witnesses. Details on the accident were sketchy because sun spot activity has virtually knocked out all high-frequency radio transmissions in the high Arctic. Resolute Bay, site of the investigating RCMP detachment, has been particularly affected by the communications blackout.

"Our report is that the man was killed by a bear, but we have no other details at all," an RCMP spokesman at Frobisher Bay said.

Vancouver Sun, Jan. 7, 1975

Polar Bear Kills Youth

Inuvik, N.W.T.—An 18-year-old Dawson Creek youth, formerly of Delta, was mauled to death by a polar bear Sunday at an Imperial Oil Ltd. exploration site in the Mackenzie River delta, 200 miles northwest of here.

RCMP reported Monday that Richard Michael Pernitzky was working outside a building when he was attacked by the bear. There were no witnesses.

Vancouver Sun, Jan. 7, 1975

POLAR BEAR KILLS OIL WORKER

Special to the *Sun*

Inuvik, N.W.T.—An 18-year-old oil worker from B.C. was killed Sunday by a polar bear near a drilling barge in the Mackenzie Delta 100 miles north of here.

Fellow workers who organized a search when the man failed to arrive at his living quarters found the bear 300 yards from camp still clutching the remains of Richard Pernitzky, of Dawson Creek.

One of them said the bear showed little fear although the men fired a flare and drove bulldozers at it. They had no firearms.

Northwest Territories law forbids anyone but an Indian or an Eskimo to kill a polar bear.

An Eskimo worker at the camp was later given a war surplus rifle brought from another camp, but the sights of the gun were damaged and he failed to hit the animal.

The bear eventually was killed by an Eskimo flown to the scene with RCMP from Inuvik.

Three metal tags were attached to the ear of the bear, indicating it had been tranquilized and removed from civilization at least three times.

Pernitzky is believed to have been attacked near the barge when he went to check its sewage disposal system in the Arctic darkness on Sunday morning.

His co-workers were not able to begin a full search until the sun rose about noon.

Other oil workers had seen the same bear at the garbage dump of a nearby camp several days earlier but did not report it either to company officials or RCMP, one worker said.

A spokesman for Imperial Oil Ltd., which operates the oil drilling rig, said Pernitzky was employed by Polar Camps of Dawson Creek, a catering firm, and is survived by his mother in Dawson Creek.

Vancouver Sun, Jan. 9, 1975

BEAR 'REPRIEVED' 2 DAYS BEFORE MAN WAS KILLED

Inuvik, N.W.T. (CP)—A worker at an oil rig north of this Mackenzie delta community says armed men were sent after a bear two days before a bear killed a man.

But, said the worker who asked not to be identified, the men decided not to shoot the animal because it didn't look hungry.

Richard Pernitzky, 18, of Dawson Creek, was killed by a polar bear Sunday about 100 miles north of Inuvik. The bear was later shot by a native flown in by the RCMP.

Jim Bourque, a game management officer, said Wednesday he and a local trapper were the two men who went looking for the bear reported Jan. 2, but they saw only tracks.

"And no one can tell if it was the same animal. Bears wander all over the Arctic: they have no natural predator."

Three tags attached to the bear's ear showed it had been tranquilized and removed from civilization at least three times.

"It was very unfortunate it happened," Bourque said. "But people in camps have to be more aware."

Vancouver Sun, Jan. 14, 1975

POLAR BEAR PATROLS TO BEGIN

Calgary (CP)—Dogs and armed patrolmen will be guarding against polar bears at Imperial Oil Ltd's northern drilling sites, company officials said Monday.

These and other measures, to be implemented "within the week," followed the mauling death Jan. 5 of an 18-year-old worker at one of Imperial's drilling sites in the Mackenzie delta.

The day after the incident, five senior employees from the company's Calgary and Edmonton offices were sent to investigate conditions at the rig site, located about 120 miles north of Inuvik.

The group returned Friday with recommendations aimed at preventing polar bears from coming near inhabited drilling areas, said Gord Willmon, Imperial's frontier manager.

He said there was no gun at the drilling site, and regulations prohibit anyone but an Eskimo from shooting polar bears.

To begin immediately are daily helicopter inspections of the drilling areas. There will also be dogs at northern camps and experienced native hunters to patrol the areas.

He said a gun will be assigned to each camp and a qualified marksman will be authorized to use it in emergencies.

Vancouver Sun, Sept. 2, 1975

TWO SURVEYORS MAULED IN CAMP BY POLAR BEAR

Ottawa (CP)—Two members of a geological survey team were mauled last week by a polar bear which wandered into their camp on Somerset Island in the Arctic, the energy department said today.

John Legault, 23, of Dorval, Que., and Bob Taylor, 27, of Ottawa, suffered severe cuts on their hands and shoulders. The two men, members of a field party of the Geological Survey of Canada, were sent to hospital in Frobisher Bay, N.W.T., and are now recuperating at their homes.

The attack occurred while the men were sleeping. The bear seized Legault by the head and dragged him away. While attempting to load a rifle, Taylor was also attacked. A third member of the survey party then managed to kill the bear, the department said.

The Province, Sept. 4, 1975

HIS HEAD WAS IN POLAR BEAR'S JAWS

Montreal (CP)—John Legault, 23, said he "didn't feel a thing," when his head was in the jaws of a 400-pound polar bear two weeks ago at a campsite 40 miles south of Resolute Bay, N.W.T.

In an interview in his Montreal apartment, Legault said: "It all happened so fast, all I felt was grinding and crunching of teeth on my scalp."

Legault was one of eight field members sent by the Geological Survey of Canada this summer to study beach erosion on the northern coast of Somerset Island.

Both he and the party's leader Bob Taylor, 27, were flown to a Frobisher Bay hospital after being mauled by the bear.

Taylor returned to his home in Ottawa and Legault to his home in suburban Dorval last Sunday to recuperate.

"We'd all gone to bed early on that particular night," Legault said. "At 3 A.M. my tent-mate Ross Cameron and I were awakened suddenly by a flapping sound outside.

"We thought it was a fox, and Ross went to check," he said. "The bear immediately began to chase Ross.

"I decided to run also and when the bear saw me, he changed directions, loped toward me, and started pawing me. He got a grip on my head with his mouth and pulled me.

"I could see his paws were dripping with blood."

Taylor came out of his tent when he heard the commotion, holding one of the party's three rifles. He tried firing the gun but it would not go off.

The bear dropped Legault and attacked Taylor, biting him about the head and shoulders.

Finally another member of the party, Jim Savelle, 25, shot and killed the bear.

When the bear's stomach was opened, nothing was found but seaweed, an indication the bear had eaten nothing substantial for some time.

Legault received over 50 stitches to his scalp, neck and back but suffered no permanent damage and said he would go on a similar expedition again.

"Only this time I'd bring a bigger gun," he said.

It should be noted that there have been polar bear–man confrontations since the final 1968 incident mentioned in the 1970 Jonkel report, and with regrettable results to the victims. The confrontations have occurred over a broader geographical expanse, but to a total degree, are now less common than at the time of Jonkel's 1970 publication.

It is hoped that the quoted items will help educate people entering polar bear country, and prevent more attacks or killings.

18

Battling a Bear and Then the Courts

Fred Sturdy was just a nice kid of nineteen years when he heard of a job in Jasper National Park, Alberta, Canada, with one of the service companies. Most of the main tourist business was over by late August, but there was still a week left for Sturdy to make a few dollars. Besides, he liked the area. This particular day was cold. The girlfriend of one of his friends was also working in the Maligne Lake area. He was going to take a walk and asked her if she would like to accompany him. They took that walk past the ranger's cabin, along a road leading to a clearing where there were a number of abandoned buildings.

On the way back, while Sturdy was being severely mauled by a grizzly the girl fainted. He was to be partially crippled for life.

Following almost a year in the hospital, Sturdy spent part of the next ten years in a suit for $75,000 against the Canadian

Government Parks organization, proclaiming their negligence.

He lost the suit. They claimed *he* was negligent.

If he appealed the decision and accepted fifty-fifty blame with the parks, his lawyer told him that he might get $35,000. The cost of the first suit was $8,500, and the projection for the appeal costs was another $8,000—or a total of $16,500.

Fred Sturdy said, "To hell with it! I've had enough."

He is now in partnership in four smart menswear stores—making it on his own.

I met him in his shop in Sherwood Park's East Gate Shopping Center, and wrote this chapter the following evening. He's a winner and projects that image even before you speak to him.

"Yes, Mr. Cramond," said the tall, dark-haired Sturdy. "You want to talk about my bear incident. Let's go and get a cup of coffee."

"But you're on duty," I replied. "I just came to set a time that would be convenient to you, when you are off."

"No matter. Nothing doing here that needs me right now."

He grinned in an infectious manner. He was a handsome young man who wore large-rimmed, tinted glasses that obscured most of the evidence of the grizzly's clawmarks on his left side of his face. He led the way across the shopping center mall to a small coffee counter and dining room. At the counter, he took a couple of cups and saucers and filled them from the steaming coffee decanter. Before doing so, he had asked me if I would prefer tea. As I dug for my wallet, he put his hand up in protest, stating that he had invited me and that he was going to get it. I said to hell with that. He laughed and told the proprietor, "His money is no good!" He then took both cups and led the way to a corner table.

His question was direct as I sat down opposite him: "Mike, what is the purpose of your book?"

He was looking directly at me, questioningly. It took me back for a moment. None of my other interviews had brought forth such a frank request.

"Well, Fred. The first purpose is to provide information that could prevent or lessen the possibility of bear attacks. Sec-

ondly, I'm hoping the book might help those who have suffered attacks."

He nodded appreciatively, saying nothing. I went on: "To
put it more concisely, I'm hoping the book will instill in people
a little more fear of bears—or at least give them an understanding of the personal danger they face when they come in contact with bears. Let's put it this way. If you said to a person,
'There are sharks out in that water,' they wouldn't swim there.
But if you said, 'There are bears out there,' in all probability
they would go into that wild element just to try to get a look
at them."

He was studying me as I spoke, and grinned at the summation.

"Yeah, you're right! *I* was one."

"I was—*still* am, Fred. But not as damn foolish about it as
I was."   ·

"No, me neither." He paused, lifted off his glasses, and
looked directly at me. For the first time, his facial disfigurement became apparent. I had the feeling he subconsciously
might have wanted to witness my own reaction—perhaps
even consciously.

"Your doctors did a good job on you, Fred," I told him.

"Yes, I had a very good cosmetic surgeon. He's the best. I
was one of his first of many with this type of injury. You'd like
to hear about my incident, I guess."

I nodded. "Yes, I would."

"Well, this friend of mine told me about a job out in Jasper
Park for the summer. I was nineteen years old. It was the kind
of thing I thought I would like. This particular night was in the
last week of August. A friend's girlfriend was there—he was at
another part of the park. I just asked her if she would like to
go for a walk," he said, hesitating. "Mike, do you have a pencil?"

He picked up one of the napkins when I handed him the
ballpoint pen, and quickly sketched the area where the bunkhouse in which he stayed was. He outlined the buildings beside
a road that transected a main road leading to the lakefront.
This offshoot road also split off to the ranger's cabin in the

direction of the lake, and went past the flattened earth platform of the garbage dump in the other direction.

He circled the dump.

"They dumped the stuff here, then pushed it over the edge —a drop of about fifty feet," he said. "I didn't think too much about bears. I'm a city kid. Heck, I used to walk down another trail that made a circle right around the area where all the garbage ended up." He drew another line along the napkin, showing that trail's relationship to where the dump was. "I never saw a bear in that area, and that's where they would have to cross to get to the dump."

He paused and lit a cigarette, offering me one. As I refused with an explanation that I'd quit twice—once for sixteen years, now for three years—he grinned and continued.

"It was in the evening—getting toward dusk. We walked around by the ranger's cabin, past the dump, and over to the clearing where the other government buildings were. It was getting dark quickly, so we turned around and headed back. We cut off onto the road that circled the dump area, and were just past the entrance."

He paused, as if trying to be fully assured of his recall. Then he said, "I remember a growling. The girl with me took off on a run—we had been walking side by side—and then tripped or fell into the ditch at the side of the road. I heard the grizzly coming and started to run into the bush on the side of the road on which she had fallen. I was scared as hell! I didn't know what had happened to her. The bear was coming right after me. I only got about fifty feet before I tripped and fell. Then the bear was right on me, before I could even think or get up. It hit me in the face, right here."

He indicated the scarred left side of his face. "I don't remember any pain from that swipe of his paw."

I interjected a question: "Were you on your back?"

"No, not on my back. More on my side, with my knee up. Like this."

He turned in the chair and lifted his leg in a half-crooked position, meanwhile pointing to the inner portion of his thigh.

"I guess I was lucky that I was in this position," he said. "The bear bit me right in here." His hand indicated the area. As his palm pressed in against his pantleg, the hollow became apparent. The sight jarred me momentarily. He went on, "If it hadn't got me there and torn out a chunk of my thigh, it probably would have got me in the stomach area and killed me."

He was looking directly at me again. He said, "There was a great deal of pain there—on that bite. I don't remember it too clearly, but I felt pain. It tore a great big chunk loose. I remember thinking, *I'm dead*. Then the grizzly was gone. It just left me."

My mind went back to Ted Watchuk (see Chapter 16), who had recently told me that the bear he fought off did exactly the same thing after tearing a section out of his calf and thigh. Both men had been very graphic in their recollection.

Fred was speaking again: "I was torn up pretty badly. My eye was hanging out on my cheek, and I couldn't see clearly because of all the blood. My leg was torn up. The bear just missed the main artery by a fraction of an inch. I got up and tried to yell. I couldn't. It also got me in the throat, and there was a hole right here, in my windpipe."

He pushed aside the collar of his shirt, indicating the scar.

"I guess that hole saved my life, though," he said. He lit another cigarette and looked at my cup: "Would you like another cup of coffee?"

"Yes, please—I'll get it," I said, trying to rise.

"You sit still, I'll get it—more cream and sugar?" He insisted again that I remain seated.

A moment later he returned with the coffee decanter, set the cream and sugar on the table, and filled both cups. He dropped back into the chair.

"Well, the girl came to and ran to the ranger's cabin. She didn't know what had happened to me, exactly. But she came back by the dump entrance road with the ranger, in his car. I was on my feet, trying to wave at them and get their attention. I couldn't make any sound because of the tear in my throat. They drove right past—didn't even see me. It was all a bit hazy. I was trying to get to the road in the darkness. I guess it took maybe ten minutes for the girl to reach the ranger's cabin, get him, then come back. Then they drove right past!"

He paused in an effort to recall. "I got out on the road, and some guys from the camp were coming back in another car. They stopped when they saw me waving. Couldn't believe what they saw. I was a mess."

He paused reflectively. I interjected a question: "Was it a sow bear?"

"I couldn't tell one bear from another. Parks and I disagreed on a few things. I think *they* were negligent. They said *I* was."

I stopped him with a statement: "I've talked with them. Many parks employees have a habit of covering their asses. They're afraid of public criticism, afraid to talk to news people. The bureaucracy seems to get to them, Fred. All I'm trying to get is actual information that will be helpful to their cause, as well as that of the public. I don't have any vendetta against anyone or anything. Hell, parks people themselves have been killed, doing their jobs. The Bambi, Smokey the Bear, Gentle Ben syndrome gets emotional idiots up in arms if Parks or Wildlife branches say they are going to kill a marauding bear. I guess they get it whichever way they go."

Sturdy was looking at me while I spoke.

"They have their problems, too," he said.

"Yeah, I've listened to some of them." I nodded.

"How long did it take you to get to the hospital?"

"Oh, a couple of hours. I was in the Jasper hospital for six days and in the University Hospital at Edmonton for a year. I remember over the weeks and months thinking, *Why me?* I wasn't too aware of this. . . ." I had been very athletic. They had a bad time with the leg. Gangrene set in deeply, and they wanted to cut the leg off. I guess my dad wouldn't sign the papers."

The shock of the aftermath was getting to me.

"Jesus Christ, Fred," I said. "You were only nineteen. At that age recuperative powers are enormous."

I thought about a motorcycle accident a friend and I were in years ago. The doctors wanted to take off his foot, and his mother came to me and asked me what I thought about it. I'd pleaded with her to stop them, and she did. Jack was forever thankful to me for that. He had a stiff foot, but it didn't stop him from being an athlete. Hell, he had saved my life by pushing the motorcycle and sidecar off my chest while I lay in the middle of the highway. I remember seeing his foot folded over beside his ankle, the bone sticking out through his running shoe. Yet he walked from where he had been thrown— 15 feet away—and pushed the motorcycle off me so I could get out of the center of the highway. And *he* had thanked *me* for saving his foot!

Fred was continuing his narration: "But it was gangrenous, Mike. The doctors operated on my leg and cut out all the gangrenous muscle and tissue. I've lost about 20 percent use of my leg. It affected some of the nerve tissue in my foot and leg, and I had no control over turning up my toes. Wore a brace for a long time. Now I wear these shoes." He indicated a pair of modern high boots. "They seem to handle it okay."

He was lifting the foot to show the muscular control. I grinned at a recollection that came to mind. When I had phoned his home, earlier during the day, his wife had answered and said he was out playing golf.

"How was your score today?" I asked.

"Oh, not bad for me. I used to play on the Jasper golf links when I was a kid. Used to see bears right on the course, occasionally. We never bothered about them, just stayed clear of them. They always went away. Now I can't play out there and feel relaxed. I always worry that a bear may come along. Funny—I guess I'm scared of them."

I nodded my head in agreement. "Hell, I'm apprehensive of them too. Researching this book is making me jumpy about just going into wild places."

He was listening thoughtfully and spoke when I became silent.

"One of the things that bothers me is taking my family camping in the wilds, which I don't do often," he continued. "I think kids enjoy that, should have it. My wife, our little daughter, and I just went out for a long weekend. I was on edge the whole time, couldn't relax."

He was searching for words. I thought I might help.

"Some people who have been through it feel that way,

Fred," I told him. "Others don't. I've had a couple of bears come after me—killed them, too close for comfort. It's natural that a guy would be nervous. I have always been jumpy in the bush—but I hunt, and carry either a rifle or shotgun with me most of the time. Being jumpy spoils some of the fun, but you forget about it, sooner or later."

He grinned and nodded. "Yes, I guess so. I guess I've got over most of my trauma. To a degree, I talked my way out of it over the years. A lot of people came to visit me there. You could see that some of them came out of curiosity—you could tell by the look on their faces, but good friends helped. Their sympathy got to me, though. I had a bad time for a while."

He was getting up to bring some more coffee—if I wanted it. I refused. He sat down and looked up at the ceiling.

"It's the way the little kids look at me that I can't handle well. They point to my face and ask their mothers about it. I don't know how to talk to them. I've had so many curious people ask me what happened that I'm fed up with talking about the grizzly attack. I've wanted to say, 'I got it in Vietnam.' Anything but tell them the story *again*."

He was looking earnestly at me. I said something about my being facially scarred when I was a kid, and being ashamed of it—just pockmarked by smallpox, but very self-conscious. Nevertheless, other people didn't really notice it.

He nodded. "Every once in a while our little girl, who is four, looks up at me and says something like, 'Why is your eye like that, Daddy?' I just answer whatever comes into my mind. She forgets about it." [Ed. Note: She now knows the real story.]

I was looking at him, comprehending the words he had just uttered. He is actually a handsome man. His personality is such that his injury is not noticeable. I remembered seeing Malcolm Aspeslet (see Chapter 6), with much worse disfiguration, playing with his three-year-old daughter—a very happy family interlude. I knew they had met.

"Malcolm Aspeslet is figuring on another operation to regain the use of the eye that was bitten," I said. "He was the one who told me about your case. He and Barbara are having their problems as a result of the attack. I'm hoping that this book's publication can help raise a fund that will send him to Scotland. There's an excellent surgeon over there who figures he can reconnect the eye's nerve system."

Fred Sturdy smiled thoughtfully. "Yes, Malcolm's parents asked me to go and see him in the hospital. That was a tough one for me. I was going to see myself, as I looked at his injuries. It was a tough thing to face. I could look at myself . . . but seeing someone else going through it . . ."

His words trailed off.

"Fred," I interjected. "One of the things I want very much to come out of this book is that those of you who have suffered bear attacks may be able to contact one another. The sharing of feelings and solutions to problems might be helpful to everyone . . . perhaps an organization . . ."

He shook his head in semi-negation.

"I think each person has to handle it himself," he said. "I'm not a sympathetic type. Well, perhaps that isn't it. I don't have the patience or tolerance for other people's aches and pains. I think the last thing you want is sympathy . . . or curiosity. You have to make the decisions to come out of it yourself."

He thought for a moment. "I think I was a rotten kid," he said. "And that experience turned me around. It made me have a greater appreciation of life."

We talked for about another hour. He explained his legal battle of nine years, trying to get a $75,000 settlement that he felt was justified. And that seemed entirely justifiable to me.

I showed him the clippings that follow:

Vancouver Sun—Aug. 31, 1965

CANADA GRIZZLY MAULS HIKER

Jasper, Alta. (CP)—A grizzly bear with three cubs seriously mauled a young Edmonton hiker Sunday, but left his girl companion alone when she fainted.

Fred Sturdy, 19, of Edmonton, was in serious condition Monday night in Jasper Hospital. Diane Davidson of Sudbury, Ont., who was walking with Sturdy high in the Rocky Mountains, was released from hospital after treatment for shock.

K. B. Mitchell, superintendent of Jasper National Park, said, "It appears the two walked right into the bears in the darkness."

Vancouver Sun—Sept. 16, 1967

GRIZZLY BEAR'S VICTIM ASKS $75,000 OF GOV'T

Edmonton (CP)—Fred Sturdy, 21, is suing the federal government for $75,000 in a damage claim believed the first of its kind to go before the courts.

Sturdy spent almost a year in hospital after being mauled by a grizzly bear in Jasper National Park in August 1965. He suffered face and skull fractures, torn thigh muscles, and cuts.

A girl with whom Sturdy was walking at dusk near a garbage dump when the mauling occurred, was not injured. The case will be heard before the Exchequer Court of Canada.

The Province—Dec. 11, 1973

BEAR VICTIM SUES

Edmonton (CP)—A federal court heard opening arguments Monday in a suit against the federal government by Frederick Sturdy, 27, of Edmonton, mauled by a grizzly bear in Jasper National Park in 1965.

Sturdy, now manager of a clothing store, still has a scarred face from the bear attack.

He testified that there were no warnings posted about bears in the Maligne Lake area where he and a friend, Diane Davidson of Sudbury, Ont., were fishing Aug. 30, 1965.

Sturdy said he and Miss Davidson were returning to a tourist camp along a shortcut past a garbage dump when they heard a low growl.

He ran about 50 feet before the bear attacked, cuffing him in the face and tearing the inside of his thigh.

Thurs., Dec. 13, 1973

PARK MAN 'LAUGHED OFF' BEAR REPORT

Edmonton (CP)—A Vancouver man said in federal court that a Jasper National Park warden "laughed it off " when told of a grizzly bear at a garbage dump where an Edmonton man was mauled in 1965.

Nicholas Jaques, 24, was testifying in a lawsuit by Frederick Sturdy, 27, who is seeking damages from the federal government for the mauling he received from a bear near the dump Aug. 30, 1965.

Sturdy has said park officials were negligent by not warning resort staff and visitors to the Maligne Lake area, about 20 miles southeast of the Jasper townsite, of dangers from bears raiding the dump for food.

Jaques, then 16, was camp boy for a chalet on the north end of Maligne Lake. One of his jobs was to haul garbage to the nearby dump where Sturdy was attacked.

Jaques testified he saw a grizzly at the dump three weeks before the attack and notified area warden Stanley (Mac) Elder.

But Jaques said Elder refused to believe him, and the camp boy did not report the bear to chalet managers for fear of losing his job.

Elder, now warden service manager for the Jasper townsite area, denied that Jaques reported seeing a bear. He testified that he had never seen a bear at the dump, although he had seen bear tracks and droppings.

Elder said his investigation of the attack indicated that a migrating mother bear with two or three cubs was involved.

Prior to the attack, the only warning he had of a grizzly in the area was a report of one seen that day at a nearby spring, said Elder. However, he added, the report was made only half an hour before Sturdy was attacked.

The owner of the chalet at which Jaques worked, Ken Lucas of Calgary, testified Tuesday that a sign warning of bears was posted at the chalet and brochures were available to visitors.

"I find it very difficult to believe that Fred wouldn't have known there were bears in the country," said Lucas.

Jim Sime of Calgary, acting chief of natural resource conservation for the western region office of the parks branch, testified that of 22 persons injured by bears in the western parks between 1929 and 1965, only six were attacked by grizzlies.

Sturdy's case was the only one involving a garbage dump, he said.

The Province—Tuesday, Feb. 5, 1974

Damages Refused

Edmonton (CP)—An Edmonton man's bid for damages from the federal government following his mauling in Jasper National Park has been rejected by a federal court which could find no evidence of negligence by park authorities.

Frederick J. Sturdy was badly mauled by a female bear with cubs as he and a friend strolled in near darkness past an open garbage dump at Maligne Lake in the park.

Sturdy glanced through the clippings thoughtfully, showing no malice or vindictiveness. I asked if he would advise people to sue Parks. He shook his head no, saying that he had wasted ten years in court. Each case was different.

I can't help thinking of Sturdy and the others. I'd just like to make one submission, Your Honor.

The man to whom you refused a petition for damages was thirty years of age.

The kid who went on an evening walk with a girl friend was nineteen years of age. He was damaged beyond any remote proportion of blame, by just being a normal young guy going for an evening walk.

It's *our* money you'd be paying out, Your Honor. We'd rather pay *him* than many the courts have compensated.

19

Both Grizzlies
Charged

Two of the three grizzlies that have fallen to my rifle had first charged. The non-attacker's skull was smashed from behind the ear, and it went down in a jellied hummock of fur. The latter two charged, or "attacked," because I interfered with them. The first of those grizzlies was wounded before it came; the second was defending its cubs, and also had a malformed front paw.

The only reason for either of them being in these pages is to show exemplary habits of men and bears. Neither incident could be considered an attack, and neither is included in the statistics that appear in the Appendix.

My freelance writing career began with fiction for national magazines, but it blossomed first in true police cases, and then in business, economics, the arts, regional history, and archaeology. It finally settled in the field of recreations, particularly in hunting and fishing. My first three stories in that latter field were all accepted in the mid-1940s by Raymond T. Brown, editor-in-chief of *Outdoor Life* magazine. Within a year my work had been published in four major national magazines, and before I quit writing for them my stories had been featured in all major national outdoor and adventure magazines of the time. It was the association with *Outdoor Life* magazine that brought me in contact with outdoors illustrator Bob Kuhn and led to the first grizzly charge.

Kuhn was a sailor in the merchant marine during World War II. He picked up assignments for magazine illustration when he was in New York and painted them in the depths of the crew quarters during off-watches at sea. My first piece for *Outdoor Life* ran in the September 1945 issue. Entitled "Happy Hunting Grounds," the story was illustrated by Bob, in full-page color plate. I wrote to him and asked him if I could buy the painting. Instead, he sent it to me as a gift—typical of him. The painting still hangs in my rumpus room, a reminder that he used to paint while a merchant seaman, and that I used to write while a territorial provincial policeman. During the next few years Bob's works always illustrated my *Outdoor Life* pieces, and he reached an early crest of success. He mailed me other illustrations he painted for my articles, as gifts.

After living in Mexico for almost a year, I moved back to Vancouver, B.C., in 1951 and offered to take Bob hunting in the Rocky Mountains. Following a post graduate English course at the University of Oklahoma, I was in the process of writing my first successful book, *Hunting and Fishing in North America,* and needed grizzly, mountain goat, and sheep photo illustrations. In a telephone call from Connecticut, Bob let me know he would arrive by plane that week. The trip was to be a joint venture: He needed background photos for his illustrations, and I needed material for future magazine articles. After a series of disappointments and setbacks on the trip (it was the first year that non-Canadians were required to hire a licensed guide and could no longer be guided by a friend), Bob and I finally managed to get an Indian guide, Louis Capello, near Invermere, B.C., on the west side of the Rocky Mountains.

Bob Kuhn was a likable guy. Although he had a football player's frame and bulk, his hands were soft from using paintbrushes. We literally had to saw and hew our way six miles up a mountain trail that Louis Capello had not used for two seasons. The route was crisscrossed with fallen timber, and Bob's hand blisters were bleeding by nightfall. It wasn't as difficult for me, as I had been rowing regularly and cutting my winter wood almost annually since I was a youngster.

But the trail, blocked by fallen logs, had kept the country on the mountains behind it free from human access for two years. Game builds back to its normal abundance when given such protection. During our second day at the 6,500-foot base camp, we shot two prize snow white mountain goats.

The following day, Bob and I hunted and actually walked into the circle of a resting herd of fifteen elk. The royal (seven point) elk bull got up from within 15 feet of Bob and me. Bob was so close that he couldn't line up the animal through his scope, and I wouldn't shoot because I wanted him to get the bull. I figured I could get one any year. Before either one of us shot, the bull and his entire harem plunged off unscathed into the surrounding forest. We both laughed about that one. Bob had been expecting me to shoot.

On the way home (Louis was in camp, recuperating from a bad fall he had with his bronco), a new fall of snow was powdering the mountainside. About a mile from camp, I noted the unmistakable tracks of a single grizzly bear. It was crossing the hill and heading to the spot where we had field-dressed our mountain goats. Showing Bob the clearly defined dots out in front of the forefoot-pad marks, I explained that those marks easily identified the animal as a grizzly. It was his first such encounter.

Early the following morning, we awakened to find two inches of powdery snow covering our Alpine-flowered paradise of the previous day. The snow was dry, flaked, and as light as goose down.

During the previous, bonfire-lit evening, I had told Louis about the grizzly tracks that Bob and I had encountered, and explained that such a trophy would fill out the hunt, particularly for Bob, who really wanted a grizzly hide for his expanding den and studio in Connecticut. A grizzly would also give me illustrations for my coming book. Louis had first questioned my eagerness to take the animal, but was satisfied with the explanation.

Shortly after dawn, we climbed the steep slopes above the base camp and headed in the direction of the goat remains. As Louis was hobbling with a makeshift crutch that slowed the pace, my eagerness pushed me 100 or more feet ahead. The snowfall had covered the wild strawberry plants so delicately that you could still see the crimson fruit beneath the thin white covering. As I climbed upward, I occasionally stopped to pick morsels of the fragrant and sweet fruit. Wild strawberries in October! No more elegant a taste can be found on earth. The actual summer of the lowlands never really comes to the 6,000- to 7,000-foot level of the Rocky Mountains. The Alpine summer is, instead, a suspended winter, often for only days or weeks at a time. Vagrant frosts come during late August, and skiffs of snowfall in September while lupine, wild hyacinth, bluebells, columbine, larkspur, and strawberry plants are still blossoming.

While bending to pick strawberries less than 50 yards ahead of Bob and Louis, I occasionally heard stones rattling down the 45-degree incline of the nearby earthen slide. My preoccupation with the unusual delicacy was almost absolute. The warmth of the early sun in the crystal air had not yet burned off all of the night clouds from this high elevation. Temperature changes induced by the snow and moist atmosphere brought curtains of mist drifting between us and the upper segments of the slide. Only occasionally were the jagged peaks high above revealed as the sun caught them. The moving mists intermittently blotted out Bob and Louis, only yards downhill. Once, when I looked back, Louis had his chin resting on the brace of his hands on his wooden staff. He was staring up beyond me, as if aware of something.

As he could not hear even loud voices without his hearing aid, his attitude momentarily caught my attention. But I went on plucking strawberries, not heeding the increasingly regular rolling of small stones from above. Mountains continuously shed from their tops as a result of erosion, and you soon grow accustomed to the sounds of rubble trundling downward. Be you hunter or hiker, you should make a point of checking out *every* unusual sound that breaks the silence of Alpine fastness —particularly if you're in grizzly country.

I did look up after I saw Louis staring intently at the hillside above me. Mists were obscuring vision, even between us. The fogs were even more dense uphill. A wisp of breeze pushed the current wraith away.

There, 50 yards above me, was a grizzly digging into the earth of the slope. Pebbles were rolling away from the cupped semicircle it had made, and were coming down the incline. A quick glance at Louis, also now visible, showed him to be staring at the area above me.

It seemed as if Louis couldn't clearly see the grizzly through the mist, but that his native sense had somehow told him the animal was there.

My own reaction to a game animal is reflex. I identify it absolutely, raise my gun, and shoot. Field studies have shown me that the usual time between mutual sightings and the animal heading into cover is 15 to 30 seconds. In that time, I have killed most of the animals I have wanted to take.

When I raised my rifle my 2½-power scope was more than filled with the grizzly's bulk. It was that close. I centered the post and crosshair just behind the front shoulder, on a level with the joint, then dropped the sights lower to allow for a still rising bullet at 50 yards. The grizzly had sensed my movement, or heard me. It turned to face me.

Just as I squeezed the pressure of the military rifle trigger, the bear took a quick step upward. The cartridge exploded a split second later. Instead of crashing down on the slope, however, the big animal sprang up onto its hind legs and started batting the air with quick, vicious, undirected swipes. Roaring loudly, it spun in three quick circles seeking the unseen attacker, bit at its own leg, then dropped to all fours.

With an unexpected speed and effort, the bear lunged upward toward a thick patch of juniper. The animal's amazingly quick reactions had deadened my own reactions as I stood and stared in fascination. I had not previously missed any animal at even five times the distance. The bear immediately disappeared into the junipers.

Impulse, not common sense, impelled my own reaction. I

ran uphill at full speed, heading for the area of the slide just opposite the junipers. Louis's warning shouts came to deaf ears.

"Don't go close, Mike!" he yelled.

Panting hard, I stopped when I was about level with the clump of green growth—close enough to clearly see the blue fruit of juniper berries. Between me and the edge of the bushes was an eroded spring freshet gully, about 8 feet deep, some 20 feet from the greenery.

Even level with the waist-high growth, I could see nothing that resembled a grizzly bear. Finally, to my desperately searching eyes, a gray-fawn patch of hair showed near to the top of a higher shrub. Then, off to either side, appeared some light fawn-hued coloration. I still couldn't make out the grizzly's outline.

It was less than 30 feet away, yet I couldn't see it.

As the inner panic of frustration lessened, my mind put together the top patch as the hump, the sides as the shoulders, no head, no eyes, no steam of its breathing. From what I could see, I believed it was facing me. I centered the scope about 12 inches below what was possibly the hump, sighed out the pent-up breath that might disturb my aim, then squeezed the trigger—point blank.

The grizzly hurtled into the air, clearing the 6-foot-high bushes and the ditch between us—a full, 20-foot vault. I vaguely remember my arms going up when it seemed the animal's jump would bring it crashing down almost at my feet.

Instead, it thudded onto the ground about 10 feet from me and struggled to rise on all fours. Then, from behind me, came a loud crack as Bob Kuhn's rifle went off. His bullet hit the bear in the short neck, the passage furrowing the long hair between shoulder and head, as the animal lay kicking below me.

Bob and Louis quickly climbed up to my level. I was standing with my rifle still aimed over the convulsing form. Louis continued remonstrating: "You damn lucky he don't get you, Mike!"

Bob looked pensively at me. "Sorry, Mike," he said. "I thought he was gonna get up. Otherwise, I wouldn't have shot. You were just standing there."

I shook my head. "I don't know what got into me," I said. "Running up on a wounded grizzly! I know better."

We moved around the carcass. I kicked it for reaction, rifle still cocked on its head, but the bear was dead. Pulling it over on the slope, I was curious to see what had happened with my first shot. It proved to be three inches below where I had aimed, but in line. When the bear had stepped up, the bullet hit the elbow above the cord and then sliced off the end of the sternum. The result was a small, ragged hole, a wound that would have healed within weeks. My second bullet, fired from across the gully, had been deadly. It had gone into the abdomen between the thick neck and shoulder and had literally pulverized the heart and lungs. Bob's bullet had pierced the neck, shearing close enough to the spine to at least stun the bear.

I turned the animal over in order to reveal the belly, preparatory to skinning it. In the center of the lower chest was another bullet puncture. *That* hole was unexpected. I looked up at Bob.

"Did you shoot twice?" I asked.

He shook his head. "I shot only once," he said.

"But there are *four* bullet entries here!" I said, scratching my head.

Bob looked at me curiously. "You shot him *three* times."

"No. Only *twice*," I said. "Once from down there, once from up here."

Kuhn's stare was incredulous: "You shot him *twice* from up here. Once *in the air!*"

I grinned disbelievingly. "Who are you kidding?" I asked.

I looked over at Louis, who was contemplating me with a deep look. He said simply, "Yes. You do it."

Bob still didn't believe that I was serious. He pointed to the top of the embankment.

"Go look on the top of the bank. Your two shells should be there. That was the fastest shot I ever saw! And you don't even remember it!"

At the top of the bank, I found two brass cartridge cases lying about three feet apart. They were mine. The last shot? It must have been instinctive—my arms going up?

Bob was staring at me. "Now do you believe me?" he asked.

At this date, no recollection of that shot comes back. I still see the hurtling form of the grizzly, higher than my head, coming directly at me. And I well remember Louis Capello's admonition, "Mike, you lucky you *'live!*"

It may be either an overstatement or an understatement. A grizzly's power to charge, even after being hit with a fatal heart and lung shot, is a well-established fact. It was to be proved to me once more.

My outdoors writing was still just a paying hobby that made possible trips that were not otherwise available. Ches Delmonico, later to become my friend, had just opened a guiding outfit and lodge in the Dease Lake area, which foots the Cassiar Plateau in British Columbia. He wanted written publicity, and invited my friend, the late Jack "Pintail" Lillington, in for a hunting-fishing trip. Jack, unable to take the time and not really a big-game hunter anyway, suggested to Ches that he might get better exposure for his lodge and safaris if he invited me instead.

It was an unexpected windfall for big game at a time when my work could be set aside for ten days.

At that point, I was trying to establish myself in the outdoor film field—on a shoestring. It seemed to me that the market for outdoor footage in the newly blossoming media, television, would be excellent. My ardor for big game hunting was subsiding as hunting pressure increased on even the farthest frontiers. Some big game species were decreasing in numbers, and I just couldn't see hunting them anymore. My family's taste for venison could easily be satisfied by the still-innumerable coastal blacktails or the interior mule deer. A moose every other year or so could give us more beeflike meat, and moose were on the increase in most areas of the province anyway.

But kill a bear? Not really. Perhaps one of the thin-horn mountain sheep, the Stonei of the Cassiar, but mainly I wanted to photograph them in their remaining natural abundance on the big plateau. Ches Delmonico understood that desire and assured me I would fill up as much color film as I wanted to bring.

After two days of fabulous flyfishing for arctic grayling on the Dease River, Ches, his assistant guide Vincent Johnny, and I rode our train of horses to the plateau top. The arrival at that 6,000-foot elevation, despite Ches's earlier statements that I wouldn't believe the colors, was a revelation in beauty. Alpine flowers of all colors grew in unbelievable abundance there. The air was crystal clear, the sun's rays brilliant, the sundowns spectacular, and the ranges of peaks set in concentric rings on all horizons simply indescribable.

And game! While stopped for lunch, we took ptarmigan with thrown rocks for a camp supper stew. The following day I filmed forty-five Stone sheep, including two magnificent rams and a dozen lambs. On one nearby mountain cliffside, I photographed fifteen brilliantly white mountain goats caught in the sun's slanting rays.

Ches was vindicated by my wide-eyed enthusiasm.

"Mike," he said, "you haven't seen anything yet. Tomorrow we'll take you to the ram country. I've seen as many as fifteen near-trophy rams in one bunch. This is an area we haven't even hunted yet."

By the fourth day we had taken the pack train 20 miles through Alpine passes, to another paralleling range of vastly rugged high peaks. Between the two ranges lay a valley at least ten miles long and five miles wide. The floor of the valley appeared to be covered with a thick green carpet, while through its center flowed a pristine glacial stream.

Ches pointed to the range of peaks on the far side and said, "*That*, Mike, is *ram* country. I've seen at least one record-breaker, or near record-breaker, over there. You and Vince will go over there tomorrow, but I have to leave you. That other party is supposed to come in at the end of the week. They may arrive early. We'll glass this valley for caribou. They generally come through here later in the fall, but sometimes they're this early."

Ches and Vince moved to opposite edges of the rock bluff upon which we had stopped with the horses. While they were lying prone, using field glasses to inspect the distant parts of the valley, I unpacked my Bell & Howell 16-mm camera and checked the film level in the magazine. It didn't have enough to take a good segment before running out. I ran off the short end filming the view of the valley.

Ches's voice suddenly interrupted my picture taking.

"Hey, Vince! Take a look at this! It's the biggest grizzly I've ever seen!"

Vince swung his binoculars to the indicated area. "Pretty big, that one," he said.

While they were watching the bear, I replaced the reel of color film. Both of them agreed that it was a large grizzly. I looked at it through my own binoculars. It seemed quite large: a very round, fat-appearing animal with a light yellow coat. At a mile distant, even 10X glasses didn't give too much detail. I looked at Ches. "Can we get close to him?" I asked.

"He's right out in the open. . . ." Then, aware of my feelings about shooting bears, "But you could take him. He looks like a real trophy."

"Can we get close enough to him for film?" I asked.

Ches shrugged and looked at Vince. He was confident. "We try!" he said.

Delmonico instructed Vince to tether the horses on the bluff where they had begun to graze. We would, he decided, stalk the whole distance to the grizzly on foot, taking advantage of the occasional willow clump and the hummocks on the valley floor. As a precaution against their clinking during the approach, I removed my loose, extra cartridges from the side pocket of my jacket and wrapped them in my handkerchief. I placed them on top of my haversack and then slipped the heavy movie camera back into its case. Ches called me over to check the route down with him.

While we were glassing the area, Vince picked up my rifle and camera and brought them over. He was ready to go. We dropped over the edge of the bluff on its blind side and began working our way to the lower levels. There was little cover in the valley. Going from low brush to brush, using grassy hummocks, we expended an hour making our bent-over, crawling stalk.

When we finally reached it, the small rise that we had seen behind the bear proved to be about six feet high. Resting for a moment, we could hear nervous snorts from the animal, a belly-tingling noise when that close. We inched to the summit of the rock hummock. I pulled out my movie camera and checked the lens. Ches slowly raised his head above the top of the hummock.

I heard his gasp of surprise: "Damn," he whispered. "It's a sow with two cubs!"

We all were well aware that a she-bear can be very unpredictable when she's with her cubs. Although the sow couldn't see us, she obviously knew that something was near her. The snorts were becoming angry.

Ches looked seriously at me. "Don't take any chances with her," he warned me. *"She might come!"*

Nodding agreement, I switched to the intermediate distance lens and checked the aperture. Then, with a cold chill in the pit of my stomach, I raised up on my elbow, the camera held on the brace of my forearms. I whispered to Vince to come alongside of me, to take the camera just in case I had to pick up the rifle to shoot. I had a sickening feeling that the big sow would be triggered into action the moment she heard the movie camera.

Ches's warning jarred my edgy nerves. "She's looking right at you, Mike," he said.

When I pushed the button to roll the film, the camera immediately emitted what seemed to be a deafening clatter. The sow reared up on her hind legs, neck arched directly at the sound like a snake ready to strike. Suddenly, she dropped down on all fours and made a short, feinting rush in our direction. (This is a common grizzly tactic intended to unnerve the adversary into giving ground. It is often used as a bluff, but just as often is the start of a headlong charge. The continuity of reaction is never certain.) She again rose on her hind legs, head thrust forward, circling for a line of scent and sound. She eyed my outline and the whirring camera for a second before dropping on all fours into a full charge.

I could see, through the viewer of the camera, that she was clearly coming directly at me. Just as my nerve gave out, Ches gritted angrily, "You'd better shoot! *Right now!*"

Vince took the camera while I grabbed my rifle. When I

looked up, the sow was once again on her hind legs about 50 yards distant. The lines of bush between us were confusing her direction when she was down on all fours. Seeing me now standing, she remained upright an instant. I lined up on her chest right between the shoulders and squeezed the trigger.

Behind her, in the still waters of a glacial pond, the water spurted up in a pillar. At least 18 inches too high, and a foot to the right.

She swung around to the sound of the splash, then whirled quickly back to face the metallic sounds of my newly injected cartridge. My second bullet smacked into the pond in the center of the concentric rings made by the first one. As the plume settled, she dropped back on all fours and rushed forward through the undergrowth.

I now realized that she kept rising to her feet so she could pick up the direction of the sound of the camera. Vincent Johnny was standing beside me, still running the camera, recording every split second. Shocked by *two* misdirected shots, I subconsciously concluded that the rifle sights must be out that much. The grizzly burst through the next hedge of bushes and went up on her hind legs again. I drew down on her *left haunch*, an unbelievable correction, and fired. Her big form went down in a heap.

"Hit her again, Mike! Hit her again!" yelled Ches.

Having just seen the sow instantly crumple to the ground, I was sure that the bullet had broken her spine. I turned to Ches to argue.

His finger went out in a rigid point: "Look out, Mike! She's up again!"

The grizzly was on all fours again, coming as if she had not even been hit. Her speed, at 30 yards, was undiminished. My hasty injection of the shell threw it diagonally across the receiver. Vince was still holding the whirring camera on her while I fumbled the shell into the breech. I fired, but the slug only threw mud up beside her.

She was 25 yards from us now.

Flicking the bolt in another injection, my finger squeezed

down again. The hammer clicked, but nothing happened. The four-cartridge clip was empty!

Ches was at my elbow.

"For Crissake, Mike! Shoot!"

The reach for the handkerchief-wrapped cartridges brought the sudden realization that my pockets were empty! My shells were a mile away—still on the hill where Vince had left the knapsack as too obstructive a burden to the stalk. Over the years, I have always kept one shell in my left back pocket, a cartridge to be used in only an emergency, never to be touched for any other reason. It was there as my fingers gripped for it. Never has a period of time seemed to have such a lengthy duration for me.

The grizzly was now surging through the third line of brush. She knew exactly where she was going, and her head was down in full charge right at me. Drawing down on her left forepaw, I fired again. The bullet hit her in the right shoulder. She went down, somersaulting hind-over-snout.

"Again, Mike!" Ches ordered fiercely.

As he spoke, the grizzly got up once more. Now carrying 400 expanded grains of high-velocity lead, slavering blood and roaring, she was within 20 yards. I was out of shells, and she was coming fast. Vince, in the meantime, had rewound the camera and was still recording the charge—and grinning!

"I'm out of shells, Vince! You shoot!"

Instead, he held the camera on the animal, eager to get every split second of the charge. I backed up, as did Ches, who now realized that something was very wrong at my end. I shouted at him, to urge Vince to pick up his rifle and shoot! Ches did not carry a rifle.

He yelled to Vincent to shoot immediately!

Believe me, I was looking for a tree. At that elevation there wasn't one higher than 16 feet in the entire valley. Switching my rifle around to use it as a club, I realized that the stock would split off like a chip of wood. If I grasped it by the wooden butt and used it as a club that way, the steel barrel might stun the animal if I crashed it across the head or snout. I inverted the gun.

Vince suddenly grasped the situation, set the camera on the ground, and levered a shell into his haywire (actually) wrapped, vintage 1894 Winchester .30-30 rifle. Bringing the barrel up, he stepped toward where the grizzly would break through the last line of low brush. It came out just 15 feet from him, saw him, and centered its charge.

The muzzle of his rifle jumped as the bullet hit the bear's head and went whining off. His second bullet screamed off the grizzly's skull in another ricochet. The third shot came so quickly that it almost blended with the second. The animal went down in a slide that brought it to within 10 feet of him. Vince quickly jumped over the convulsing body, and rapidly placed a fourth bullet into the base of its skull. The animal's movements ceased.

I stood ashamed, contrite, and very grateful for a courageous young Indian. He grinned triumphantly.

Bending to the animal, he pointed to the perfect X where the first two bullets had cut knifelike furrows in the skull and then slid off the bone shield in ricochet. The third shot had entered one eye.

Examinations of my own rifle showed that its special, gold-tipped front sight was half sheared off and bent aside, and that the buckhorn rear sight was bent upward and over, with a residue of aluminum left on the barrel. It had obviously been dropped or thrown about during the rough plane trip into the north country. I hadn't noticed the damage because I'd been so preoccupied with getting my camera and lenses in perfect order. The gun had been dead on when last shot, and I hadn't even thought of checking it.

The grizzly had also been damaged before our encounter. Her right forepaw had been severed across the toe joints, leaving only the round base pad. That old injury alone was enough to make her an uncertain, possibly belligerent, animal. Ches suggested that the toes had been sheared off, or bitten loose when she was younger, perhaps caught beneath a large boulder that dropped down as she was digging for marmots beneath it. Who knows? I felt guilty about causing her death.

"Vince, you sure have a lot of guts. You saved our lives!" I exclaimed.

He grinned a broken-toothed rejoinder, and shook his head.

"Grizzly bear *good* bear, Mike. You shoot him, he come toward you. Not like black bear, go run in the bushes where you gotta go after him. Grizzly bear, he *always* come *toward* you."

I'll vouch for that statement . . . now.

20

Killer Grizzly Capital of the World

It had been somewhat of a shock to discover that there had been six major grizzly attacks right along the route I was presently driving to the inner west coast village of Bella Coola. That would make it the "Killer" Grizzly Capital of North America—the entire world!

Following months of poring over news clippings, scientific reports on bear attacks, book after book, and official documents, and after sorting them according to location, file number, type, name, place, and date, I found that specific individual items had become blurs to me. All 523 news items, which encompassed at that date 244 attacks and killings, had become a conglomerate. I had been working and waiting months for the hard winter of the Chilcotin District to pass.

Spring break-up was almost through by this May 7 in Williams Lake, 300 miles north of the U.S. border. Jack Mackill, retired B. C. Fish and Wildlife Conservation Officer, and my

274

old friend, had two days earlier picked up the telephone at his Pine Valley home just five miles north of Williams Lake.

"Sure, Mike," he had said. "Come up around 6:00 P.M. We can spend the evening talking about some of the attacks." That phone call began the revelation.

When I had dug out the filed items from the cases in the camper, in order to check them with Jack, I had discovered that six of the attacks by the big silvertip bears had occurred in the Anahim and Bella Coola districts. The area's major city, Williams Lake, is the focal point of the Chilcotin District. Even today, it is very much a frontier of the West, where cowboys and loggers constitute the bulk of the population. Beaded jackets are for Sunday best, moccasins are still the favored winter footwear, and characters straight out of Eric Collier's book *Three Against the Wilderness* and Rich Hobson's *Grass Beyond the Mountains,* both bestsellers, still live and work here. I'd written of the country and its people, thirty years previously, for both national magazines and newspapers, ever since the year that Eric Collier had invited me to his Meldrum Creek cabin for a fall duck and goose shoot. I had incited him to write his book, and I'd returned again and again. Then, somehow too occupied elsewhere for ten years, I'd gotten away from the area's rugged beauty.

Now driving the gravel road 200 miles to Anahim Lake, I thought it strange that I'd not recognized the area as site for many grizzly attacks. One of my own encounters with a grizzly bear had even occurred right in the heart of the Chilcotin's higher levels! More than forty-five years ago, a story had been related to me by Joe Ciancci, entomologist, friend of my youth, and fellow student in my Spanish language classes. Joe had told me of a trip he had taken up an old pack trail used by the native interior Stick Indians before the arrival of the white man. The Indians used to go to the coast on that trail, and trade their furs for fish oils there. Joe's trip, lasting two weeks, had been an arduous backpack through the mountains from tidewater. I remember my utter amazement when Ciancci told me that he and his partner encountered fourteen grizzly bears while studying the flora and fauna along the way.

"What kind of guns were you carrying, Joe?" I had asked.

He hesitated for a moment at the question. "We didn't have any gun at all, Mike. Too much other stuff to carry—with our packs and gear."

Knowing the reputation of the area, even at that time, I was surprised.

"Did any of those fourteen bears bother you?"

He thought for a moment before answering. "Well, we had a bad moment with a couple of them. At one point it looked as if they were going to charge. We just stood still . . . and prayed a little!"

Joe Ciancci, a highly intelligent and studious man, suddenly reached another and greater dimension in my respect. Even now, the primitive trail that he and his partner had taken cuts only slightly deeper into the cliffs, precipices, rock slides, and rubble of glaciers. Today, it is one of the two most precipitous mountain highways in the world. (The other such road, also in killer-grizzly country, is the Going-to-the-Sun Road in Glacier National Park, Montana.) The mountainsides rise more sheerly from the fjords of the coastline and in actual bulk are higher than the Rockies; the coastal giants rising 9,000 to 11,000 feet elevation right from sea level, while the Rocky Mountains begin rising from the adjacent land levels of 2,500 to 3,000 feet to attain their greater peak elevations. At the levels of their Alpine regions, both mountain ranges are unquestionably grizzly country.

At the recent evening at Pine Valley, with retired conservation officer Jack Mackill, we had recalled our mutual experiences, both as game wardens (as a territorial policeman I was ex-officio game warden) and as police constables. In particular, we talked about our own experiences with grizzly and black bears. I had told Mackill that my present trip was to contact former hockey great, Connie King, at Anahim Lake, where King has a small frontier cattle ranch.

Now, as that frontier town approached along the gravel highway, I realized that not more than a few miles from where King had been so badly mutilated was the spot where a grizzly bear had contemplated coming into my tent while I was sleeping. Mackill had laughed at my recollection of the incident as had many others, because it was actually funny in retrospect (mainly because nothing tragic actually happened).

To get that into perspective, I should mention that most of my life in the outdoors has been spent either in canvas tents or without any cover at all. My wife and I, with our two children, from diaperhood to their degrees, lived at least two or three weeks of each summer in tents that we pitched in the wilderness. I didn't ever give much thought to a bear coming into the cloth house that shut out everything wild from the area where we slumbered. No bear had *ever* made such an offer. Still, I always kept a loaded rifle or shotgun beside my sleeping bag—just in case!

We always took our dog with us on such outings. First there was our old springer, Trudy, a bitch with fine blood lines, and then her male offspring, Blaze, whom I derisively called "Huckleberry Bear Hound Dog." That epithet came from the fact that he was scared as hell of bears, even blacks, and that he actually loved to pick and eat huckleberries with us. Mountain huckleberries and blueberries are bear fodder that we picked every autumn. I could always tell when a bear was around on such occasions, because Blaze's nose would suddenly be tucked almost between the backs of my knees.

But I suppose Blaze is the real reason why that grizzly didn't actually get a chance to come right into my tent, that night at Pelican Lake in the Bella Coola–Anahim country.

Pelican Lake held some of the finest and largest rainbow-cutthroat trout (mystery trout) known anywhere. I wanted to flyfish for those five- to six-pounders, and had taken Blaze along for company. After driving down a barely passable trail to the lake's edge, I set up the umbrella tent on a flat, grassy spot. I then launched the boat and went fishing. Success was almost immediate; I caught five rainbow-cutthroats weighing from two to five pounds each. After bringing them in, I put them on a block of ice in the cooler. Blaze and I shared one of them, fried in butter, for lunch.

Afterwards, I wandered about 50 feet along the shoreline to examine a gray patch that I had spied from the boat. It turned out to be the remains of a moose killed the previous fall; most of the hide was still intact, with the hair on it. I pulled off a handful of hair and carried it back to the tacklebox in my Jeep. During a previous trip, I'd found that flies tied with moose hair often brought in the largest trout. At the time, the only thought I gave to that kill was that it was a fortunate find for my fly tying.

The following day, having left the tent in place, Blaze and I went on a trip with a friend at Anahim Lake. When we returned at dusk, the Jeep's headlights picked up something moving on the forest edge, near our tent site. It had been a tiring day, though, and the only thing that crossed my mind was that I'd spooked a deer or moose. Having fed Blaze, I patted his bed of sacks and told him to *stay.* This was a ritual: He was not allowed into house or tent. His sleeping quarters were in outside kennels year-round, although he was allowed into the basement on severe winter nights. While camping out, his bed consisted of two sacks or an old blanket that I always placed outside the tent, right alongside my camp cot and sleeping bag. Except for the canvas wall between us, he slept right alongside me.

This particular night he *woof-woofed* a bit, then tried his usual tactic of attempting to get inside before the zipper was pulled down on the door flaps. He whined a bit more than usual, but was told to shut up. His *woof*s grew less complaining as he settled in alongside my side of the tent. Before climbing into the down sleeping bag, I had checked the bolt on my rifle to ascertain if the action was on "safe." Then I set my flashlight beside the rifle and promptly went to sleep.

Deep in the night, my bed suddenly started to push up from under me! My body was raised up, and the whole tent seemed to shudder under the impact of an earthquake. I was actually being lifted off the ground, and my bed was shaking. In the depth of slumber, my reaction was immediate.

"Christ! An earthquake! Here! Right under me!"

My foot flew out of the unzipped bag as I attempted to get out of the cot. It struck something warm and furry! As my hair stood on end, I yanked my foot back into the covers so hard that my knee hit me under the chin. Now I was awake.

A whimper came from beneath me, and along with it the sounds of continued struggles and heaving. From outside the tent came the deep growl of an animal, and then the sounds of restless movement.

What the hell was all this? Not an earthquake, that's for sure.

But how did Blaze, who was outside, get beneath my camp cot when the tent zipper was still down? It had to be *him* under there. My consciousness was returning. There was something else moving near the tent flap. I reached for my rifle and flashlight, only to find Blaze's legs straddling both.

"Get away, you bastard!" I roared at both Blaze and the animal intruder.

The low growling continued outside as I fumbled with the switch on my flashlight, then the bolt and safety on the gun. The whole tent jerked suddenly as whatever was outside struck the guy ropes. As I flashed on the light, the rays hit the mesh of the mosquito screen and reflected the light, totally obscuring any vision to the outside. I slid up the zipper and shoved the gun ahead of me.

The face of a grizzly appeared less than 10 feet in front of me. The animal was shuffling backwards while I yelled blue-bloody murder. My flashlight fell out of my nervous hands while I attempted to place it alongside the barrel of the gun.

There was a gut-wrenching sound of feet outside—but in which direction, I couldn't tell. I fumbled for the light.

When it came on again, the grizzly had backed off to 15 feet. I held my gun over it, wondering.

"Go on, you old bastard! Get! Get!"

It moved backward and sideways reluctantly, wagging its head. *Just what did this bear have in mind?* I did not wish to kill it. And if I shot at the bear and wounded it, it could probably reach me before I could shoot again. What to do? There were four shells in the rifle magazine. One over its head might serve to turn the animal.

Pointing the flashlight right into the bear's red-rimmed eyes, I leveled the rifle muzzle over its head and squeezed on the trigger. The resultant explosion and flash of flame made the bear swivel about in a quick movement and break into flight. It disappeared into the darkness.

I didn't have the heart to put Blaze outside again. The cloth wasn't much resistance against the slashing claws and teeth of a grizzly, but the tent canvas seemed, at least to him, preferable to the open air. I felt the same way about it, although I did momentarily consider an uncomfortable night in the Jeep.

In the morning, the unmistakable claw marks of the grizzly showed where its pads had swiveled and torn aside the earth at the crack of the rifle. I had the feeling that the bear would not be back. It didn't return during the two nights before our departure.

This incident wasn't in any manner an attack; it was simply an incident in my own life that related to my pursuit of more knowledge about bears.

Now, years later at Anahim Lake, with sundown approaching, my stop there was only long enough to alert Connie King by "bush telegraph" (that is, passed along by word of mouth) that I wanted to see him. Then I was back on the road, driving through a growing timber parkland. A section of the road's dirt windings became abruptly, but only vaguely, familiar. A road to the left led into the forest as I drove past at 35 mph. As the dust billowed up in my rearview mirror, I recognized the road I'd used 15 years earlier.

"That! *That* side road is the road to Pelican Lake. I'll be damned! Just as I had been thinking about it."

The road appeared as it had years ago, when Blaze had been my companion. Poor dead and gone Blaze. He'd actually been a wonderfully courageous dog and unbelievably defensive of our family against any and all odds, except bears. He left all bears to me, particularly grizzlies.

The end of a lagoonlike lake appeared beside the main road as I continued on my way. My eyes, casually drawn from the country gravel road, picked up the silhouette of a familiar black figure. There, standing where the timber ended abruptly, was the form of a cow moose. Her head was up in my direction, her stern quarters semi-crouched in readiness to bolt. Her fat belly hung pendantlike between her slender long legs, and made me think that she had wintered well to have a bulge like that.

"Hell! She's full with calf!" I said to myself. "Wonder when she'll drop that one? It's May 8 right now. Well, within the

month, I'd bet. When I reached Bella Coola, I'll have to ask
Tony Karup at what period they calf in this colder climate."

Her silhouette stood out against the lake's reflection as I
looked in my rearview mirror. Then she was gone.

The road ahead became rougher as the mountains of the
coastal barrier intruded onto the plateau of the Chilcotin.
Frost heaves began to appear regularly, some partly refilled
with gravel by the highway crews. Then, farther along in the
mountains, I passed the crews trying to keep the road passable
for the thrice-a-week bus that somehow navigated it. After a
couple of bad mudholes, where the Jeep high-centered, the
pull of the positraction in the rear end shoved the scraping pan
and axles ahead onto harder surface. Then it was over and the
mountains were scraping snow off the black clouds coming in
from the coast. The weather change came in a light drizzle of
needlelike splinters, then in rounded globules of compacted,
wetter hail, and then in sleet. The snow patches beside the
road lay among the timber, looking like white sections in a
dark, pieced-together quilt. Past them, I hit the downgrade
leading to the coastal fjord.

At first, the rough highway wound sharply over fairly wide
gravel, a steep swath carved between the trees. Then it narrowed to a rockcut on one side of a steep mountain valley. The
pathway abruptly narrowed to a hand-cut, overhanging ledge
in a rockface of tortuously steep mountain cliffs, broken by
switchbacks, upon which the rear end of the vehicle seemed
to be pushing at an angle from above and behind. The belly-
jerking, awe-inspiring drop to the rocks thousands of feet
below, the 12-foot-wide cut into live rock, and the sounds of
rubble rolling under the power braking of the back wheels had
sweat beading on my forehead, my hands slick and slippery,
my gut tensed, and my teeth clenched.

God almighty! How much more of this?

More yawning canyons, rocks slipping under my wheels, the
road edge directly beneath showing miles of depth down into
the distant valley. Then a switchback, which was almost a
corkscrew into the side of sheer precipitous rock, and a graffito
scrawled on the rock wall into which the car would smash, if
not kept in the lowest of its gears.

There, spray-painted onto the rough cliffside were the words, "Relax, Tony!"

The rest of the message had been worn off by the weather.

I smiled as I thought of the man who got out to write that message. Who the hell was Tony? He sure wasn't any more scared than I was. Yeah! Relax, Tony!

The road continued tortuously down, but the humor of that message had relaxed me. New hope sprang with each second. Then I realized that I would have to climb this road again on the way out.

"Hell, I'd almost rather face a grizzly!"

The road abruptly took a more moderate descent into timbered slopes. A river appeared beside the road. It was the upper Adnarko, a steelhead stream *par excellence,* from which anglers also took 50- to 60-pound spring salmon on rod and reel. No time in the schedule for fishing on *this* trip. What a relief to be down that bloody hill!

At the village, four miles from the port of Bella Coola, Tony Karup's pleasant greeting welcomed me to his B.C. Fish and Wildlife office, an extension of his neat bungalow. He told me he was extremely busy at the moment, but that he could see me in the morning. If I went back a quarter of a mile along the road, there was an officially abandoned campsite—unofficially still open. The suggestion was excellent. The 300 miles of driving on endlessly winding gravel roads had been enough excitement for one day.

The next morning, Tony and I sat down in his office. Tony's cultured English accent wasn't exactly what you would expect to find in a game warden-conservation officer located 300 miles off the main highway, in such rugged and remote country.

"What in hell is an educated Englishman doing as conservation officer in Bella Coola?" I asked.

Tony Karup grinned and shrugged.

"It's a long story, Mike. I was a commercial fisherman: It started from there."

"*That*'s even harder to believe," I said.

We both laughed. You don't prepare for commercial fishing in these northern coastal waters by going to an English college or public school. That occupation is a tough one, certainly no tea party. In a way, though, the demands of being a conservation officer in an outlying district can be as tough as commercial fishing. I asked him about recent grizzly attacks.

Tony nodded to the filing cabinet. "I can show you the case histories of at least a couple of bear attacks," he said.

"Good! Do you have the details on Scholtes and Harestad?"

"Scholtes, yes. I have it right here," he said as he pointed to the file already on his desk. "Leo Van Tyne told me that you were interested in the details. I was on duty here when it happened."

"Can you give me a little background on Scholtes?"

"Yes. He's European, and has made a couple of trips out here. He's an excellent person, and a good hunter—interested mainly in trophies that might place in the record books. He's coming out again this year."

"He's not now grizzly shy?" I said, jokingly.

"No. Nor is he vindictive. He just hasn't accomplished what he set out to do—to take a good class trophy animal."

I flipped open my own file and handed Karup the following news clipping, my only source of details.

"This doesn't give much background as to what actually happened," I noted.

Tony looked at the item.

MAN SURVIVES BEAR MAULING
Special to *The Sun*

Bella Coola—An Austrian visitor was in satisfactory condition in hospital Monday after being mauled by a grizzly bear 58 kilometers southwest of here.

Fred Scholtes, a chemical engineer from Villach, was attacked by a female grizzly with a cub, as he was returning to a logging camp after a day of fishing on the Kwatna River.

Tony Karup, fish and wildlife branch conservation officer, said Scholtes managed to walk more than a kilometre to the camp where he was given first-aid treatment before being taken to hospital.

Karup said the unarmed Scholtes heard a squeal from the cub

before the mother knocked him down and mauled him. Scholtes got to his feet but was knocked down and mauled a second time.

Tony put down the clipping with a nod. "This is accurate— as far as it goes," he said.

"What about your end of it?" I asked.

"Well, this is the official file on the case."

He fished into the folder, bringing out the statement taken from Scholtes at the time of the incident.

Problem Wildlife Complaint Form 001344   Sept. 11, 1978

Grizzly Attack, Kwatna River

Subject: F. E. Scholtes
           A 95 VILLACH
           Treffner Strasse 54
           Austria   Ph: 94242-279693

Occupation: Chemical engineer
D. O. B.: December 3, 1929
Entered Canada at Vancouver August 21, 1978. Arrived Bella Coola Aug. 22, 1978.

Personal Statement:

On Saturday, August 26, 1978, Scholtes left Bella Coola with guide-outfitter K. Stranaghan for Kwatna River, where he would do some fishing while waiting for the mountain goat season to open on September 1.

Then, the actual statement of the survivor.

On August 29th at about 18:00 hours, I took Stranaghan's pickup truck and drove about six miles up the river on the logging road, where I made some observations of Bear and to photograph. When the light deteriorated for photography, I returned to the vehicle and drove back down the road. I stopped some two miles short of the camp at a good fishing spot. I fished there for a half-hour or so and then decided it was time to return. I was unable to start the truck this time, about 20:30

hours, so I decided to walk the remaining two miles to camp.

I was somewhat concerned for my safety, as I was well aware of the many bears in the general area of the river, so while walking I deliberately made as much noise as I could—by talking out loud, whistling, coughing, etc. At a point some one-hundred meters from the logging camp garbage dump, which I knew to be frequented by bears, I stopped for several minutes while I clapped my hands, knocked rocks together and generally made as much noise as I could in order to let any bears in the dump be aware of my presence, and to allow them to depart before I proceeded.

At about 21:20 hours, having assured myself that I had taken all the precautions I could, I started on my way again. I had just about passed the area of the garbage dump when I was surprised by hearing the squeal of a bear cub. I turned around to face in the direction of the sound when I saw a bear rapidly advancing in my direction. I raised my arms and advanced toward the attacker while shouting in a vain effort to deter it. The bear pressed home the attack on all four feet and knocked me on my back, biting my knee first. I struggled with the bear, trying to protect my face and fend off its jaws with my feet. The bear continued to bite my body and, while this was happening, I could distinctly hear the cub squealing in the background. The bear, hearing her cub, left me. I hoped that she would depart so that I started to get up from the ground, but who once again returned to the attack, biting me again and again on the body and shaking me. I was conscious that the bear, while mauling me, was still concerned for her cub, as she left me again but returned very shortly for the third time. This time she got her teeth into my chest area, and although I tried to protect this spot with my forearm, she tore that limb away, and I realized that any defense was futile and went limp. Shortly afterwards she left me and departed with her cub into the dense undergrowth, not to return.

Once I was sure she and her cub were finally gone, I rose to my feet and—not knowing how badly I was injured or how much blood I had lost—made my way slowly the remaining mile to camp. There, the first-aid attendant dressed my wounds, and I was carried to a stretcher and put on a small craft to take me to Bella Coola. We were met some eighteen miles from Bella Coola by Fisheries patrol vessel *Francis M*, on board which were Doctor Peter Barg of the Bella Coola hospital,

guide-outfitter K. Stranaghan and Conservation Officer A. G.
Karup. I was taken to the Bella Coola hospital at about 4:00
hours.

The report had the normal ring of a departmentalized document: precise, accurate, to the point. Mentally, the reader has
to dramatize, improvise, judge, and assess according to his own
interpretation. But the facts are there, impersonal, correct,
and detailed.

What about the character of the man, F. E. Scholtes?

It was too early to ask. I wanted to know about Tony Karup,
the man who attended the incident, his feelings, assessments,
opinions. He had been answering the phone and had referred
to other reports while I was reading. He was still talking to a
caller, reassuring the person of his early attention. I looked
around the office again.

On the clean, natural-wood walls were the mounted racks of
a white-tailed buck and a comparable black-tailed deer, a
mounted grouse, the fanned tail feathers of a grouse, and other
items primarily for identification purposes. Behind his desk
was a rack of shiny, well-oiled guns. One of them was unusually
beautiful. It was a "drilling," comprised of side-by-side 12-
gauge shotgun barrels, over which was fitted the barrel of a
rifle. The stock and forepiece were beautifully figured black
walnut of the finest quality, the chasing and engraving sharp
and jewel-like. Not only a prestige piece, but the kind of gun
any fine-arms fancier often waits his whole life for and doesn't
get.

I pointed to it. "Your grizzly gun, Tony?" I asked.

He smiled a trifle self-consciously and took it from the rack.

"As a matter of fact, it is—somewhat. I have a very deep
respect for the double-barrel big-game guns—the main ones
used on large animals in South Africa. They have enormous
stopping power, as you know."

He handed me the gun, a beautiful piece. After wiping my
palms on my pants, I reached out.

"Looks like a Sauer," I commented.

"No, it's a Krieghoff. I had it made to order."

As I handed it back to him, he broke the breach open to

reveal the barrel's mechanism. One 12-gauge barrel was open. The other was fitted with a 220 tube insert, the upper barrel being a 7×65 mm. rifle. On top of the rifle barrel was mounted a top-quality Bausch & Lomb scope.

Just handling this excellent example of gunsmithing gave me a deep appreciation for the fine craftsmanship that went into it.

"It cost you a bundle. About as much as a new automobile, I bet!"

He smiled. "Yes, about that. It's very effective."

"Do you carry it for bear?"

"Yes, it's a good measure of protection, but I don't shoot *any* animal unless I have to."

"How many grizzly bears do you encounter in a year? And any problems with them?"

He looked thoughtfully up at the ceiling. "Oh, I'd say ten to twelve grizzly encounters a year. Perhaps one of those would be aggressive. They usually avoid you unless you create the problem. I remember one particular big bear. Two of us were going to cross the river on a fallen log. The man behind me said, 'Tony, look down below you!' I did, and about six feet away was a big grizzly bear looking up at me. I was so shocked I just stared back at it. It turned its head away and grabbed a salmon out of the water. They all have different natures."

My next question was a bit loaded: "You're protective of grizzlies, then?"

He answered without subterfuge: "Yes, I am. *We* enter *their* domain. They have a right there, and we interfere with it. They require protection."

"Would you kill one that was bothering people?"

"Only if there was no other out. Protection of human life is also important. One has to be sensible."

His answers were frank, unbiased, logical. I said so.

"Tony, I have done some dumb things with bears earlier in my life. Actually fed by hand, a black bear sow with three cubs, in Yellowstone Park many years ago. I even stepped between her and her cubs and fed them individually. Now, knowing what I do, I realize that it was a preposterous act, even for a man who doesn't know their potential. But for a man having my experience at that time, with both wild and so called 'tame' bears, it was outright poor, even foolhardy, judgment. I hope the book I'm writing will get this point across to the public. If it does only that, it will be a success."

He was looking at me with an evaluating glance.

"I'm glad to hear you say that, Mike. It's difficult to get the public to understand."

He stopped for a moment, looked out the window at some feeding hummingbirds, then turned back to me.

"I remember one complaint I had from a woman who was camped upriver, in regard to grizzly bears," he said. "When I got up there, these people were camped right next to a gravel bar. As I walked down the beach to their camp, a grizzly bear sauntered right past me—about twenty feet away—and went down to the river. Just going about its business. I went over to the camp, and introduced myself as the conservation officer in answer to her complaint, and asked what the trouble was."

He paused with an amused smile at the recollection.

"The woman said, 'Officer, I want you to do something about that bear. It's a nuisance. It keeps bothering us.' I asked her for an example. She said, 'It keeps coming about the camp. It simply can't be hungry. The children fed it all of their lunch sandwiches just yesterday!' "

My laughter was tinged with my incomprehension of such a mentality.

"Actually? Tony, did she really say *that?*"

He nodded with a still-mystified half grin.

"As you sit there, she did. Just that! There have been many others, almost as bad. One of them was from a man who was catching fish for drying. He was gutting them in the river, and then hanging them around his camper. He was right on the river where grizzlies commonly came down to fish. One of the bears got on top of his camper one night and apparently tried to get in. Did a little damage, too. Obviously it smelled the food in the camper. The man wanted me to shoot it. I argued that he was inciting the animals to such activity by camping right in their usual domain. He could move his camp away from the river and avoid such conflict. He got quite huffy and insisted that I kill the grizzlies."

Tony Karup looked at me a little helplessly. I was shaking my head as the story unfolded.

"What did you do about it?" I asked.

"Well, there was certainly no reason to kill any grizzly. All the man had to do was move to a spot that wasn't in the way of the grizzlies' entrance to the river. I asked him if he knew the route back toward Anahim Lake. He stated that he did and asked, 'What the hell kind of question is that?' I said, 'I suggest you avail yourself of your privilege of using it!' "

I was laughing. There were many times, in my own experience as a cop, or peace officer, that such a straightforward approach had been the only reasonable way to deal with such a recalcitrant.

"Did you hear any more from him?" I asked.

"No. And he must have taken my advice, because he wasn't around when I went to check up again."

Karup told me of other incidents that a conservation officer normally has to deal with. I asked him about the Scholtes case, in particular. Were there any contributing circumstances?

"Not too many, Mike. Scholtes describes it pretty graphically in that report. There wasn't any investigation really necessary. I went out and checked the area and circumstances. There was only one contributing factor. We felt that the logging company had placed its garbage dump improperly, too close to the road and right by the river. We took departmental action that made the company move the location to a better area."

"Did you shoot the animal concerned?"

"No. Scholtes described it as a quite small sow grizzly with a cub. The cub was bawling continuously. He was trying to get his pack off his back when the bear hit him. She bit him in the knee first. When she got him down, she went for his face and chest. I have some photos, taken in the hospital, if you'd care to see them."

"Yes, I certainly would."

"What about Scholtes? Was he conscious?"

"Oh, yes. We had the call here in Bella Coola, that he had

been badly mauled and injured. I went out on the forestry boat —it was foggy, and flying was impossible. We traveled down the inlet about 25 miles, met the boat carrying him, and brought him aboard. The doctor got to him about 2:30 A.M. He had been given first aid in camp, and we brought him into the hospital here. Here are the photos."

Karup sorted through a pack of color prints until he found the ones he wanted. He handed them to me.

A healthy, tanned, smooth-muscled man with black hair and a handsome, intelligent-looking aquiline face was sitting upright on the edge of a hospital cot. Both of his arms were swathed in bandages, his open pajama top revealed most of his chest. The teeth and claw marks seemed to be penciled onto his tanned skin, yet the indentations and swellings already showed evidence of healing. The wounds were the unmistakable ripping, biting, tearing results of a grizzly attack—just as recognizable as the tri-corner biting made by a man-eating shark.

Strangely enough, Fred Scholtes was smiling, upright, obviously in good health. I said so to Karup.

"Yes, he was in excellent shape. The doctor said that it contributed to his quick recovery. He trains for months before he comes out to hunt. You need to be in good shape for the climbing and packing that is required.

"Has he had enough grizzly hunting now?" I queried.

Tony shook his head. "No, he's booked again to come out this year. He believes that the incident is part of the game, a chance he must take in going after a record animal. He won't shoot anything but an outstanding trophy. He doesn't have any regrets, and he's not vindictive toward grizzlies."

I was nodding my head. There are few men such as Scholtes among hunters. The Europeans have a traditional "code" that gives actual ceremonial respect for a downed animal. A friend of mine, Rudi Bauer, always used to place a fresh sprig of fir in a deer's mouth following the kill. He used to say it was in respect for the majesty of the animal, "the last meal" for it. Rudi died last year in a plane crash while flying among the mountains near where another man was mauled and nearly killed by a dwarfed grizzly bear. Bauer would have liked Fred

Scholtes. I can't help respecting such men, even though I don't condone trophy hunting as it is often practiced. My own pursuit of any animal is a simple primitive urge to take it and put it to culinary or other uses. Any trophies I have accidentally or incidentally taken have been given away, only the flesh and hide being personally utilized.

Fred Scholtes will be back in known killer grizzly country, to kill or be killed by a grizzly on his own terms.

21

Assorted Thoughts on Bears and Man

Bear-man problems traditionally result from man's intrusions. The bear is in its place, and has been in its place ever since bears evolved. On the other hand, man has expanded his territories, usurping the territory of anything that has stood in the way. One solution to the conflict would be to keep man out of bear territory. Unfortunately, such a simple remedy is not practical.

Man will continue to consider it his *right* to enter bear habitat, rather than looking upon his intrusion as a privilege that should be treated with wisdom and caution. The laws of nature are harsh, with beast pitted against climate and ecology. The beast, be it man or wildlife, fights in self-defense and to protect other values. Thus, men die fighting off bears, and bears die fighting off man. How best to ensure survival of both bear and man?

Most bear-man confrontations occur in public parks. The

292

majority of the others occur in wild or unsettled territory, though a small number take place in sparsely settled areas and even in heavily inhabited areas.

In Parks

A park is a partly wild sector of land that has no distinguishable boundaries to a wild animal. It may have poorly defined boundaries, even to humans. Parks are usually set aside by farsighted people with the hope of preserving the land in its original condition.

A park's natural features or its recreational opportunities become the prime attraction for people from whose depredations the park was originally protected. Parks of all kinds annually attract people by the millions. As I've noted in earlier chapters, the excessive people-to-bear ratio in parks causes a large share of the confrontations. Easy access by road, trail, or airlift brings visitors whose wants and needs are catered to. This, in turn, results in more tourist accommodations and more park personnel.

Experience managing big popular parks can play a role in a park administrator's climb up the executive ladder. So some administrators feel compelled to increase visitor levels, which in turn can help maintain and increase budgets and staffing. Parks personnel know this, evidenced in their almost universal reluctance to divulge unfavorable data. For example, the visitor statistics are readily available, even promoted in park advertising, but any detail that could discourage visitors becomes classified as "not available" (for any reason), "as yet uncalculated," or "restricted to personnel." This is particularly true when any action or suit may result from the exposure of information that—after all—*should be available to the public.* Especially guarded are the details of a bear-man confrontation not yet passed beyond the statute-allowed time for lawsuit.

Researchers can sometimes obtain "within-house" opinions from parks personnel, but usually only if the purveyor thinks that his identity or even his opinions won't be made known, or won't "get his tail in the gate." Such leaks of information can be revealing and sometimes arise from resentment. Only rarely are they brash and untrue. They serve like pressure releases for parks personnel who have kept quiet in spite of their desire to let the facts be known.

Ironically, the truth is that the parks don't really have much to hide. Parks management is earnestly seeking solutions to bear-man problems. Unfortunately, sometimes earnest efforts are shortsighted.

Environmentalist Meddlers

It is doubtful that the public itself is doing its best. The public has been blinded by what might be termed the Bambi syndrome on one hand and by man's supposed inherent rights on the other.

Many people have been brainwashed by so-called environmentalists when it comes to wildlife. Largely, this has been the result of a belated sense of guilt over man's devastating role in the environment. This devastating role sometimes resulted from questionable concepts—some biblical. Phrases such as "Go forth and multiply," "It's my right," and "Have dominion over the beasts of the field" have been used to justify rampant "progress."

Some environmentalists want to turn things around. And some self-serving, sometimes deluded, and often calculating individuals and corporations have ridden the tide of popular ecological causes, such as antihunting, gaining fame and clout while making a few bucks for themselves in the process.

Bears as Kindly Critters

For decades, Smokey the Bear was exploited as Nature's beneficent spokesman for caution against accidental cause of forest fires. His challenge is a good one, but using a bear as a symbol here is as baseless as associating an owl with profound wisdom.

Bears are actually inappropriate symbols of beneficence. They are willful, playful, purposeful, intelligent, occasionally aggressive, and above all acquisitive and territorial. They will kill and eat each other, just as humans have done, and they will kill and eat humans. But this does not deter opportunistic or misinformed people from representing bears as kindly critters.

Grizzly Adams established the notion that bears can make good pets—a very questionable and perhaps profit-motivated idea. But the lovable-bear notion is still embraced by modern writers and other media people. And the concept is supported by all manner of talking animals in advertising. The Gentle Ben characterization on television may lead children to believe that a wild bear will not attack them, let alone eat them.

Immersion, from a tender age, in any doctrine tends to instill life-long beliefs. Thus, the eloquent person who grew up on misinformation regarding bears finds himself criticizing parks personnel for killing a bear. Well-meaning perhaps, this person is certainly naive.

Again, I suggest the surest way that people can avoid bear problems: *Stay away from bears and their habitat!* But perhaps *that* is unrealistic.

The Value of a Gun

Man has traditionally entered bear habitat prepared to deal with bears or suffer the consequences. This is usually the outlook with which the hunter, the geologist, and the trapper enter the wild. But this is usually not the outlook with which other people enter.

A gun is the preferred insurance for those who know bears. But most parks and preserves prohibit the carrying, use, or even possession of guns. This leaves park visitors and staff quite vulnerable to attack.

A gun actually does something for the psyche of the man who carries it. It allows him to feel more confident and convey confidence in "body language" to a bear. Thus a man standing firm, believing in the infallibility of his gun, has a greater edge for bluffing a bear off. Anyone who has observed group interactions of animals has seen the threat displays with stiffened stances of the animals prior to contact. Such displays, or language, including the fixed gaze at the eyes of the other animal and the ready attitude itself, are part of the bluff.

Here are added factors to think about: (1) bluffing works for man only sometimes, (2) an armed person is more readily recognizable to the animal as either a threat or as a prepared opponent, and (3) exhibited confidence—even if it's an act—will sometimes turn an animal away. However, the statistics from my study of bear-man confrontations show that, even with a gun on the ready, men have been attacked and killed.

Men who have either studied or hunted bears often claim that most bears run as soon as they recognize a human. These men have had many experiences of that kind, so their opinions are worth noting. On the other hand, many hunters say, "But, I never see a bear when I have a gun." This may suggest that bears know or sense when a man has a gun, whether it is hidden or not.

I've spent a long lifetime, hunting animals every year. While in the bush, on the plains, in the mountains, and in the marshes, the first thing that has alerted me to the presence of another man has been the reflection of light off a gun barrel. I usually see this flash long before I see the man. Natural objects that reflect light are usually quite still. Bears too may associate intermittent flashes of light solely with man.

I don't think any researchers have proven that a wild animal has known that a man was carrying a gun. Few other instruments transported in the wilds are carried in so many different positions as the gun. Even though a gun is quite probably the first visible warning to an animal, I believe it's the man's confident bearing, rather than his gun, that makes the animal flee.

Men, despite their claims of being silent in the bush, are actually noisy, even when stalking. Modern man has neither the constant need for stealth, nor the physical ability to stalk his quarry silently. Noisy movements of any kind indicate to another animal that the approaching animal could be one of the following: (1) a predator, (2) a dominant animal, or (3) a belligerent animal. Only the dominant animals in any species disregard the pecking order, and many of these animals establish their dominance by a noisy approach, purposefully even biting on trees, swatting at bushes, or rattling antlers against trees. It is logical that a noisy approach can convey a confident, dominant attitude. However, a display of dominance may also trigger an attack.

Author's Bear Bluff

One of my bear confrontations illustrates some of the points above. While walking in front of Clive Cope, a fishing companion, on a narrow trail along the Seymour River in British Columbia, I noticed a large black bear coming down the path in our direction. We were walking toward the bear, which was just 60 to 70 feet ahead. The bear kept up its approach, though with hesitation, its eyes directly on me. I stopped dead. Over my shoulder Clive, a former boxer with well-known guts in the ring, said, "What the hell, Mike! *Go ahead!* It will probably back off." Clive was a good fisherman, but not a hunter.

The big black slowed down. Its contours told me this was a male. The hair on his shoulders stood up like a mane, a sure sign that he was aroused. He eyed me with less than kindly intent. I said, quietly to Clive, "That one won't back off. It's angry. Just wait a minute, then back up, very slowly—*facing it.*"

Clive knew when to accept advice. The big black stopped when he was within 30 feet of us, wagged his head, shuffled his feet, and growled. But he stopped. "Now," I whispered to Clive, "in step, back up slowly."

We had not taken two full steps when the bear shuffled again, came a couple of steps closer (at which point we stopped), then in an uncertain posture once more wagged its head and shuffled sharply. He looked toward the steep bluff alongside the path, and back at us, then whuffed and shuffled again. Then, with a show of disdain—a show of face—he turned his head and took one reluctant step toward the screen of bush between the path and the rock bluff. Having taken that one step he hesitated and looked back malevolently. Then, in one graceful leap, he mounted the rock outcrop above the path. The big bear once more turned his head and again stared threateningly back at us, before disappearing silently into the surrounding growth.

Clive said, "Jeez, he was a belligerent bastard! Shall we go ahead now?"

My reply was emphatic: "No goddamn way! That was a dominant male. He bluffed us back—just enough. But we bluffed him just enough to turn him. He may suddenly decide that he didn't like that loss of face."

"How the hell would you know all that, Mike?" Clive asked, grinning.

"Did you see the hair on his back?" I asked.

"Yeah. It was standing straight up. I thought only dogs and cats acted like that."

"That was enough for me. We'll go back."

We backtracked. Within ten days of that confrontation, a report came in to our news office that a Game Department warden had killed a large male black bear that had chased two steelhead anglers right into the river where Clive and I had met that big fellow. It is a matter of record.

The only means of defense Clive and I had were fishing rods—plus experience. Facing the bear wasn't a matter of guts on my part. It was a matter of necessity. Clive had the guts. His earlier ring superiority was based less on dexterity than on plain old guts. When I was in the ring, I learned to back up, because I had more dexterity and less guts.

Connie King (see Chapter 15) also had Clive's raw courage. He fought a grizzly hand to hand without weapons and survived. In that same territory where Connie fought this grizzly, I put a shot over a grizzly's head to discourage it. I am sure my stock of courage would have run out under the circumstances Connie faced. And after an initial attack like Connie or Ted Watchuk suffered, I would either have retreated or lain down to play dead. Thank God I have never had to make such a decision.

A Final Note

You, the reader, may someday have to face a bear if you go into bear country. I hope that the contents of this book have better prepared you.

Remember, don't accept the one-sided viewpoint of self-proclaimed "experts," that you can walk into the realm of bears, face them down, and come off scot-free. Much depends upon your own personality, your wits, and your knowledge of wild animals to assure that your reactions or defenses will have the desired effects. What works for some people, on many bears, can fail for others. There is *no* sure way of gauging how an individual bear will react in a given situation.

Quite simply, *there is no sure behavioral defense against bears.*

Appendix

Bear-attack Statistics

During twenty years of gathering items about attacks and killings by bears, I found a plethora of lore, legends, and tall tales. In many cases, fiction was related as fact. To prevent this fiction from being entered as evidence, I compiled the statistics that follow, not from word of mouth or hearsay, but from items I could certify by news clipping, official documents, or actual contact with a person involved in the incident. I personally researched and investigated all stories I've recounted at length in this book, either by visiting the scene of the confrontation, by interviewing the persons involved in the incident, or by whatever other method necessary to get the real story.

Beyond the actual statistics that follow, there are no doubt hundreds of incidents involving attacks that are not tabulated. A rough personal estimate of the additional items, which could be considered to be attacks, would put that total figure at a good 50 percent more attacks than are tabulated. It is quite possible that the actual total is nearly 500 incidents since the earliest used date of 1929. Killings and attacks that are related in the dozens of historically based books have not been included, however. These incidents would at least double the probable incidents to be considered as attacks by bears. With only one or two exceptions, the incident used must have had the element of severe injury to a person or persons. Those attacks to myself or my family are not included in the list either. They are related only to indicate my experience with bears has been more extensive than that of the ordinary person.

In all tabulations of the past, there are chances for miscalculation, or an occasional misstatement or misconception. Then too, some facts weren't available. The date of each incident, for example, was taken from the item announcing or verifying it (date published in a periodical, official documents, etc.). It may not be the actual date of the incident, but it *is* the date of its *official* exposure. Anyone wishing to correct or add to the incidents described herein is encouraged to write me at 4875 The Dale, West Vancouver, B.C., Canada V7W 1K2.

Appendix: Bear-attack Statistics

Name/Origin	Date	Place	Situation	Action	Bear Sex
Kills by Black Bears in Wild					
BAINES, Alan Russell, B.C.	7/21/80	Ft. St. James	Fishing	?	M?
DUCKITT, Suzanne, B.C.	8/9/67	Vernon, B.C.	Playing	Ran	M
GAIER, Rudolph H., AK.	?	Anchorage, AK.	In cabin	Fought	?
MARSHALL, Carrol N., Alta.	8/21/80	Zama, Alta.	Oil worker	Pulled from tree, fought	M
MATHEWS (2 brothers), B.C.	6/23/61	Kaslo, B.C.	Farming	Shot bear	?
MORRIS, Lee Randal, Alta.	8/17/80	Zama, Alta.	Oil worker	Found dead	M
OTTERTAIL, Jack, Ont.	10/2/68	Atikikan, Ont.	?	?	?
RICHARDSON, John, CO.	7/26/71	Grand Lake, CO.	Hiking	?	?
SMITH, L., B.C.	9/19/64	Schefferville, Que.	Prospecting	Fought	?
VALDEZ, Victoria Lee, WA.	7/9/74	Glendale, WA.	Playing	?	M
WIGG, Nelson, B.C.	10/22/66	Nelson, B.C.	Farming	Ran	?
Attacks by Black Bears in Wild					
ARRIT, Bryan, CA.	10/20/53	Yuba City, CA.	Shot and Killed bear	?	?
CARSWELL, Gil, Ont.	?	Haileybury, Ont.	Trapping	Fought	?
CLEMENT, Sean, Ont.	8/31/77	Wawa, Ont.	In house	Ran, mother shot it	S & cub
CORBETT, Scott, Ont.	7/20/66	Sandstone Lake, Ont.	Near home	Fought	?
CRAIG, Curtis, Alta.	9/6/77	Smoke Lake, Alta.	Camping	Climbed tree	?
DAY, Maurice, MI.	?	?	?	?	?
DUSEL-BACON, Cynthia, CA.	8/13/77	Fairbanks, AK.	Prospecting	Lay still	M

Name	Date	Location	Activity	Reaction	Sex
ELLIS, Martin (with Marshall, C.N.), Alta.	8/17/80	Zama, Alta.	Working oil	Climbed tree	M
FOURNIER, Alex, Alta.	9/21/67	High Level, Alta.	Sleeping	Dormant	?
HILBOURN, Lloyd, MN.	?	Barbeau, MI.	?	?	?
JONES, Frank E.	?	Westbank, B.C.	A previously wounded bear	Killed bear	?
LEGAULT, Art, MI.	6/?/50	Engadine, MI.	Cutting wood	Fought	?
LYPKA, Fred, Alta.	5/31/66	Yellowknife, Y.T.	Prospecting	Fought	?
McANDREWS, John.	7/8/78	Chilliwack, B.C.	Swimming	Lay still	S & cub
McISAAC, Douglas, B.C.	7/4/69	Kitimat, B.C.	Playing	Ran	?
McLEAN, Sylvester, B.C.	?	B.C.	?	?	?
MASSOP, Joe, B.C.	9/21/64	Alberni, B.C.	On road	Fought	?
MAZZA, Giorgio, Italy	5/30/78	Ft. Nelson, B.C.	Cycling	Fought	?
MOORE, Linda, CA.	7/26/71	Grand Lake, CO.	Hiking	?	?
NORFOLK, Lance, Ont.	9/2/75	Sault St. Marie, Ont.	Walking	Dog fought	S & cub
QUIRING, Paul, CA.	8/22/67	Prince George, B.C.	Sleeping	Fought	?
RADACH, Mike Age 21, WA	9/26/77	Wenatchee, WA.	Stream survey	Ran, swam	?
SAPRIKEN, Mrs. Nic, B.C.	6/11/68	Nelson, B.C.	In house	Author drove bear away	?
SEFTEL, Steve, UT.	7/15/77	Flathead River	In sleeping bag	Fought	?
TASKINEN, Chad, B.C.	10/7/77	Kitimat, B.C.	Near home	Neighbor shot	F
THEXTON, David, B.C.	?	Pringston, B.C.	In kitchen	Fought	?
WOODSWORTH, Alg., Ont.	9/17/57	Dryden, Ont.	Walking	Ran	?

Kills by Grizzlies in Wild

Name	Date	Location	Activity	Reaction	Sex
CARDINAL, Harvey, B.C.	1/17/70	Fort St. John, B.C.	Hunting	Was ambushed	M
REEVES, Ray, AK.	6/8/74	Izembeck, AK.	Photographing	?	?
WANTJOFF, George, B.C.	6/23/51	Castelgar, B.C.	Ranching	?	?
WILKINSEN, Bryan E., Y.T.	F	Whitehorse, Y.T.	Trapping	Fought	?

Appendix: Bear-attack Statistics (cont.)

Name/Origin	Date	Place	Situation	Action	Bear Sex
		Attacks by Grizzlies in Wild			
BONE, Joe, B.C.	?	B.C.	?	?	?
CALLINSON, Leash, B.C.	?	Toad River, Ft. Nelson, B.C.	Hunting	Fought	?
CARLSON, James, NB.	10/25/75	Valdez, AK.	On pipeline	Fought	?
CHURCHILL, Sheila, Age 21 B.C.	10/30/79	Whitehorse, Yt.	Near bear kill	Man fought with rocks, flare	?
COLE, Ronald, AK.	5/31/75	Skwetna, AK.	Surveying	?	?
CRAWFORD, Don, Alta.	9/18/65	Hinton, Alta.	Hunting	Shot it	?
CURTIS, Edward, MT.	?	Libby, MT.	In tent	?	?
DIXON, Edward, B.C.	10/29/63	100 Mi. House, B.C.	Hunting	Fought, shot it	?
ECKENSTAM, Marilyn, B.C.	9/5/80	Mica Creek, B.C.	Hunting	Rifle shots	Six ?
FISHER, Ray, B.C.	10/18/56	Gray Creek, B.C.	Camping	Hid in truck	?
HANNA, Andrew, AK.	?	Whitehorse, Y.T.	?	?	?
HARESTAD, Carl, B.C.	9/24/79	Bella Coola, B.C.	Farming	Hid, ran	?
HART, Dominique, Alta.	9/18/65	Hinton, Alta.	Hunting	Fought, shot it	S & cub
HARVEY, Halbert, MT.	12/10/64	Golden, B.C.	Hunting	Lay still	?
HELEGESON, Monty, Alta.	8/15/66	Waterton Lakes, Alta.	In tent	Parent fought	?
HOGAN, Dr. Gerald, PA.	?	Spruce Lake, B.C.	Hunting	Shot it	S & cub
HUBL, Hank, B.C.	?	Iron Ridge, B.C.	Hunting	Lay, fought, shot it	?
JACK, Mattie, B.C.	5/?/63	Anahim Lake, B.C.	Ranching	Lay still	?
JOACHIM, Kelly, Alta.	9/14/68	Grand Cache, Alta.	Hunting	Fought, shot it	?
JOHNSON, Axel, B.C.	?/?/63	Bella Coola, B.C.	?	Fought, lay still	?
JORGENSON, Harold, ?	?	Horsefly Lake, B.C.	Hunting	Shot, fought	?

Name	Date	Location	Activity	Action	Sex
KING, Connie, B.C.	5/6/68	Anahim Lake, B.C.	Ranching	Fought	S & cub
KLIENSHROT, Paul, B.C.	7/2/60	Bralorne, B.C.	Hiking	Lay still	S & cub
LARSON, Axel, B.C.	6/23/51	Canal Flats, B.C.	Hunting	?	?
LE NOBLE, Neil, B.C.	6/2/75	Richmond, B.C.	Surveying	Climbed tree	S & cub
McKELVIE, Robert, B.C.	9/9/63	Kamloops, B.C.	Hunting	Fought, lay	M
MACK, Clayton, B.C.	9/16/46	Bella Coola, B.C.	Hunting	Fought	M
MARKUSICH, Mike, B.C.	10/21/68	Fort St. John, B.C.	Hunting	Lay still	?
MILLER, Dick, WA	10/25/78	Kitten River, B.C.	Fishing	Fought	?
POWELL, Tom, B.C.	5/23/51	Northern, B.C.	Hunting	Partner shot it	?
SCHERLING, Donald, B.C.	9/13/61	North Cranbrook, B.C.	Hunting	Fought, shot, lay	?
SCHMIDBAUER, John, B.C.	5/25/60	Bralorne, B.C.	Hunting	Fought	?
SHOLTES, Fred, Austria.	9/5/78	Bella Coola, B.C.	Walking	Fought, lay	S & cub
TAUSCHER, Hubert, WA.	7/31/68	Noxon, MT.	Fishing	Fought	S & cub
TURNER, Alvin, B.C.	11/5/68	Invermere, B.C.	Hunting	Fought	?
WATCHUK, Ted, Alta.	5/2/75	Bennett Dam, B.C.	Surveying	Fought	S & cub
WISEMAN, Ed, MT.	9/28/79	San Juan, Mt.	Hunt-bow	Fought and killed	F
WOOD, Gordon, Ont.	8/30/69	Whitehorse, Y.T.	Geo. survey	Ran, lay	F
ZIMMER, Bill, WA.	10/25/78	Kiteen River, B.C.	Fishing	Fought	?

Kills by Polar Bears in Wild

Name	Date	Location	Activity	Action	Sex
MEEKO, Paulosie, Que.	11/18/68	Churchill, Man.	Stalking	?	?
PERNITZKY, Richard, B.C.	7/1/75	Inuvik, N.W.T.	At garbage dump	?	?
UNIDENTIFIED (Austrian) Sweden	7/22/77	Spitzenbergen, Sweden	Camping	?	?
YLAND, Franciscus, Alta.	9/8/72	Devon Is., N.W.T.	Hunting	?	?

Attacks by Polar Bears in Wild

Name	Date	Location	Activity	Action	Sex
LEGAULT, John, Que.	9/2/75	Somerset Is., N.W.T.	Asleep in tent	Ran, fought	?

Appendix: Bear-attack Statistics (cont.)

Name/Origin	Date	Place	Situation	Action	Bear Sex
NALGE, Adele, Man.	11/20/67	Churchill, Man.	Walking	Fought	?
OVERTON, Tony, Canada.	5-6/?/61-62	Norwegian Bay, N.W.T.	In sleeping bag	?	?
SPENCE, George, Canada.	5-6/?/66	Patrick Isle, N.W.T.	Near cabin	Fought	?
SPENCE, John, Man.	3/16/69	Rupert Creek, Man.	Trapping	"	?
TAYLOR, Bob.	9/2/75	Somerset Is., N.W.T.	Asleep in tent	Fought, shot it	?
THORASSIE, Adolph.	11/20/67	Churchill, Man.	Walking	Ran, fought	?
ULRICH, S. H., Man.	11/19/68	Ft. Churchill, Man.	In house	Fought	?
UNIDENTIFIED (Russian), Sweden	4/25/77	Gronfjorden, Sval	Working	?	?
WHYTE, Bradley, Man.	?	Ft. Churchill, Man.	Walking	?	?
Kills by Unknown Bear Species in Wild					
FARR, Dalton, Y.T.	8/16/67	Demster, Y.T.	Hunting	Shot, fought	?
INKSTER, Robert, B.C.	7/13/70	Wells, B.C.	Trapping	Lay	?
LAYBOURNE, Janice.	8/30/76	Fairview, Alta.	Berrypicking	?	?
OLSON, Harold, B.C.	?	Toneko Lake, B.C.	Walking	?	?
PRINCE, Carl, B.C.	7/13/70	Wells, B.C.	In sleeping bag	Lay	?
Attacks by Unknown Bear Species in Wild					
ARMSTRONG, Eric, B.C.	8/21/67	Lac LeHache, B.C.	Ranching	Fought, climbed	S & cub
ARNOT, Ernest.	7/3/73	Bear Valley, Alta.	?	?	?
AUGER, Anna, Alta.	8/21/80	N. Slave Lake, N.W.T	In tent	Fought, screamed	?
AUSKESLIS, Nancy, MT.	9/16/72	Jasper, Alta.	Hiking	Fought	?
FURLONG, Pat, MI.	?	Newbury, MI.	?	?	?
PATTERSON, Michel.	?	?, MI.	?	?	?
SNOW, Peter.	8/9/68	Raton, NM.	In sleeping bag	Lay	?

Kills by Black Bears in National Parks

Name	Date	Location	Activity	Circumstance	
COATES, Barb, Alta.	8/9/58	Jasper, Alta.	Playing	Mother fought	?
HALFKENNY, George, Ont.	5/17/78	Algonquin, Ont.	Fishing	?	M
HALFKENNY, Mark, Ont.	5/17/78	"	"	?	M
POMERANKY, Carol, MI.	7/7/48	Hiawatha, MI.	Playing	?	?
RHINDRESS, William, Ont.	5/17/78	Algonquin, Ont.	Fishing	?	M

Attacks by Black Bears in National Parks

Name	Date	Location	Activity	Circumstance	
BELL, Mrs., (?).	8/11/78	Jasper, Alta.	In tent	?	?
BROWN, Jerry, MT.	8/26/67	Glacier, MT.	In sleeping bag	?	?
BROWN, Lee, Alta.	7/27/74	Beauvais Lake, Alta	Hiking	Climbed	S & cub
CAMERON, Paul, MI.	7/?/75	Pork Mt., MI.	" "	Lay, fought	?
CAMPBELL, Blair, Ont.	6/3/76	Banff, Alta.	?	?	?
COPEN, Maxwell, Alta.	5/23/71	Banff, Alta.	Jogging	?	?
CORNELIUS, Robt., Alta.	8/24/78	Jasper, Alta.	In tent	?	?
CREORE, Jo Anne, Alta.	5/29/76	Jasper, Alta.	In sleeping bag	?	?
CUMBERLAND, Hilda, Alta.	8/15/76	Jasper, Alta.	In tent	?	?
DISSER, William.	8/27/75	Glacier, MT.	?	?	?
DOUGLAS, Kenneth, OR.	8/12/69	Mt. Rainier, OR.	In tent	?	?
DYKES, R. L. (Mrs.), Alta.	5/16/70	Banff, Alta.	Feeding bear from car	?	?
FEENEY, Mike, Alta.	8/29/78	Jasper, Alta.	In sleeping bag	?	?
FLORIS, Jacobi, B.C.	7/6/76	Whitehorse, Y.T.	Photographing	Men fought	M
GARDNER, Eugene.	8/18/72	Jasper, Alta.	Hiking	?	?
GOEBEL, Cameron, Alta.	7/27/74	Beauvais Lake, Alta.	Hiking	Fought, climbed	S & cub
HEYER, Steve, Mt.	8/26/67	Glacier, Mt.	In sleeping bag	?	?
HOLDENRIDE, Dieter, Germany.	8/9/68	Yoho, B.C.	In tent	?	?

Appendix: Bear-attack Statistics (cont.)

Name/Origin	Date	Place	Situation	Action	Bear Sex
KLIEN, Mary, WA.	6/21/77	Waterton, Alta.	In tent	?	?
LAUTERBACK, Mrs., IL.	8/26/77	Waterton, Alta.	In trailer	?	?
LINKS, (Mrs.) Frank, B.C.	?	Manning, B.C.	Photographing	Stayed still	?
MARTIN, Sylvia, Ont.	8/15/77	Whistler, ?	In tent	?	?
MORGAN, Gerald, England	5/18/76	Jasper, Alta.	?	?	?
ST. PIERE, Richard, Sask.	8/5/75	Waterton, Alta.	In tent	Lay, fought	?
SHEARER, Mary, Alta.	7/4/66	" "	" "	?	?
SMITH, Paula, RI.	8/5/78	Jasper, Alta.	" "	?	?
Unidentified, Female	6/10/62	Kootenay, B.C.	In car	?	?
" ?	8/27/76	Yoho, B.C.	In tent	?	?
" Male	7/1/64	Kootenay, B.C.	Photographing	?	S & cub
" "	5/23/64	Banff, Alta.	Walking	?	?
" "	8/29/?	Kootenay, B.C.	Feeding	?	?
" "	7/29/62	Kootenay, B.C.	In car	?	?
" "	9/6/62	Kootenay, B.C.	In car	?	?
" "	7/8/61	" "	"	?	?
" Female	7/8/61	" "	" "	?	?
" Female	6/22/61	" "	" "	?	?
" Male	7/8/60	" "	Photographing	?	?
" "	6/22/60	Banff, Alta.	Hiking	?	S & cub
" "	9/22/51	" "	Feeding	?	?
" "	7/9/59	Kootenay, B.C.	In tent	?	?
WALLEY, Randy, B.C.	6/6/76	Kootenay, B.C.	In tent	?	?
WASCHUK, Ms. J., Sask.	8/15/75	Jasper, Alta.	Photographing	?	?

Kills by Grizzlies in National Parks

Name	Date	Location	Activity	Response	Type
...jane, MN	7/25/80	Glacier, MT.	Unauthorized camp	?	M
CHAPMAN, Barbara J., B.C.	7/28/76	Glacier, B.C.	Observing nature	Lay still	S & cub
COHOE, Ernest, Alta.	8/24/80	Banff, Alta.	Fishing	?	M
EBERLY, Kim, OH	7/25/80	Glacier, MT.	Unauthorized camp	?	M
ETHERINGTON, Wilfred, Alta.	9/25/73	Banff, Alta.	Photographing	Ran	M
GOODAIRE, Percy, Alta.	9/26/29	Jasper, Alta.	On duty	?	?
GORDON, Laurence, TX	10/6/80	Glacier, MT.	Hiking	Found dead	F
HELEGESON, Julie, MN.	8/13/67	Glacier, MT.	In sleeping bag	Cried out	S
KOONS, Michele, CA.	8/13/67	" "	" "	" "	S
MAHONEY, Patricia, IL.	9/23/76	" "	" "	" "	2 cubs
MUSER, Allison, Sask.	7/1/77	Waterton, Alta.	Playing	Ran	?
WALKER, Harry, AL.	6/26/72	Yellowstone, MT.	Chasing it	?	M

Attacks by Grizzlies in National Parks

Name	Date	Location	Activity	Response	Type
ASPESLET, Malcolm, (with Beck), B.C.	10/1/71	Glacier, B.C.	Hiking	Fought	S & cub
AUSEKLIS, Avis (Mr.), MT.	9/14/72	Jasper, Alta.	Hiking	?	?
BANTON, Audrey.	8/7/72	Banff, Alta.	Near lodge	?	?
BECK, Barbara (with Aspeslet), B.C.	9/1/71	" "	"	Fought	S & cub
BLACK, Rosco.	9/9/76	Glacier, B.C.	Hiking	?	?
BRADBERRY, Phillip, AL.	6/26/72	Yellowstone, MT.	Camping	Ran	M
BRAMER, Kevin, Alta.	5/2/68	Lake Louise, Alta.	Walking dog	?	S & cub
DAUBNEY, John.	8/9/39	Glacier, MT.	Photographing	?	?
DUCAT, Ron, OH.	8/13/67	" "	In sleeping bag	Lay still	S & cub
GARDNER, Noel, MT.	8/27/62	" "	Doing research	Fought, climbed	"
GATES, Kenneth, MN.	9/1/71	Glacier, B.C.	Hiking	?	?
HOPE, Robb, Alta.	7/15/76	Jasper, Alta.	"	?	?
HUGHES, H.C.	?	Tweedsmuir, B.C.	Mining	Lay still	?

Appendix: Bear-attack Statistics (cont.)

Name/Origin	Date	Place	Situation	Action	Bear Sex
JECKS, Len, Alta.	6/5/68	Jasper, Alta.	Hiking	?	S & cub
JORDAN, Doreen.	8/7/72	Banff, Alta.	At lodge	?	?
KADOWSKI, Norm, B.C.	6/13/74	Tweedsmuir, B.C.	Fishing	Fought, ran	?
KELVER, Brian, Ont.	9/5/80	Banff, Alta.	Hiking	?	?
KRAMER, D., FL.	8/1/73	Banff, Alta.	In sleeping bag	?	S & cub
LEUTHOLD, Andre, (with Toblar), Switzerland	9/3/80	Banff, Alta.	Photographing beaver	Lay still	?
LULU, Wilfred, B.C.	8/30/69	Whitehorse, Y.T.	Mining	Fought, fell	?
MUSKETT, Bob, Alta.	9/5/80	Banff, Alta.	Fishing	Ran	M
NELSON, Alan.	6/19/60	Glacier, MT.	?	?	S & cub
PARRATT, Smith.	6/19/60	" "	?	?	?
PETERSON, Harold, IL.	8/7/75	Glacier, MT.	Hiking	Fought	?
PETERSON, Karen, IL.	8/7/75	" "	"	Father fought	?
PETERSON, Seth, IL.	8/7/75	" "	"	"	?
ROGERS, James, CA.	8/31/69	Jasper, Alta.	Hiking	Ran	?
ROGERS, Ken Jr., CA.	8/31/69	Jasper, Alta.	"	Ran	?
ROGERS, Ken Sr., CA.	8/31/69	" "	"	Decoyed	?
ROSE, Stephen, CA.	6/7/68	" "	?	?	S & cub
ROWED, Genevieve, B.C.	9/1/72	" "	"	Lay still	2 cubs
ROWED, Harry, B.C.	9/1/72	" "	"	Fought	2 cubs
SCHWIEGHOFER, Wm.	7/16/76	Glacier, MT.	In tent	Fought	?
SHEA, Tom.	7/7/60	Glacier, MT.	?	?	?
SKJONSBERG, Terry, Alta.	9/16/76	Banff, Alta.	Observing	Climbed	?
SLUTKER, David L., Alta.	6/7/68	Jasper, Alta.	Biking	?	S & cub
STEPNIEWSKY, Andrew, B.C.	7/28/76	Glacier, B.C.	Observing	Lay still	S & cub